Advocacy, Activism, and the Internet

Also available from Lyceum Books

Advocacy, Activism, and the Internet

Community Organization and Social Policy

edited by

Steven F. Hick and John G. McNutt
Carleton University   Boston College

LYCEUM
BOOKS, INC.

Chicago, Illinois

LYCEUM BOOKS, INC.
5758 S. Blackstone Ave.
Chicago, Illinois 60637
773+643-1903 (Fax)
773+643-1902 (Phone)
lyceum@lyceumbooks.com
http://www.lyceumbooks.com

Printed in Canada

Library of Congress Cataloging-in-Publication Data

Advocacy, activism, and the internet : community organization and social policy / edited by Steven F. Hick and John G. McNutt; foreword by Norm Chomsky.
    p. cm.
Includes bibliographical references and index.
ISBN 0-925065-60-9 (alk. paper)
    1. Social service—Computer network resources. 2. Social advocacy—Computer network resources. 3. Internet. I. Hick, Steven, 1959– . II. McNutt, John G., 1951– .
HV29.2 .A38 2002
361.3'0285'4678—dc21   2001057983

Contents

Foreword

The Internet, Society, and Activism

The following is a compilation of comments by Noam Chomsky from an informal discussion with the volume editors and a variety of other sources.

Noam Chomsky

THE INTERNET, AS A RECENTLY EMERGED TECHNOLOGY, RAISES A NUMBER of important concerns for social activists. The first is that we must analyze the Internet in the historical context of other communications media, such as radio, print, and television   media that at one time, like the Internet, were both new tech nologies and potential forces for liberation. Knowing their history is critical because, in the end, their potential was unfulfilled. Second, we must realize that the Internet alone will not organize people. Social activism will still involve painstaking, face-to-face, grassroots work. The Internet may make this easier, but the careful process of organization will remain a human effort, and the only guide for this powerful tool will remain human judgment. No technology is inherently democratic, and no technology is inherently oppressive. A fairly neutral thing, it cares little whether it is used for oppression or liberation—or whether it is used at all. We must choose whether to use technological tools in our grassroots organizing efforts. Third, we must consider the atomized, isolated nature of Internet communities—an ironic feature, given the Net's unprecedented ability to connect individuals around the world. Key questions are whether this isolating quality can also be a uniting force; and whether its effect on those it reaches will be democratic or commercial, simply providing corporations with new ways to invent needs for unwanted products and new online venues for selling them. The corporate world would like nothing more than for all of us to become glued to an interactive tube to watch advertising and shop online.

The Internet's development is reminiscent of that of radio in the 1920s and 1930s. When radio first emerged, it was a fixed resource, the users of which understood would ultimately be regulated by government. People of the day asked whether the radio would be devoted to the public interest, and be essentially a democratic instrument, or would it be turned over to private power, and be essentially a commercial instrument.

There was a struggle over the answer. Activist groups, such as public-interest groups, church groups, and labor unions, wanted the radio to be a public-interest entity. They were, however, extremely weak and divided, and when radio emerged they essentially lost the battle. This was during a very repressive period following Wilson's Red Scare, which had shattered the whole society; those who tried to organize to guide radio into becoming a kind of public-interest phenomenon were largely destroyed. Radio use became completely commercial, handed over to corporations under the pretext that this was more democratic than public ownership. In the United States, only limited public radio, such as student radio stations that could reach three blocks, was allowed. The rest of the world went the other way. In almost every other country the medium became public; radio was as free as the society in which it operated. It was free to the extent that people could affect their governments.

When television broadcasting emerged in the United States, it wasn't even a battle. By then business dominance was so overwhelming that the question over private versus public ownership never arose. Business simply took over the medium.

In the 1960s the government allowed public radio and television, but in an interesting way. Congress had imposed conditions on public-interest requirements for the big networks. These conditions were seen as a nuisance by the large media corporations, which realized it would be better to allow a marginally public system.

We are now facing a similar situation with the Internet, and the direction it takes will be crucial to the future of society. It could turn out to be a democratizing force, with public participation, or it could end up being only a mechanism for corporate propaganda, creating artificial wants, enabling us to buy things more quickly, and so on. If individuals and communities do not act quickly to counter the corporate push to control the Internet's future, it will likely take the latter path, due to the balance of forces.

The Internet was a public creation, although the public didn't know about it and it did not happen democratically. For the roughly thirty years during which the medium was being developed, the initiatives, the ideas, the funding, and the risks were almost entirely within the state sector. The Internet was developed by the Pentagon, the National Science Foundation, universities, and private corporations (usually under government contract). The World Wide Web was created in an international laboratory, the IAUG Physics laboratory in Geneva. In the early days, the Internet and the World Wide Web were the monopoly of relatively privileged sectors of people with access to computers in universities, government, and research centres. In the academic world it became a useful means of sharing scientific results. In 1995 these largely public creations were then handed over to private corporations—but no one seems to know how this was done.

Once the system was given to the private powers, they immediately began to find ways to control it and orient it toward profit-making activities. A survey of certain U.S. newspapers carried out by Norman Solomon at the end of 1999 revealed that the term *information superhighway* had been used 842 times in 1999, while *e-commerce received* 20,641 mentions. This contrasts with figures from 1995, dur-

Table 1:   Mentions of the terms *information superhighway* and *e-commerce*

	Information Superhighway	E-Commerce
1995	4,562	915
1996	2,370	1,662
1997	1,314	2,812
1998	945	6,403
1999	842	20,641

Source: Adapted from N. Solomon, "What Happened to the 'Information Superhighway'?" Distributed via the Media Beat distribution list 2000.

ing which 4,562 stories had discussed the information superhighway, compared to 915 mentions of e-commerce (see Table 1). This change illustrates a shift from a publicly based institution to a privately based institution.

The corporate structures that are increasingly controlling the Internet are attempting to suppress its liberation. They quite naturally want it to be used as a tool for pursuing increased profits, to subjugate people and separate them from one another. They want to focus our attention on "the more superficial things in life, like fashionable consumption," to satisfy what are called *invented wants* or *created wants* in the business literature.

Anyone who is alive knows that a goodly part of life is devoted—essentially subjected—to such artificial efforts from infancy, when advertising aimed at children begins. And if the corporations get their way, the Internet will become a large part of this.

Although the future of technology is unpredictable, it is likely that there will be a further corporate takeover. Those in the business world want to cut large parts of the Internet out of the public domain altogether, turning it into *Intranets* that are fenced off with firewalls and used exclusively for internal corporate operations. They also want to control access to the Internet to ensure that users are guided to the commercial areas; their intention is to trap the public in e-commence, advertising, and other profit-making activities. Alternative sites will continue to exist, but finding and accessing them will become progressively more difficult.

Corporations will surely undertake to make it difficult for people to use the Internet in ways that are subversive of concentrated power. Even today, access is largely controlled through a small number of portals or entry points, and those are controlled by major corporations such as AOL TimeWarner. Such control will not make it easy for those who want to use the Internet for social activism. Although corporations probably can't make it impossible—the nature of the system is such that it is technologically impossible to block all such use—they can create the conditions whereby it is difficult to escape e-commerce and to use the Internet for other purposes, by distributing fast and slow channels, by leading users through particular paths, and so forth. Numerous techniques can make it extremely difficult to use the free resources of the Internet in ways other than those intended by the corporate owners. In fact, one could say the same about the print media. It is not illegal in the United States and Canada to publish a newspaper to compete with the corporate media; anyone is legally entitled to do so. But the organization and structure of the system are such that it is impossible. Media corporations will make every effort to move the Internet in this direction as well. Whether they are successful depends on the reaction of citizens.

The Internet need not become a tool for corporate control and propaganda. It can instead be a significant instrument for promoting human rights and social justice. The future of the Internet is something that people ought to fight about—it does not have to turn out to be mostly negative. Internet access is a new freedom that will require nurture and protection just as our other freedoms required. Through active struggle, society can create a public entity that can be kept under public control. But that will mean a lot of hard work at every level, from Congress down to local organizations, unions, and other citizens' groups that will struggle against it in all the usual ways. The Internet itself will be an important component of this struggle.

Clearly the Internet has liberating potential. The Internet retains its capacity to be used independently for activism and social change, and there are numerous positive consequences of this new technology for grassroots organizing. For example, IGC Internet with PeaceNet, EcoNet, WomensNet, and Anti-RacismNet strategically use the Internet by providing relevant information, action alerts, and specialist Bulletin Boards at which groups with particular interests and concerns interact and discuss all sorts of things. *Z Magazine,* an independent leftist journal, has a Z-bulletin board to which activists can subscribe; it is now bringing in a readership from around the world, on many issues it has been an invaluable tool, enabling organizers to disseminate information on issues that would not normally be picked up by the mainstream media. For example, information about East Timor came mainly from Australia, but with the Internet available, it came at once. That made an enormous difference. Information is spread quickly, bypassing the mainstream media. The use of the Internet in organizing protests against the World Trade Organization meetings in Seattle is another success story; the organizing against the Multilateral Agreement on Investment was also substantially Internet based. Internet organizing assisted the overthrow of the Suharto government in Indonesia, in which students played a large role.

There are, however, several downsides to the Internet. One aspect, which is hard to quantify, is the depersonalizing and isolating nature of online communication. This is a reflection of a global society in which people are very atomized and feel very much alone. The individual often thinks that he or she is the only one who thinks in a particular way. Society has become so atomized, broken down, and depersonalized that the normal bonds of association and communication are lost. People turn to e-mail and chat rooms to gain a sense of community belonging. This is the one aspect of the Internet that is troublesome. People do not gain the social skills they need to function properly when their friends and communication are primarily virtual.

Efforts by large corporations to control the Internet are predictable. We all need to be aware of these efforts. Whether the corporations succeed depends on the forms the popular struggle takes. It will be a battle. The corporate concentration of power will not readily allow the Internet to be a democratic technology. Corporate efforts in the past century have been to stop such developments. Yet corporate dominance is not inevitable. The struggle over Internet control is a worthwhile one.

Preface

Be ashamed to die unless you have won some victory for humanity.

Horace Mann

IN THE PREVIOUS CENTURY, THE FIELD OF SOCIAL WORK STRUGGLED against the ill effects of new technology and of the new economic system it permitted. The social fallout from this system was horrific; those on whom it fell were those on whom the abuse of power has always fallen: children, women, the elderly, the poor and uneducated. Social workers fought for the rights of these groups and tended the needs of the disenfranchised and the socially dislocated. One of their most powerful—and empowering—tools was the organizing of communities, which were both a source of support for the socially weakened and an opportunity for the reaffirmation of the individual's social worth.

This commitment to social and economic justice continues in the social work profession today, and in the educational programs from which its practitioners emerge. Students graduate from BSW and MSW programs with an understanding of the profession's commitment to advocacy and social change, a knowledge of the issues that face our society and the people we serve, and the methods of community organization and policy practice that make social change possible. These social workers and their abilities are needed no less today than they were 100 years ago—perhaps even more so. For all that the global information economy has simply reinvented the old problems of social dislocation and disenfranchisement, the context of these problems is entirely new. We desperately need new tools in our social work arsenal to meet this challenge. Technology—the very technology whose use has exacerbated such problems in the name of profit—can provide many of those tools, of which the Internet is only one.

The volume you are holding is, in a sense, such a toolkit. This is the first book-length treatment of activism and advocacy over the Internet from a social work perspective; its authors, cutting-edge practitioners and researchers. Their insights will guide your search for the skills you—and those who look to you for help—need. This is not a dry technical manual on how to build a Web site (although it may spark good ideas for the content of one). Instead, you will find here:

- A brief history of the role of technology in the emergence of the present economy;
- Current theory on the role of information and communications technologies (ICTs) in social work;
- An overview of "teledemocracy," and the social worker's role in it;

◆ Discussions of the nature and meaning of the so-called digital divide, and of how to close it;
◆ Interventions using the Internet and other ICT at the group, local, state, national, and international levels; and
◆ Discussions of real-life successes and—equally as important—failures in this new field.

In short, this is a thoughtful, stimulating look at a new and vibrant form of practice.

Now is an exciting time to be a social worker. We face both the same challenges our profession has always faced, and others entirely unlike those our predecessors ever encountered. Not only can we shape the present, we can also build the profession of the future and embed in it the knowledge that the commitment will be what it has always been: the struggle for justice.

Steven Hick
John McNutt

Part **I**

Community Organizing and Advocacy on the Internet: An Introduction

Chapter 1

Communities and Advocacy on the Internet

A Conceptual Framework

Steven Hick

John McNutt

INTRODUCTION: WHAT IS THIS BOOK ABOUT?

The Internet has affected all areas of social, economic, and political life. It is having a powerful impact on organizations that are committed to social change and social and economic justice. Electronic, online, and Internet-based advocacy or activism have become forces to be reckoned with in the new area of cyberpolitics. This book is the first major treatment of this new and exciting form of social work practice. This book presents a systematic description and analysis of the Internet as a tool for political advocacy and social activism in social work throughout the world. It will also examine the problems faced by activists and advocates using the Internet.

Many questions remain concerning the impacts of the Internet on society and on social work advocacy and activism. For example, who is using the Internet for social activism and how are they using it? What are the benefits of this new technology for social work advocacy? What is the impact on community organizing, both globally and locally? Can you truly have a sense of community on the Internet? What dangers does the Internet pose for activists and society in terms of the digital divide, isolation, and community building? Does the Internet confer a new potent force that by itself will encourage democracy and empower communities? These are just a few of the questions that this book will raise and discuss.

This three-part book comprises a wide variety of views on important issues concerning the use of the Internet for social work advocacy and activism, as well as the dangers and challenges the Internet poses. Both experts and practitioners provide their unique perspectives and diverse experiences. The authors present both a review of critical issues as well as an advanced and in-depth examination of central problems, such as limited access and information skills for numerous countries and sectors of society (the digital divide), North/South issues, commercialization of the

Internet, success stories and lessons learned in online organizing, and a variety of opportunities, challenges, and dangers for grassroots activists.

This book will

◆ Discuss current theoretical perspectives on community organizing, advocacy, and the Internet;
◆ Present a systematic description of the development of the Internet as an advocacy and social activist tool in social work;
◆ Explore the digital divide and its global consequences for social work;
◆ Discuss how to use the Internet for social work activism and advocacy;
◆ Feature the use of the Internet by a variety of community, nonprofit, and advocacy groups;
◆ Examine the impact of the advocacy and activism on the Internet on different places in the world and on different groups of people in society; and
◆ Discuss current issues and future trends related to the Internet as a tool for social work practice with larger systems.

CHALLENGES AND OPPORTUNITIES

The development of information and communications technology (ICT) has vastly transformed the capacity of social work agencies, community organizations, social movements, and groups of concerned people to build coalitions and networks and to advocate for causes, principles, and other people. Social work organizations frequently advocate and initiate action dealing with health care, child welfare, poverty, human rights, environmentalism, physical and sexual abuse, suicide prevention, substance abuse, homelessness, and all the other human problems in modern society. Community groups may organize around issues relating to access to services or cutbacks in social programs. Other groups may oppose free trade, developing-world debt, or globalization. Direct-action groups may use electronic civil disobedience, or "hackerism," to impart a message or disrupt unjust behavior. As we move into the new century, the social work profession is faced with a number of new threats to social and economic justice. In addition, many of the traditional threats have not gone away. Although an exhaustive treatment is not possible here, some of the more significant challenges seem to be the following.

◆ *Globalization and a world information economy.* The transformation of the world economy has created a number of issues that promise to have a negative impact on large segments of the population. Increased competition among nations and even subnational units has created forces that discourage taxation and thus funding for social welfare programs. This same competition has disempowered workers and made industrial jobs more insecure. In some nations, it has led to mass unemployment. Other societies have experienced growing economic inequality.
◆ *Threats to the physical environment.* The destruction of the physical environment continues, despite years of environmental activism. Although most

industrialized nations have adopted laws to protect the physical environment, there are significant pressures to discourage enforcement from industry groups and free-trade advocates. In the United States, passage of the NAFTA treaty reduced the ability of federal and state governments to enforce existing laws. In the face of legislation, multinational corporations have moved facilities that do not meet environmental laws to nations that either do not have or are unable to enforce these standards. With the competition to court economic activity, this is usually not difficult. The growth of toxic wastes, global warming, species extinction, and other problems is likely to continue unless activists are successful (Hoff & McNutt 1994).

◆ *The digital divide.* As the industrial economies give way to information economies, a new social underclass has emerged: the *information-poor.* These are groups of people who will be denied inclusion in the future (Ebo 1998). There is strong evidence that a significant portion of those who are currently excluded will be excluded in the future economy; in addition, a significant group of people will newly enter the ranks of the poor as economic transition eliminates the industrial jobs they now hold and pushes them out.

◆ *Devolution.* The move toward lower levels of government and greater use of privatization is worldwide in scope and promises reduced enforcement of national laws and the reduced protection of powerless groups. In social welfare, competition has led to service cutbacks and the creation of a two-track system of care whereby wealthier clients experience better treatment than those who do not have their own funds.

◆ *Reduction of social welfare efforts.* Years of conservative government in many industrial nations has led to a reduced level of social welfare. In the United States, welfare reform, managed care, and other recent policy initiatives have led to a decline in both access and service quality. With only a few exceptions, governments throughout the world are reducing their commitments to social programs, privatizing service delivery, tightening eligibility requirements, and eroding entitlements.

All of these trends, and others, lead one to conclude that social work advocacy and activism is as important as it has ever been. In many ways, we owe it to ourselves, our clients, and our profession to become the most effective advocates possible. One way to accomplish this is to become proficient in the use of new technologies.

SOCIAL WORK ACTIVISM AND ADVOCACY IN CYBERSPACE

Social work advocacy and activism in cyberspace are really not much different from such activities elsewhere. The same skills and knowledge are necessary. The Internet merely introduces new possibilities using e-mail, newsgroups, listservs, Web sites, chat rooms, virtual communities, computer conferencing, and online publishing, to name a few. They all, in many ways, either replace or augment activities that were previously done using other means. For example, e-mail action alerts are the electronic version of flyers that grassroots organizers hand out on street corners or at rallies. The key difference is that the Internet enables rapid response and is less costly to implement. In fact, the same advantages that the Internet brings to global corporations to facilitate global expansion and influence can be used by social workers to fight injustice and advocate for change.

Before we explore the use of the Internet in electronic advocacy or activism we must define the terminology and the conceptual and theoretical landscapes. We begin this chapter with a definition of electronic advocacy and activism and an examination of how the Internet is an important part of activists' strategies. Next, a theoretical discussion presents the issues faced by online activists, including an examination of critiques of the Internet, which view the medium as "progress without people"[1] or as a destiny itself.[2] We present a critical theory of the Internet that sees people not as abstracted from the Internet, but instead formed—and informed—by it. With this theory the medium can create locations that empower social activists to change both the Internet and society for the better.

The Internet can enable social workers to accomplish tasks more effectively, more quickly, at a lower cost, and on a global scale. Part 2 of this book discusses activists' strategies and tactics for using the various tools. This discussion includes concise overviews of the tools and how they can be used, as well as discussions of possible pitfalls and dangers.

WHAT IS "ELECTRONIC ADVOCACY AND ACTIVISM?"

Providing a straightforward definition of electronic advocacy and activism is not an easy task. First, we must define what we mean by *electronic,* which is the topic of the next section. Then we must define the terrain intended by the terms *advocacy* and *activism.*

The Internet

The Internet is, put simply, *a global pool of information and services, accessible locally through individual computer stations, each of which is part of a global system of interconnected computer networks.* The Internet is the major component of the emerging information and communications technology (ICT). The Internet is independent of physical geography, and no single person, government, or business owns it. The Internet is not subject to any global regulation. Virtually any information can be posted on the Internet, depending on the local national infrastructure, and made available to anyone who wishes to access it. There is no global legislation, although efforts to develop legislation are underway in several multilateral forums. Still, the Internet of today is often described as being an anarchic environment, unrestrained, unregulated, and accessible—at least theoretically—to all. In many ways, the Internet can be likened to the advent of printing in the fifteenth century, when information became freely available. The impact on society at the time was huge, much like that claimed of the Internet today.

The full depth and breadth of the Internet are hard to quantify, having grown exponentially from the original four networked computers known as ARPANET in 1969 to approximately 16 million hosts or sites in 1997 (Hafner & Lyon 1996; Grobman & Grant 1998). A *host*, or *site*, is not a user but a "node" at which information is stored, accessible by the Internet user. Of the estimated 16 million sites, 96 percent are found among the twenty-seven nations of the Organization for Economic Cooperation and Development (OECD). The World Wide Web (WWW) has roughly 30 million home pages available to users of the Internet worldwide. (By 1996, the Internet already had an estimated 60 million users globally [Halpin & Fisher 1998]. This number is doubling each year.) The Internet has thus evolved from solely government and academic networks to become a vital element of society, as well as a source of advocacy and activism opportunities.

A wide range of tools can be used on the Internet; the principal ones available include e-mail for communication and the World Wide Web (WWW) for accessing information. Other tools include newsgroups, online conferencing, video conferencing, bulletin-board systems, Internet telecommunications, real-time chat, discussion groups, and listservs, among others. Moreover, the Internet has made the exchange of information both faster and cheaper. Through e-mail, it is possible to communicate simultaneously with many people, in many different locations, rather than having to contact them individually. This aspect of the Internet is clearly a major benefit for networking by social work activists.

Traditional means of communication have changed rapidly and significantly over the past two decades. Such communications technologies will continue to change rapidly, both as technology advances and as the global pressure grows for instant and comprehensive communication. The personal computer has forever transformed the way we work. Many believe that the future belongs to the knowledge workers—those who have the tools to build a world in constant information transformation. Electronic communications cuts through barriers of time and distance. It helps people work together who normally would or could not do so. The Internet facilitates the finding and retrieval of information in a way that was impossible before. It is also a great catalyst and tool for decentralization, including the decentralization of power.

Advocacy and Activism

Under the rubric of *activism*, social work authors examine a wide variety of issues and topics (see Epstein 1981; Ezell 1991, 1993, 1994; Haynes & Mickleson 2000). Other terms such as *community organizing/community practice, policy practice,* and *social action* are also used in place of activism—frequently with different meanings. Furthermore, any one term may have different meanings in different countries and regions. In the United States, the term *advocacy* is often used as a broad concept to include social action and lobbying; in other parts of the world the concept refers to specific social work practices whereby practitioners advocate for services or resources for a particular client or group of clients. In other parts of the world where social services are less developed, the term *community development* or, more recently, *community participation* is used to refer to a range of activities. We do not intend to settle these contested terms, except to provide a definition of the terminology that we will use in this book.

Frequently, social workers distinguish among three levels of practice: (1) the *micro* level—working one-to-one with an individual; (2) the *mezzo* level, working with families and other small groups; and (3) the *macro* level—interventions with organizations and communities, or seeking changes in policies, procedures, legislation, or other institutional arrangements. This distinction provides us with the boundaries of what this book will address. We intend to examine macro-practice and the Internet.

In this book we will use both terms—*advocacy* and *activism*—to capture a range of activities being accomplished by macro-practice using the Internet. Advocacy and activism have been seen as parts of professional practice since the early days of social work (Specht & Courtney 1994; Trattner 1994). Throughout the profession's history, social workers have fought for the rights of groups that could not advocate for themselves and have organized both their own activities and those of others to change policy and politics. As even the social workers come increasingly from disadvantaged sectors of society they find themselves within groups advocating for change.

Electronic techniques, particularly those that make use of Internet-based technologies, are changing the way that advocacy and activism are practiced (Bowen 1996; FitzGerald & McNutt 1999; Grobman & Grant 1998; Hick & Halpin 2001; Hick, Halpin, & Hoskins 2000; McNutt & Boland 1998, 1999; Schwartz 1996; Turner 1998). New techniques are a means to make the aspects of lobbying, campaigning, and organizing more effective and efficient.

Electronic advocacy refers to the use of high technology to influence the decision-making process, or to the use of technology in an effort to support policy-change efforts. In some contexts its definition has been restricted to acting on a client's behalf to obtain needed resources and services. *Activism* is generally defined in broader terms to include organizing groups of people with common interests or concerns to gain support for an issue, change policy around an issue, or undertake direct action to change a situation. It often involves getting involved in political affairs by taking part in such actions as protests and demonstrations to call attention to injustices and gain support for issues. The term is often used to refer to the activities of grassroots protest movements. The lines between advocacy and activism are not always clear, and many practitioners will use both in an intervention. We will use both terms here to ensure that we examine the full range of macro-social work actions enabled by the Internet.

Numerous interventions can be considered to be using new technology, including television advertising, radio announcements, fax campaigns, Web sites, e-mail, and video conferencing. FitzGerald and McNutt (1999) have differentiated between two categories of electronic advocacy. The first, called *traditional electronic advocacy,* involves the use of television, radio, fax, and other similar types of technology. The second division, *emergent electronic advocacy,* uses Internet-based technologies to influence policy. These include Web pages, e-mail, discussion groups, newsgroups, and so forth. This book is concerned solely with the emergent Internet technology.

While the use of the Internet for advocacy and activism is of fairly recent vintage, there is clear evidence that this use is growing (McNutt 2000a). The practice is alternately called NetActivism (Schwartz 1996), e-advocacy (Bennett & Fielding 1999), cyberactivism (Price 2000), and electronic advocacy (FitzGerald & McNutt 1999; West & Francis 1996). These labels describe a practice that (1) makes use of Internet-based technologies; (2) represents a move toward "new media" and away from traditional media approaches, including mass media (television and radio); and (3) complements more traditional approaches to advocacy.

As with any innovation and significant developments in technology-related practice, when the general state of technology increases or advances, some of the new techniques eventually diffuse into the expected skill set of players within the social system (McNutt & Boland 2000). The development of electronic advocacy as an area of practice—that is, the diffusion of technologically supported advocacy techniques within the third sector—is well documented. The leading edge of technology advances as new tools are developed. The earliest efforts were largely e-mail based (Schwartz 1996). These techniques used e-mail to connect with other activists and to communicate with decision makers. An interesting case study is the OMBWatch campaign against the Istook Amendment[3] (Schwartz 1996).

The second phase of e-advocacy development followed the growth of the World Wide Web. One of the best-known examples of this new approach is Move On [http://www.moveon.org], which relied on Web-based strategies (Bennett & Fielding 1999). Early Web-based interventions consisted of simple pages, which eventually gave way to more sophisticated Web-based technologies.

We are currently in the third stage: the growth of sophisticated Web-based technologies and new organizational types. Online fund-raising, geographic information systems, and teleconferencing are the current leading-edge techniques (Norris 1999). McNutt (2000b) found that a number of nonprofits were using these techniques. In addition, following the example of MoveOn, a number of Internet-based organizations are now being developed.

Although the next step is unclear, it will probably involve wireless technology and more skill in the use of artificial intelligence techniques, such as neural networks. Organizations will become more sophisticated in their use of these tools. We will begin to see more empirically grounded research on effectiveness and more formal training for cyberactivists.

The evolution of electronic advocacy might be seen as a series of transitions or steps, with each new technology displacing, but not eliminating, older methods. In addition, organizations change the way they use the techniques, and activists become more proficient in using the tools.

Currently, the techniques used by online activists include

◆ E-mail
◆ Newsgroups
◆ Discussion groups or listservs
◆ Web pages
◆ Chat rooms
◆ Online fund-raising
◆ Virtual communities
◆ Alternative news and information services
◆ Online petitions
◆ Online surveys
◆ Videoconferencing
◆ Banner ads
◆ Targeting and mapping software
◆ Virtual civil disobedience (hacktivism)

THEORETICAL FRAMEWORKS FOR UNDERSTANDING THE INTERNET AND SOCIAL WORK

The introduction of new technology has always had important impacts on so-cial work advocacy and activism. Profound changes are occurring in the way advo-cacy and activism take place. Historical analysis illustrates that each time a new technology is introduced into society and drastically changes the status quo, there is strong resistance and resolute advocacy. In many ways, this dynamic was present in the founding of the profession as a response to industrialization and the problems that ensued (Garvin & Cox, 2001).

Whether we like it or not, technology has always had an impact on how activism takes place worldwide. To be able to act and struggle with technology in our society we need a theoretical framework to guide our actions and analysis. How we ap-proach the introduction of new technology in social work depends largely on how we view the relations between technology and the people in our society. Too much of the debate on technology and social work is based on sentiment and passion, which are either for or against technology; in many cases the debate is based on a technological determinist framework, which sees technology as determining the social world. The technological determinist view of social change sees technology as "the prime mover" in history. *Technological determinists* view particular techni-cal developments, communications technologies, or media—or more broadly, technology in general—as the sole or prime antecedents of changes in society; that is, they see technology as the fundamental condition underlying the pattern of so-cial organization.

Strong resistance against the disruption of the usual way of doing things that is introduced by new technology tends to occur at the outset, as understanding and knowledge of the new device or technique and how it can be used emerge. There also tends to be considerable debate between the two extreme positions, often with little common ground in the middle. Santana (1997) refers to this as the *technophilia/technophobia debate:*

> Studies dealing with the relationship between technology and society tend to fall into two extreme positions: technophilia or technophobia. The latter sees technology as an evil element that is taking society to a process of dehumanisation, not recognizing any benefit that it might bring to human life. The former takes the opposite position, placing on technological advances the solution and the means to improve performance in different kinds of activities. (1)

This type of dualistic analysis is common when active resistance, or promotion, of new technologies threatens the status quo. In this book we have attempted to position ourselves in the middle of the debate, while encouraging active discussion and debate by presenting what we believe to be the full range of opinion on the subject.

These somewhat dichotomous attitudes toward the Internet helps to introduce the debate found in sociological approaches to technology. Do we take a utopian, or technophilic, view? Or a dystopian, or technophobic, view? Is technological determinism or social/cultural constructivism the correct philosophy? There are many well written and insightful publications that further pursue these debates (Feenberg 1991; Smith & Marx 1994). The following view (Loader 1997) might be useful when considering the merits of technological determinism versus social or cultural constructivism:

> The former generally overlooks the social context in which the technology becomes embedded, whereas the latter attempts to reduce technological advancement to social or cultural forces. These extremes can be avoided by means of a realist viewpoint which takes into account both the growth of scientific knowledge and the material make-up of technological artefacts, on the one hand, and the social settings in which they become embedded, on the other. (14)

The utopian sees cyberspace and such tools as the Internet as almost "other-worldly." The dystopian, on the other hand, holds that this technology simply hides the reality of our failing society.

We attempt to avoid either position, believing instead that we should think critically about the role that technology plays in advocacy—and in human evolution and everyday life, for that matter. We must go beyond polarized thinking and excited tales of either high-tech doom or cyber-elation. The goal here is to systematically examine the technological transformation of advocacy—neither to champion nor dismiss technology, but rather to research it, understand it, and apply it in a manner consistent with our goals as social work advocates. This perspective examines what social workers can do to ensure that we influence the emergence of advocacy techniques that use new technologies without compromising values and principles important to us. Given the impact of emerging technology on the lives of the people with whom we work (our clients), it is imperative that all social workers understand technology.

WHY IS THE INTERNET IMPORTANT TO SOCIAL WORK?

The Internet is a powerful mechanism of collective action and communication. It has the potential to become the most powerful tool for political organizing developed in the past fifty years. If you surf the online discussion groups you will find that one of the most popular topics of discussion is the interaction of politics and social issues. People log on to the Internet primarily to communicate with each other, and increasingly they are discussing what needs to be done to make societies and the world a better place. Social activists who argue that the today's youth are not concerned with social change simply do not see what is said in Internet discussions. It would not take much to turn these rapidly developing discussions into new forms of organizing.

In addition to the potential, there is a very real threat from other quarters. Other groups are using the Internet effectively to advance their agendas—agendas that are very different from and may conflict with our own. Social work advocates and activists can use the Internet, but so too can the enemies of social justice disseminate their information and propaganda in the same way. If they succeed in limiting our ability to use the Internet, the ramifications will be considerable.

UNDERSTANDING ELECTRONIC ADVOCACY PRACTICE

It is remarkable that working for social change online has developed into so many different advocacy techniques, given the short time that the Internet has been in existence. This says much about the vitality of and interest in the field. It also suggests the degree to which technological change has affected our ability to reach out to others in the social change community. The work of social work advocates and activists can be divided into six different categories or types[4]: community networking, electronic democracy, electronic government relations, virtual communities, online social action organizing, and civil disobedience. This typology is useful to structure our discussions of how the Internet is changing our work and provides the basis for the development of our conceptual framework.

- ◆ *Community networking.* Community networks, or FreeNets, are locality-based systems designed to serve their immediate communities with ways to communicate and deliberate virtually (Schuler 1994, 1996). They also provide online services for their communities. Their role in electronic advocacy lies in the fact that they provide the ability for civic discussion and debate as well as the opportunity for small organizations to have an online presence. This is a consensus-based strategy in most cases.
- ◆ *Electronic democracy, or e-government.* Another consensus-based strategy that involves the creation of electronic town halls and similar forums for public debate. These are generally provided by local governments but can, in some circumstances, be sponsored by local nonprofit organizations. They provide a political free space for dealing with public issues. A related development is the electronic-government movement (Milward and Snyder

1996). Because citizen participation is often a part of these systems, they provide another opportunity for organizing, activism, and advocacy.

♦ *Electronic government relations.* This area includes predominantly legislative advocacy (McNutt 2000a,b; McNutt & Boland 1999). It has been an important area for both major organizations and small, grassroots programs. Techniques include petitions, letter-writing campaigns, and similar efforts. International campaigns of conscience can also be included in this category.

♦ *Virtual communities.* This category of practice is a community of people that exists only online; the individuals do not meet face to face. This category functions both as an entity that is removed from most standard descriptions of a "community" (geographic, acquaintanceship, etc.) and as a supplement to a more traditional community. For example, Virtual Sisterhood [http://www.igc.apc.org/vsister/] creates and facilitates a global network of women committed to enhancing their own and other women's activism through effective use of electronic communications. Through this virtual community of women, whose members may be anywhere in the world, Virtual Sisterhood is expanding and strengthening the impact of global feminist organizing through the use of electronic communications.

♦ *Online social action organizing.* This type of use aims at bringing communities, groups, and individuals together to redistribute power. This type of effort tends to be more conflict oriented in nature.

♦ *Civil disobedience.* This is the final, most conflict-oriented type of electronic advocacy (Langman, Morris, Zalewski, Ignacio, & Davidson 2000). It involves interfering with the operation of an opponent's materials—or even stealing from their computers or destroying their technology. This type has also been referred to as *hacktivism* because it can include efforts to hack into an opponent's computer system.

A Conceptual Framework

It is useful to have a model of electronic advocacy that is compatible with similar, nonelectronic approaches to macro-practice. This allows us to apply what we know from more traditional forms of community, organizational, and policy practice, and to integrate traditional and online methods. In this book, we use a modification of a formulation offered by McNutt and Menon (2001).

Social change theory tends to use a formulation that proceeds from *consensus-based* activity through *contest-based* activity to radical, *conflict-based* social action (this approach can be found in the work of Warren 1972 and Rothman 2001). Furthermore, because we are discussing technology-related practice, the degree of technology infusion is also critical; we use Queiro-Tajalli and McNutt's (1997) breakdown of *technology-enhanced* versus *technology-dependent* here. The former is traditional practice aided by technology, whereas the latter is practice that cannot be performed without technology. These are two points on a continuum, with most interventions falling somewhere in the middle.

Together, these two dimensions form a conceptual tool for understanding variation among the types of strategies used in online advocacy. It is reasonably complete but does not overly complicate the process so that it becomes useless in practice. In all probability, this framework will serve more as a transitional step than as a definitive formulation as this part of the field matures.

Using the *quadrant continuum matrix,* social workers can locate their practices in any one of four quadrants formed by these two dimensions (see fig. 1.1).

The vertical axis in the matrix represents the continuum of technology reliance, with technology-enhanced practices at the lower end and technology-dependent practices at the upper end. The horizontal axis represents the continuum along which an activity's basis—whether consensus or conflict—falls. The four quadrants formed by the intersection of these two continuums are as follows:

♦ *Consensus-based/technology-enhanced* approaches refer to social work techniques that use the Internet to help increase the effectiveness and efficiency of traditional advocacy methods. At the same time, the methods do not challenge power relations in society, but instead work to influence policy decisions or delivery.

♦ *Consensus-based/technology-dependent* approaches take the same perspective on power relations in society as above, but the work is fully dependent on the technology. Items of practice—such as virtual communities—that do not challenge the status quo fall into this category because they could not be formed without the technology, but do not aim for substantive social change or conflict.

♦ *Conflict-based/technology-enhanced* approaches use the Internet to aug-

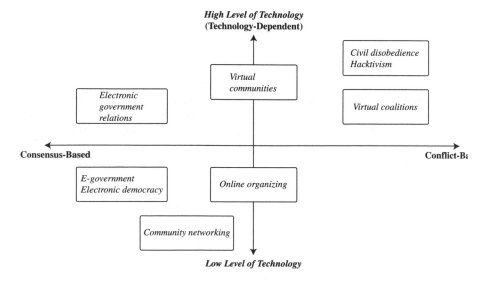

Figure 1.1   Electronic advocacy and activism matrix

ment traditional practice techniques that are aimed at redistributing power in society. Because disadvantaged social groups lack resources and power, they use the strategies available to them, such as demonstrations and protests. Increasingly, these groups are using the Internet to spread the word, organize, and mobilize others for such activities.

◆ *Conflict-based/technology-dependent* approaches challenge power relations, but involves actions that are dependent on the Internet. Grassroots organizations with limited budgets are linking with other groups in other countries using the Internet in ways that was not possible before the Internet existed. This approach may also include actions such as virtual sit-ins, hacktivism, and other virtual civil disobedience methods.

The practitioner, when approaching a practice situation, can use the framework to orient his or her strategy. He or she can evaluate the level of technology and degree of conflict and arrive at the appropriate choice of action.

This book is an introduction to an exciting new form of social work practice that has important ramifications for the future of the profession. It includes cutting-edge research, important theoretical contributions and ideas and thoughts from practitioners.

COMMUNITIES AND NONPROFIT ORGANIZATIONS ON THE INTERNET: THE STATE OF THE ART

Is it possible to have a sense of community on the Internet? Can groups of people who meet only in cyberspace survive as viable communities? What are the consequences for society, and for our sense of belonging? What are the implications for social work practice, and in particular, for advocacy and activism?

With the information highway's restructuring of our society and economy, social work advocates and activists are faced with new challenges. In many ways we have to reinvent our practice knowledge and skills to be effective in the new economy. Just as the early social workers emerged and defined their practice within the Industrial Revolution, today's social workers must reinvent their practice to work within the Information Revolution.

Social work has come to a crossroads. If we are to continue the profession's long commitment to political activity for the goals of social and economic justice, we must develop and adopt techniques to support our practice. Part 1 of this book will illustrate why new technology is an important ingredient of modern social change strategies and how this dovetails with our notions of community. It will go on to explore the state of the art of Internet use in advocacy, both for communities and for nonprofit organizations. We conclude that extensive research is needed to establish and develop this field.

Katherine Boland, Jennifer Bartron, and John McNutt outline the importance of establishing practice wisdom, foundation knowledge, and practice knowledge for Internet use in advocacy in chapter 2. This establishes the grounds for discussion of how social workers can build a foundation of general knowledge for advocacy practice. They conclude that the development of new technology-based and technology-enhanced practice methods is important and timely. Generally, however, they find that the field of electronic advocacy lacks research, and that this research is necessary in order to propel electronic advocacy.

Chapter 3 provides a quick tour of the history of our notions of community, bringing us to its latest development, the Internet. Steven Hick and Emily Reich explore the questions "Can we have community on the Net? What does it mean? What does it look like? What trade-offs and gains have been made?" They see the emergence of a new "public sphere" online, and the promotion of the Internet as both an elixir for all our ills and an harbinger of many more. They believe that the ability to develop a sense of community through the new medium is key for virtual activism or electronic advocacy. As the other chapters in this book will illustrate, the tools of the Internet clearly are priceless to an advocacy campaign. If electronic community activism is going to succeed, however—if communities of people are going to come together with shared concerns to act for social change—then it must be possible to develop a sense of community on the Internet. In the end, the authors conclude that although online communities may provide a way to recapture some of the bonds among people in our society, those connections are still not as valued as those made face to face.

In chapter 4, Ryan Turner examines the role of nonprofit organizations in engaging Americans in the use of new technology. He believes that the nonprofit sector serves as the main valve for American public discourse and civic activity.

Turner's chapter explores how nonprofit agencies use technology to enhance their capacity to fulfill their missions and address organizational needs. He details how nonprofits are using newer information- and communications-technology tools, including e-mail and Web sites, every day to leverage limited resources and increase their scope, visibility, and influence.

He concludes that most of the nonprofit field's emphasis concerning technology has been on its use for various operational and administrative tasks, with relatively little emphasis on its intersection with public policy activities. Finally, Turner outlines how his organization, OMBWatch, is examining this intersection of technology and public policy to gain knowledge about and inform research into this area.

The purpose of chapter 5 is to discuss the role of the Internet in educating social work practitioners as advocates. Steve Wernet believes that practitioners need a full array of skills upon which to draw to be successful as advocates for social change. Technology skills—Internet use in particular—is but one practice skill for social workers. In conjunction with other skills, technology skills are becoming increasingly important for the competent social worker. In this chapter, Wernet discusses advocacy as an area of professional practice, the concept of community, and curricular design for educating advocates.

Notes

1. David Noble, in *Progress Without People: New Technology, Unemployment and the Message of Resistance* (1997), discusses how the information highway and "labour saving" technology have deskilled and displaced human labor.

2. Andrew Feenberg, in *Critical Theory of Technology* (1991), discusses how instrumental and substantive theories share a "take it or leave it" attitude toward technology, and hence seek only to place a boundary around it, rather than to transform it and use it in ways that provide something of positive human value.

3. The Istook Amendment was an attempt to reduce the ability of nonprofit organizations to engage in advocacy.

4. This is a modification of a typology developed by McNutt and Menon (2001).

Suggested Readings

Bennett, D., & P. Fielding. 1999. *The Net effect: How cyber-advocacy is changing the political landscape.* Merrifield, Va.: E-Advocates Press.

Bowen, C. 1996. *Modem nation: The handbook of grassroots activism on line.* New York: Times Books.

Ebo, B. (ed.). 1998. *The cyberghetto or cybertopia: Race, class, gender and marginalization in cyberspace.* New York: Praeger.

Epstein, I. 1981. Advocates on advocacy: An exploratory study. *Social Work Research and Abstracts* 17 (1): 5–12.

Ezell, Mark. 1991. Administrators as advocates. *Administration in Social Work* 15 (4): 1–18.

———. 1993. The political activity of social workers: A post-Reagan update. *Journal of Sociology and Social Welfare* 20 (4): 81–97.

———. 1994. Advocacy practice of social workers. *Families in Society* 75 (1): 36–46.

Feenberg, A. 1991. *Critical theory of technology.* New York: Oxford University Press.

FitzGerald, E., & J. G. McNutt. 1999. Electronic advocacy in policy practice: A framework for teaching technologically based practice. *Journal of Social Work Education* 35 (3): 331–41.

Garvin, C., & F. Cox. 2001. A history of community organization since the Civil War with special reference to oppressed communities. In *Strategies of community intervention* (6th ed.), ed. J. Rothman, J. L. Erlich, & J. E. Tropman, 65–100. Itasca, Ill.: F. E. Peacock.

Grobman, G. M., & G. B. Grant. 1998. *The non-profit Internet handbook.* Harrisburg, Pa.: White Hat Communications.

Hafner, K., & M. Lyon. 1996. *Where wizards stay up late: The origins of the Internet.* New York: Simon & Schuster.

Halpin, E. F., & S. M. Fisher. 1998. *The use of the Internet by the European Parliament for the promotion and protection of human rights.* Luxembourg: European Parliament.

Haynes, K. S., & J. S. Mickelson. 2000. *Affecting change.* (4th ed.). Needham, Mass.: Allyn and Bacon

Hick, S., E. F. Halpin, & E. Hoskins. 2000. *Human rights and the Internet.* London: Macmillan.

Hick, S. & E. Halpin. 2001. Children's rights and the Internet. *The Annals of the American Academy of Political and Social Science* 575: 56–70.

Hoff, M., & J. G. McNutt (eds.). 1994. *The global environmental crisis: Implications for social welfare and social work.* Aldershot, U.K.: Avebury.

Langman, L., D. Morris, J. Zalewski, E. Ignacio, & C. Davidson. 2000. *Globalization, domination and cyberactivism.* Paper presented at Internet Research 1.0: The First Conference of the Association of Internet Researchers, 14–17 September, Lawrence, Kan.

Loader, B. 1997. *The governance of cyberspace: Politics, technology and global restructuring.* London: Routledge.

McNutt, J.G. 2000a. Coming perspectives in the development of electronic advocacy for social policy practice. *Critical Social Work* 1 (1). Available at http://core.ecu.edu/socw/csw/. Retrieved on 26 November 2001.

————. 2000b. *The Internet and non-profit advocacy: Patterns of Web-based on-line advocacy in different organizational fields.* Paper presented at the International Society for Third-Sector Research biennial conference, "The third sector: For what and for whom?" 5–8 July, Dublin, Ireland.

McNutt, J. G., & K. M. Boland. 1998. Teaching about advocacy and the Internet: Strategies for social welfare policy courses. *Social Welfare Policy: The Newsletter of the Social Welfare Policy and Practice Group* 4 (1): 3–6.

————. 1999. Electronic advocacy by non-profit organizations in social welfare policy. *Non-Profit and Voluntary Sector Quarterly* 28 (4): 432–451.

————. 2000. *Nonprofit advocacy in the cyber-commons: A study of technologically sophisticated non-profit organizations.* Paper presented at the twenty-ninth annual meeting of the Association of Voluntary Action Scholars, 15–18 November, New Orleans, La.

McNutt, J. G., & G. Menon. 2001. *A conceptual framework for classifying electronic advocacy: Implications for social work education.* Paper presented at the Council on Social Work Education annual program meeting, 8–11 March, Dallas, Tex.

Milward, H. B., & L. O. Snyder. 1996. Electronic government: Linking citizens to public organizations through technology. *Journal of Public Administration Research and Theory* 6 (2): 261–275.

Noble, D. 1995. *Progress without people: New Technology, unemployment and the message of resistance.* Toronto: University of Toronto Press.

Norris, D. F. 1999. Leading edge technologies and their adoption: Lessons from U.S. cities. In *Information technology and computer applications in public administration: Issues and trends,* ed. G. D. Garson, 137–156. Harrisburg, Pa.: Idea Group.

Price, T. 2000. *Cyberactivism: Advocacy groups and the Internet.* Washington, D.C.: Foundation for Public Affairs.

Queiro-Tajalli, I., & J. G. McNutt. 1997. Varieties of technology-related practice. Unpublished manuscript, School of Social Work, Indiana University, Indianapolis.

Rothman, J. 2001. Approaches to community intervention. In *Strategies of community intervention,* ed. J. Rothman, J. L. Erlich, & J. E. Tropman, 27–64. Itasca, Ill.: F. E. Peacock.

Santana, B. 1997. Introducing the technophobia/technophilia debate. Some comments on the information age. Available at http://www.gsels.ucla.edu/courses/ed253a/beatriz.htm. Retrieved September 21, 1998.

Schuler, D. 1994. Community networks: Building a new participatory medium. *Communications of the ACM* 37 (1): 39–51.

————. 1996. *New community networks: Wired for change.* Reading, Mass.: Addison-Wesley.

Schwartz, E. 1996. *NetActivism: How citizens use the Internet.* Sebastopol, Calif.: O'Reilly.

Smith, M. R., & L. Marx. 1994. *Does technology drive history? The dilemma of technological determinism.* Cambridge: MIT Press.

Specht, H., & M. Courtney. 1994. *Unfaithful angels.* New York: Free Press.

Trattner, W. 1994. *From poor law to welfare state* (5th ed.). New York: Free Press.

Turner, R. 1998. *Democracy at work: Non-profit use of Internet technology for public policy purposes.* Washington, D.C.: OMBWatch.

Warren, R. L. 1972. *The community in America* (rev. ed.). Chicago: Rand McNally.

West, D. M., & R. Francis. 1996. Electronic advocacy: Interest groups and public policy making. *PS: Political Science & Politics* 29 (2): 25–29.

Chapter 2

Social Work Advocacy and the Internet

The Knowledge Base

Katherine M. Boland

Jennifer Bartron

John McNutt

INTRODUCTION

Advocacy has been a proud aspect of the social work tradition, as social workers have always been involved in the struggle for a socially and economically just society. Internet-based advocacy techniques have the potential to transform this area of social work practice. This chapter will develop an appreciation of the role of advocacy within the social work profession and will discuss of the methodology of Internet-based advocacy. It will discuss the current knowledge base following Siporin's (1975) framework for describing the knowledge base of practice (practice wisdom, foundation knowledge, and practice knowledge) and drawing on recent research findings.

ADVOCACY IN SOCIAL WORK PRACTICE

Social work has a long-standing commitment to the goals of social justice and equality. Much of our work to relieve human suffering and enhance community conditions involves challenging the dominant social, political, and economic forces. Critical examination of societal values and institutions (and efforts to reshape such norms) "is a logical outgrowth of social work practice" (Haynes & Mickelson 2000, 2).

Some critics have questioned our loyalty to this component of social work practice. Specht and Courtney (1994), in condemning the profession's trend toward private psychotherapeutic practice, argue that "social work had abandoned its mission to help the poor and oppressed and to build commonality" (4). Other voices within the profession disagree. Ezell (1991, as cited in Saunders 1998), for example, found that half of the clinical social workers he studied engaged in lobbying activity occasionally, whereas one in fifteen reported lobbying decision makers frequently. Additionally, 55 percent of macro-level practitioners reported conducting advocacy practice on the job (Ezell 1991, as cited in Saunders 1998). Jansson (1999) also argues that policy practice is part of social work practice and that all social workers need these skills.

Social work advocacy practice can take many forms, commonly denoted as case advocacy, legislative advocacy, and public policy education (Saunders 1998). *Case advocacy* involves working with individuals (clients) to enforce legal rights or ensure access to service. *Legislative advocacy,* also known as *lobbying,* is characterized by efforts to promote a particular point of view on pending legislation. It can include direct appeals to decision makers as well as appeals to the public. The latter is referred to as *grassroots lobbying* while the former is called *direct lobbying* (Smucker 1999). Lobbying activity can target legislative bodies, formal and informal groups, administrative agencies, staff, and individuals (Arons 1999; Jansson 1999; Saunders 1998; Smucker 1999) *Public policy education* focuses on distributing documentation intended to inform the political process. Whereas lobbying involves promoting partisan views, public policy education is restricted to nonpartisan views. It encourages legislators and the general public to draw their own conclusions from relevant research, impact analysis, and expert testimony (Saunders 1998). The remaining category (usually referred to as *cause advocacy*) is more clearly tied to public policy.

Advocacy is not a form of practice restricted to social work. Nonprofit groups, social activists, governmental organizations, and profit-making entities act to protect their interests in the policy process. The advocacy approaches employed by these groups vary, from traditional strategies such as telephone calls, letter writing, and face-to-face meetings with policy makers, to innovative strategies involving the Internet. Sturtevant's (1998) study found, through in-depth interviews with executive directors of charitable nonprofits in Michigan, that personal and professional relationships with policy makers and their staffs, as well as the synergy made possible though working and networking with other nonprofit organizations, is key to the success of advocacy. Therefore, regardless of whether the Internet is used, relationships and networks continue to be key ingredients of advocacy.

THE RISE OF INTERNET ADVOCACY

Internet-based advocacy, which includes e-mail–based strategies, Web-based tactics, and other approaches, is a relatively recent addition to the methodological toolkit. The shifting dynamics within the political landscape and the availability of new tools are significant factors in the emergence and growth of this new form of practice.

A thorough discussion of the shifts affecting the political or policy process is beyond the scope of this paper (see FitzGerald & McNutt 1999; McNutt 1996). In broad terms, however, the economic sphere is transitioning from a service-based to an information-based orientation in the context of a global marketplace (Wilson 1996). The social sphere is characterized by the erosion of traditional patterns of family and community involvement (Snyder 1996) and calls for the abolition of historical systems of social support and the enforcement of "personal responsibility" (Wilson 1996). The political environment has undergone striking changes as the governments around the world have devolved the funding and administration of social programs to lower levels of government (FitzGerald & McNutt 1999). In short, the welfare state is rapidly being eroded. State and local decision-making bodies have inherited significant authority over critical administrative processes they lack the technical expertise to manage (Sherraden, Slosar, Wakefield, Sherraden, & Huhn 1999).

Electronic advocacy is increasingly being used to link people around the world to address this changing political and policy landscape. It is revolutionizing the ways people engage in advocacy, including community organization and policy practice. Currently there are three classifications of techniques that social workers and others are using to facilitate advocacy and organizing work.

- ◆ *Web-based techniques* include Web sites and Webcasting. Web sites, which are passive strategies, can serve as "virtual libraries." As resource sites for news, advocacy alerts, information, and related links, or as extensions of organizations' fund-raising activities, they require the constituents' initiative to access the information. Webcasting, a more active Web-based approach, requires the recipient to install software on his or her system to receive material transmitted over the Internet.
- ◆ *E-mail–based tools* are active strategies. Discussion lists, distribution lists, e-mail to individuals, and Internet-relay chat are especially effective for quickly distributing and exchanging materials with a targeted audience.
- ◆ *Other approaches* consist of the remaining applications. Some are more commonplace, such as fax, fax on demand, and conference calls. Others are more emergent: video-teleconferencing, streaming video, and so forth. Future methodologies include neural networks, data mining, and data warehousing. The common factor among all of these tools is the use of technologically advanced equipment to facilitate communication with constituencies and stakeholders.

The implications of developments in the political realm and the advent of Internet-based tools are changing how advocacy and organizing work is accomplished. The restructuring of the policy milieu compromises the potency of our traditional advocacy tools and techniques (FitzGerald & McNutt 1999; McNutt 2000c). Our most enduring practices, which were largely developed and tested in fundamentally different economic, social, and political contexts, are no longer sufficient to achieve our goals (FitzGerald & McNutt 1999). The availability of the Internet as an instrument for communication is transforming the ways in which people network and exchange information and ideas. The resulting synergy signals the opportunity for the "creation and transmission of a new practice technology" (McNutt, Caron, Domingo, & McDonough 2000, 1).

Within this context it is essential that practitioners develop a system of advocacy practice in cyberspace that is based on research and builds on the knowledge of past experience. The nature of the political environment and the social policy enterprise are changing. If our interests and values are to prevail, we will need to be effective in the coming debate on the nature of social welfare.

TOWARD A KNOWLEDGE-BASED SOCIAL WORK ADVOCACY PRACTICE

Siporin's (1975) framework for describing the knowledge base of practice includes practice wisdom, foundation knowledge, and practice knowledge. This establishes the base for the discussion of how social workers can work toward a knowledge base for advocacy practice. Generally, the field of electronic advocacy is lacking research, and what is available tends to be case studies. Given this, it is necessary to formulate the knowledge base from practice wisdom.

Practice Wisdom

Siporin (1975) identified the accumulation of *practice wisdom* as a key step in the formation of knowledge-based practice. Most of the current knowledge base consists of practice wisdom, which is likely to remain the case until more research is done on electronic advocacy. Practice wisdom, or lessons learned in the field, tends to revolve around three primary issues: efficiency, civic engagement, and inclusiveness.

Numerous case studies have documented the efficiencies of using the Internet for advocacy (Bennett and Fielding 1999; Schwartz 1996). Technological advances allow for cheaper, faster, more manageable avenues of conducting the work of advocacy twenty-four hours a day, seven days a week. Fax and e-mail techniques can facilitate the distribution of written materials to supporters. Online databases and discussion groups can be used to gather tactical information with relative ease, while mapping and geographic information system (GIS) programs, community databases, and statistical packages are powerful tools for supporting complex data analysis by small groups or individuals (McNutt 2000a,c). Web sites can be used to conduct online fund raising, to attract volunteers (McNutt 2000a,c), and to post information, best practices examples, position papers, and other materials from groups throughout the world (Krause, Stein, & Clark 1998; Jansson 1999; Schwartz 1996).

The potential of conveying complex information to a large number of geographically dispersed recipients creates opportunities for civic engagement in political activities (Schwartz 1996). Community organizing and outreach activities, as well as campaign work such as coordinating strategy, issuing calls to action, and distributing legislative alerts can be strengthened by combinations of e-mail and Web-based efforts (Turner 1998). Internet communication also shifts attention from the speaker to the content of his or her message, which might ultimately refocus the political discussion on ideas and issues (Johnson & Codron 1998). These tools create avenues for individuals and groups who have not historically participated in the policy process to have a voice.

Representatives from minority groups, and people who have not have participated in the past, may join the computer-mediated dialogue. While Johnson and Codron (1998) spoke of electronic advocacy's enabling greater political participation
from typically underrepresented groups, the Mellman Group (1999) noted that "the
potential for online activism and fundraising is vast, bringing a new and diverse
generation to the effort" (4). Breslau (2000) commented that "partisanship, religion,
geography, race, gender, and other traditional political divisions are giving way to a
new standard—wiredness—as an organizing principle for political and social attitudes" (10).

Indeed, "wiredness" may be a critical factor in our advocacy practice. Queiro-
Tajalli and McNutt (1998) caution that information poverty, or the digital divide,
threatens to exclude groups who lack either the opportunity to develop computer
skills or access to advanced equipment and networks. Data from the U.S. Department of Commerce (McConnaughey, Everette, Reynolds, & Lader 1999) suggest
that the seriousness of the problem cannot be overemphasized. These marginalized
groups will not be positioned to participate fully in emerging political activity
(Queiro-Tajalli and McNutt 1998). Breslau (2000) described research indicating that
despite "limited access to computers and the Net, nonwhites are on the whole more
optimistic than whites about the future benefits of technology" (8). This information, which was gathered from nonwhite, low-income youth, suggests that young
minority people recognize the opportunities accessible through new media.

Clearly, practitioner-generated wisdom adds to our understanding of the strategies that can be successful. These examples also provide much-needed inspiration
to continue our work. However, these lessons do not comprehensively enhance social work practice because they fail to contribute to a systematic body of knowledge
and theory to guide our practice (Specht and Courtney 1994).

Foundation Knowledge

Social scientists (Bimber 1998a,b; Davis 1999; Hill & Hughes 1998; Selnow
1994, 1998) have begun to create a base of foundation knowledge that supports this
new practice. This growing body of literature is too extensive to reviewed here in
full, but we will consider some of the more pertinent literature.

As the empirical foundation has grown in the areas of the use and effectiveness
of electronic advocacy techniques, so too has the research regarding the context in
which these methodologies are applied. There is some disagreement among scholars as to the degree of influence that the Internet will have on the political system.
Some argue that politics will be changed but the major features of the current system might not be completely altered (Davis 1999; Hill & Hughes 1998; Selnow
1998). Others disagree, arguing that politics as we know it is a thing of the past
(Morris 1999). The Internet will fundamentally alter the relationships and behavior
within our political institutions. Some scholars have considered the ways in which
innovations in technology have fueled new ways for citizens to become involved in
social issues (Breslau 2000; Katz 1997; Mellman Group 1999).

In 1997, *Wired Magazine* conducted a "Digital Citizen survey" (Katz 1997) in order to "attempt to understand and quantify how technological changes are transforming our political attitudes" (Breslau 2000, 2). The survey sought to understand the degree to which the general public was "connected"; the researchers sought to find a relationship between subjects' connectedness and their opinions, knowledge, and involvement in political issues (Breslau 2000). The results demonstrated that those who were

> classified as "superconnected" or "connected" turned out—by stunning margins—to be better educated, better informed, more opinionated, and more likely to believe in democracy, diversity, and the power of markets. They were also more likely to have faith in the future and to vote. (Breslau 2000, 4)

Katz (1997) called these connected individuals *Digital Citizens* and predicted that they would become a growing political force. Based on more recent research, Breslau (2000) has indicated that this indeed seems to be occurring, as political institutions and officials are making progress in assimilating technology. This finding seems to be corroborated by the online fund-raising success of some candidates, as reported in the media. In addition, a survey by Dataquest (Pastore 1999) found that "By Election Day, November 7, 2000, 70 percent of voting age individuals will have Internet access . . . [furthermore,] 12 percent of Web users regularly visits sites about political candidates" (1). Not all of this is completely positive for activism, but there are some positive implications.

Public opinion about technology also seems to have changed over the past few years (Breslau 2000). Although Katz's 1997 research reflected ambivalence toward the benefits of technology, more recent research has shown that the majority of those surveyed reported moderate to high personal advantages due to technological advancements of the past decade (Breslau 2000). Growing acceptance of the benefits of technology among the public mirrors the increasing use of electronic advocacy techniques described previously in this chapter.

The Mellman Group's (1999) study of "socially engaged Internet users," individuals who report contributing time, talents, or money to organizations working on social issues, identified numerous salient issues for online philanthropy and activism. The Group found that the pool of potential socially engaged Internet users is at least as large as the direct-mail pool, and that these users tend to be younger than those in the direct-mail pool. Online activists also tend to reflect greater political diversity than those in the direct-mail universe, which tends to be composed mostly of Democrats (Mellman Group 1999). Despite this large, growing pool of socially engaged Internet users, most organizations in the study had not recognized the opportunities in fund raising, activism, volunteer recruitment, and communication made possible by the new media (Mellman Group 1999).

Research by Selnow (1994, 1998) addressed the change in election results caused by the new techniques. Although his analysis is cautious, he nonetheless documents the way in which stable political institutions can be altered by technological change.

The foundation knowledge base for electronic advocacy will continue to grow as cyberspace gains in credibility as a topic of research. This knowledge must be repackaged for use in social work practice. The Internet is having an impact on political participation and opening new avenues for citizens to become politically involved. Social work advocates must recognize this trend and realize that the people who may support their issues are likely online, and that the political and policy decision makers are increasingly responsive to Internet-based initiatives.

Practice Knowledge

Establishing practice knowledge is the third stage of Siporin's (1975) framework. Social work, as a profession, has endeavored to build a research-based practice since Abraham Flexner's scathing criticism in 1915 (Specht & Courtney 1994). We have generated a considerable body of research literature concerning the contexts of practice and the worth of practice interventions (Austin 1991, 1998). Building from collective intelligence and experience, we can develop a body of practice knowledge: a set of "empirically validated principles that are derived through careful specification, testing and evaluation" (McNutt, Caron, et al. 2000, 2) that will support the continuation of our advocacy efforts.

Literature pertaining to social work's use of these techniques is largely descriptive, exploring the presence or absence of various techniques in the practice arsenals of specific organizations. In fact, many of the strongest voices within the field of electronic advocacy are not members of the social work profession. To develop a richer understanding of the use of electronic advocacy techniques in policy work, we must draw upon findings from other fields within the advocacy tradition. For the sake of analytical clarity, we will divide the works into the categories of studies of utilization, studies of effectiveness, and studies of process.

Studies of Utilization

McNutt and Boland (1999) examined the use of these techniques by state and local chapters of the National Association of Social Workers, a national professional membership association in the United States. Data generated through this effort support the hypothesis that techniques that are more familiar, less complex, and more compatible with the organization's activities were more likely to be incorporated into the affiliate's practice. Furthermore, expertise, expense, and equipment present barriers to the use of technological innovations in the chapters' policy work. At the time the data were collected, only 27.7 percent of the chapters maintained Web sites, one of the most advanced and expensive tools discussed in this piece of research. Interestingly, almost two-thirds of the chapters (63.8 percent) reported plans to develop Web sites in the future. This finding suggests that the respondents understood the value that this tool would add to their work, and were preparing to commit the required fiscal and human resources to the effort (McNutt & Boland 1999).

A study of the Public Interest Research Groups (McNutt & Boland 2000) revealed a similar pattern. Less sophisticated techniques (particularly e-mail–type techniques, fax transmittals, and simple Web sites) were more likely to be used than more sophisticated techniques. Subsequent studies of child advocacy organizations (McNutt, Keaney, Crawford, Schubert, & Sullivan 2001) and local advocacy organizations in Boston (McNutt, Burke, Boland, Barton, & Rice 2001) obtained comparable results. McNutt (2000b) found little difference among various sectors' Web-based advocacy technology use.

Zelwietro's (1998) investigation of the Internet's importance in the work of environmental organizations found that these groups had recognized the utility of these techniques, but had not yet taken steps to maximize their potential. Turner's (1998) examination of the use of technology for nonprofit public policy activities determined that nonprofit groups are currently using only a small number of the existing technologies and applications.

Researchers have also studied other electronic advocacy techniques, such as the practice of Web-based electronic fund raising. McNutt, Bartron, and Boland (1999) used content analysis to examine the online fund-raising activities of 183 United Ways with individual Web sites. They found that each of the Web sites incorporated at least fund-raising appeals or advertising strategies. Far fewer demonstrated use of mid-level strategies, such as offering download-ready pledge forms, or more sophisticated processes of accepting online contributions. Generally, the larger, more well-connected organizations tended to use more sophisticated techniques (McNutt, Bartron, et al. 1999).

Studies of Effectiveness

Several studies have addressed perceived effectiveness, as well as other aspects of effectiveness. Rees (1998, 1999) focused her attention on organizations known for effective advocacy. Looking at the techniques used at the national level by these groups, she noted the current use of Internet-based techniques by some organizations and predicted the expansion of the use of online advocacy techniques to influence policy.

Research data supports Rees's suggestion. Studies conducted by Bonner and Associates/American University (Bonner 1998), OMBWatch (Lemmon & Carter 1998) and Davis (1999) looked at the reactions of congressional offices to e-mail messages from stakeholders. The three studies appeared to agree that e-mail was not yet as effective as traditional techniques and that nonconstituents' e-mail was less effective than that of constituents.

OMBWatch's 1998 survey of congressional offices explored how modes of constituent communication were viewed by the offices. Respondents indicated that the most effective communications were, in descending order, personal posted letters, in-person meetings and telephone calls, and facsimile and e-mail communications. At the federal level, data indicate that e-mail communications were not considered to be as powerful as more traditional advocacy techniques (Lemmon and Carter 1998).

At the state level, a slightly different pattern emerged in McNutt, Lima, et al.'s (1999) study of acceptance of Internet-based technologies by Massachusetts's legislative offices. Asked to rate the importance attributed to e-mail messages, the offices gave greater weight to electronic messages than traditional letters. This effort also revealed that although legislators do believe that the Internet is impacting the legislative process in Massachusetts, lawmakers often do not appear to completely trust the material they find online. Furthermore, most of the legislators failed to use their state-supplied Web sites to convey more than superficial information to constituents (McNutt, Lima, et al. 1999).

If Massachusetts lawmakers made little use of Web sites, candidates in the 1998 congressional election took a different position. Ninety-two of the 133 candidates included a Web site in their campaign strategies. Studying these Web sites, Goff and Dulio (no date) found that 72 percent used their sites to solicit campaign contributions. The sophistication and distribution of the fund-raising techniques used by political candidates were fairly consistent with McNutt, Bartron, et al.'s (1999) findings pertaining to the United Way.

Johnson and Codron (1998), who conducted a textual analysis of the use of the Internet, have also studied the effectiveness of electronic advocacy techniques by politicians and committees. Studying 120 political sites viewable during January 1996, these researchers found that home pages can be invaluable for political promotion as well as for recruiting membership. Home pages create opportunities for the dissemination of in-depth information and explanation that simply are not possible through more traditional forms of mass media. By featuring factual information rather than persuasive mass-media messages on their sites, organizations provide users with targeted information that may be otherwise difficult to access.

Another electronic advocacy tool, banner advertisements, has been studied in the contexts of political campaigning and the promotion of social engagement (Bennett & Fielding 1999; Mellman Group 1999). For instance, E-Voter 98 studied the effect of negative banner ads on candidate approval ratings in the 1998 Pataki-Vallone race. They found a relationship between the use of these banner ads and the decline of Pataki's approval ratings in opinion polls. Banner ads were found to be less effective at driving traffic to new sites than word of mouth, search engines, and offline advertising strategies (Mellman Group 1999).

Studies of Process

Menon (2000) studied the process of advocacy in a content analysis of an issue-focused discussion group. This group of geographically diverse consumers, caregivers, and mental health professionals transformed from "just another discussion group" to a "virtual community" through the targeted use of electronic advocacy techniques. The group made effective use of the new media to mobilize a campaign for case advocacy, while it also raised awareness of mental health issues (Menon 2000).

Another study, by Wittig and Schmitz (1996), traced the course of online advocacy for homeless persons through a community network, providing an examination of the issues and stages of development. The study demonstrated that affected groups and advocates can work together using network resources and suggested that these efforts can result in community change.

Brainard and Siplon (2000) studied health care advocacy groups. They found important differences between traditional, health-related advocacy organizations and those that were more emergent in the use of cyberspace. The latter used the medium in a more sophisticated manner.

CONCLUSION

The present body of knowledge lends support to Turner's (1998) assertion that "the line between *use* of technology and *effective use* is a thin one" (3; emphasis Turner's). Advocates are using technology to advance their missions. Organizations have demonstrated growing knowledge of these techniques, and groups of all sizes are gaining competency in applying Internet-based techniques to execute familiar activities. Larger, more well connected organizations tend to use more sophisticated techniques, yet few entities have explored the application of these tools to novel activities. This suggests that we have not yet fully embraced the essential advantages of newer forms of electronic communication.

Social work has come to a crossroads. If we are to continue the profession's long commitment to political activity for the goals of social and economic justice, we must develop and adopt techniques to support our practice. Electronic advocacy methodologies are surely important ingredients of modern social-change strategies. However, if we are to integrate electronic tools into our advocacy toolbox, we must take steps to overcome the profession's aversion to technology and develop a social work–focused knowledge base.

A number of pioneers have begun the work of building this knowledge base. The continuing growth of this body of practice will require further study in a number of areas. These areas include

- Development of mechanisms to gauge accurately the impact of Internet-based tools on civic participation;
- Measurement of the extent and variety of direct and indirect advocacy techniques;
- Exploration of similarities and differences among efforts at local, state, and federal levels of government;
- Documentation of advocacy activity in nonpolitical environments;
- Comparison of the efforts of for-profit entities, government organizations, and formal and informal third-sector groups;
- Scans of emerging methodologies and political situations; and
- Research on the dissemination of these technologies within organizational fields and within individual organizations.

We are entering a new era of social work practice. The development of new technology-based and technology-enhanced practice methods is important and timely. Theoretical and empirical advanced in telehealth and administrative computing must be matched by similar developments in policy and advocacy practice.

Suggested readings

Arons, D. F. 1999. *Nonprofit management and advocacy: Examining barriers to democracy.* Paper presented at the twenty-eighth annual meeting of the Association for Research on Nonprofit Organizations and Voluntary Action, 4–6 November, Arlington, Va.

Austin, D. M. 1991. *Building social work knowledge for effective services and policies: A plan for research development.* Austin: University of Texas School of Social Work.

———. 1998. *A report on progress in the development of research resources in social work.* Washington, D.C.: Institute for Advancement of Social Work Research.

Bennett, D., & P. Fielding. 1999. *The Net effect: How cyber-advocacy is changing the political landscape.* Merrifield, Va.: E-Advocates Press.

Bimber, B. 1998a. *The Internet and citizen communication with government: Does the medium matter?* Paper presented at the 1998 meeting of the American Political Science Association, 3–6 September, Boston, Mass.

———. 1998b. The Internet and political mobilization. *Social Science Computer Review* 16 (4): 391–401.

Bonner, J. 1998. The Internet and grassroots lobbying: The next wave. *Campaigns and Elections* 19 (9): 46–48.

Brainard, L. A., & P. D. Siplon. 2000. *Cyberspace challenges to mainstream advocacy groups: The case of healthcare activism.* Paper presented at the annual meeting of the American Political Science Association, 31 August–2 September, Washington, D.C.

Breslau, K. 2000. One nation interconnected. *Wired* 8 (5): 136–154.

Davis, R. 1999. *The Web of politics: The Internet's impact on the American political system.* New York: Oxford University Press.

Ezell, M. 1991. Administrators as advocates. *Administration in Social Work* 15 (4): 1–18.

FitzGerald, E., & J. G. McNutt. 1999. Electronic advocacy in policy practice: A framework for teaching technologically based practice. *Journal of Social Work Education* 35 (3): 331–341.

Goff, D., & D. Dulio. n.d. *Untangling the Web: Internet use in the 1998 election.* Available at [http://www.american.edu/academic.depts.spa/ccps/article.htm]. Retrieved on 1 May 2000.

Haynes, K. S., & J. S. Mickelson. 2000. *Affecting change: Social workers in the political arena* (3rd ed.). White Plains, N.Y.: Longman.

Hill, K. A., & J. E. Hughes. 1998. *Cyberpolitics: Citizen activism in the age of the Internet.* Lanham, Md.: Rowman and Littlefield.

Jansson, B. S. 1999. *Becoming an effective policy advocate: From policy practice to social justice* (3rd ed.). Belmont, Calif.: Brooks/Cole.

Johnson, C., & A. Codron. 1998. Toward a cyberdemocracy: Political promotions on the Internet. *Journal of Non-Profit and Public Sector Marketing* 6 (1): 105–118

Katz, J. 1997. The digital citizen. *Wired* 5 (12). Available at [http://hotwired.lycos.com/special/citizen/index.html]. Retrieved on 26 July 2001.

Krause, A., M. Stein, & J. Clark. 1998. *The virtual activist: A training course.* Netaction. Available at [http://www.netaction.org/training/]. Retrieved on 26 March 1998.

Lemmon, P., & M. Carter. 1998. *Speaking up in the Internet age.* Washington, D.C.: OMBWatch.

McConnaughey, J., D. W. Everette, T. Reynolds, & W. Lader (eds.). 1999. *Falling through the Net: Defining the digital divide.* Washington, D.C.: U.S. Department of Commerce, National Telecommunications and Information Administration.

McNutt, J. G. 1996. National information infrastructure policy and the future of the American welfare state: Implications for the social welfare policy curriculum. *Journal of Social Work Education* 6 (3): 375–388.

————. 2000a. Coming perspectives in the development of electronic advocacy for social policy practice. *Critical Social Work* 1 (1). Available at [http://core.ecu.edu/socw/csw/]. Retrieved on 10 April 2001.

————. 2000b. *The Internet and non-profit advocacy: Patterns of Web-based online advocacy in different organizational fields.* Paper presented at the International Society for Third-Sector Research Biennial Conference, "The third sector: For what and for whom?" 5–8 July, Dublin, Ireland.

————. 2000c. Organizing cyberspace: Strategies for teaching about community practice and technology. *Journal of Community Practice* 7 (1): 95–109.

McNutt, J. G, J. Bartron, & K. M. Boland. 1999. *An empirical study of electronic fundraising activity in a group of non-profits.* Paper presented at the twenty-eighth annual meeting of the Association for Research on Nonprofit Organizations and Voluntary Action, 4–6 November, Arlington, Va.

McNutt, J. C., & K. M. Boland. 1999. Electronic advocacy by non-profit organizations in social welfare policy. *Non-Profit and Voluntary Sector Quarterly* 28 (4): 432–451.

————. 2000. *Nonprofit advocacy in the cyber-commons: A study of technologically sophisticated non-profit organizations.* Paper presented at the twenty-ninth annual meeting of the Association of Voluntary Action Scholars, 15–18 November, New Orleans, La.

McNutt, J. G., K. Burke, K. M. Boland, J. Bartron, & D. Rice. 2001. Wired in Beantown: A study of online advocacy by non-profits in the greater Boston area. In *The impact of information technology on civil society: Working papers from the independent sector's 2001 Spring Research Forum,* 229–244. Washington, D.C.: Independent Sector.

McNutt, J. G., C. Caron, M. H. Domingo, & C. McDonough. 2000. *Reinventing practice for the information age: Implications for social work education.* Paper presented at the Council on Social Work Education annual program meeting, 26–29 February, New York, N.Y.

McNutt, J. G., W. F. Keaney, P. Crawford, L. Schubert, & C. Sullivan. 2001. Going on-line for children: A national study of electronic advocacy by non-profit child advocacy agencies. In *The impact of information technology on civil society: Working papers from the independent sector's 2001 Spring Research Forum,* 213–228. Washington, D.C.: Independent Sector.

McNutt, J. G., J. Lima, K. Penkaukaus, & M. Russoff. 1999. *A study of the impact of Internet-based technologies on the legislative process at the state level.* Paper presented at the twenty-eighth annual meeting of the Association for Research on Nonprofit Organizations and Voluntary Action, 4–6 November, Arlington, Va.

Mellman Group. 1999. *Socially engaged Internet users: Prospects for online philanthropy and activism.* Arlington, Va.: CMS Interactive.

Menon, G. 2000. The 79-cent campaign: The use of online mailing lists for electronic advocacy. *Journal of Community Practice* 8 (3): 73.

Morris, R. 1999. *Vote.com.* Los Angeles, Calif.: Renaissance Books.

Pastore, M. 1999. The Net and the 2000 election. Available at [http://www.cyberatlas.internet.com]. Retrieved on 25 July 2001.

Queiro-Tajalli, I., & J. G. McNutt. 1998. *Information poverty and the Latino community: Implications for social work practice and social work education.* Paper presented at the Council on Social Work Education annual program meeting, 5–8 March, Orlando, Fla.

Rees, S. 1998. *Effective non-profit advocacy.* Washington, D.C.: Aspen Institute/Non-Profit Sector Research Fund. Available at [http://www.aspeninst.org/dir/polpro/NSRF/enpatoc.html]. Retrieved on 8 November 1998.

————. 1999. Strategic choices for nonprofit advocates. *Nonprofit and Voluntary Sector Quarterly* 28 (1): 65–73.

Saunders, M. C. 1998. *Nonprofit advocacy and public policy education.* Paper presented at the twenty-seventh annual meeting of the Association for Research on Nonprofit Organizations and Voluntary Action, 5–7 November, Seattle, Wash.

Schwartz, E. 1996. *NetActivism: How citizens use the Internet.* Sebastopol, Calif.: O'Reilly.

Selnow, G. W. 1994. *High-tech campaigns: Computer technology in political communications.* Westport, Conn.: Praeger.

———. 1998. *Electronic whistle stops: The Impact of the Internet on American politics.* Westport, Conn.: Praeger.

Sherraden, M. S., B. Slosar, H. Wakefield, M. Sherraden, & S. Huhn. 1999. *Innovations in social policy: Faculty, students and practitioners collaboration.* Paper presented at the Council on Social Work Education annual program meeting, 13–16 March, San Francisco, Calif.

Siporin, M. 1975. *Introduction to social work practice.* New York: Macmillan.

Smucker, R. 1999. *The nonprofit lobbying guide* (2nd ed.). Washington, D.C.: Independent Sector.

Snyder, D. P. 1996. The revolution in the workplace: What's happening to our jobs? *The Futurist* 30 (2): 8–13.

Specht, H., & M. E. Courtney. 1994. *Unfaithful angels.* New York: Free Press.

Sturtevant, D. 1998. *Spectator or participant? A study of nonprofits' political advocacy, Part III: Implications.* Paper presented at the twenty-seventh annual meeting of the Association for Research on Nonprofit Organizations and Voluntary Action, 5–7 November, Seattle, Wash.

Turner, R. 1998. *Democracy at work: Non-profit use of Internet technology for public policy purposes.* Washington, D.C.: OMBWatch.

Wilson, W. J. 1996. *When work disappears: The world of the new urban poor.* New York: Knopf.

Wittig, M. A., & J. Schmitz. 1996. Electronic grassroots organizing. *Journal of Social Issues* 52 (1): 53–69.

Zelwietro, J. 1998. The politicization of environmental organizations through the Internet. *Information Society* 14: 45–56.

Chapter 3

Can You Have Community on the Net?

Steven Hick
Emily Reich

ALONE, IN THE MIDDLE OF THE NIGHT, IT IS POSSIBLE TO GAIN AN AMAZING sense of connectedness with seemingly infinite numbers of people around the world and around the corner. In a few simple steps, one can be inundated with information about international, national, and local issues and presented with a number of ways to get involved and take action. In a matter of minutes, one can lobby elected representatives about foreign policy and advocate for a proposed expansion of the local elementary school. Communities coming together to address local concerns or advocate for broad policy changes constitute the foundation of every nation, and now individuals can do all of those things without ever leaving home—or can they? Does participation in online, "keyboard" communities fulfill the same needs as real-life communities? Is the Internet a valid third space for us to grow a healthy public sphere intended to support real community, activism, and advocacy? Is it possible to have real community on the Net? These are a few of the questions this chapter will address.

Despite the ways in which people are coming together through the new mass media, in many other ways, the trends into consumer culture seem to have pulled us farther apart or eroded our sense of community. To begin with, there is less need to be together physically any more. To be entertained, we no longer have to come together at the neighborhood bar or even sit with a group of other people in a movie theater. We can now watch television at home, by ourselves—often with family members watching by themselves on another set in another room!

Similar technologies are making even the nonentertainment areas of our lives—such as working, shopping, and banking—less an experience of interaction with other people. We can work from home via modem without the social interaction of the workplace; we can shop by catalog and even fax our orders in to avoid talking to the live operator; we can bank using automated teller machines instead of waiting in line for a live teller. These used to be realms in which we interacted socially, at least in a minimal way. In general, we are much less connected to our fellow citizens. These changes have given rise to serious questions about the interactions that take place in the forms of communities we have today. Robert Putnam (1995) discusses the decline in connections and civic life, describing how U.S. "social capital" (which he defines as those features of social organization, such as networks, norms, and social trust, that facilitate coordination and cooperation for mutual benefit) seems to be eroding. The title of Putnam's article ("Bowling Alone") comes from the statistics he cites—that from 1980 to 1993, league bowling declined by 40 percent while the number of individual bowlers rose by 10 percent.

The changing nature of community is nothing new. The "good old days" seem only a memory, whatever it was they looked like or whatever we envision as having been a better time. To begin, we can look back over the last centuries and examine how the rise of mass culture and changes in technology have altered our notions of community. We can argue that, although we may gain or lose connections and intimacies with each change, or make trade-offs in the depth and breadth of our relationships and involvements, it is clear that things will continue to change (Doheney-Farina 1996; Smith & Kollock 1999).

Following a quick historic tour through our notions of community, we arrive at the latest development: the Internet. Can we have community on the Net? What does that mean? What does that look like? What trade-offs and gains have we made? We see a new public sphere emerging online and see the Internet promoted as both an elixir for all our ills and the harbinger of many more. The ability to develop a sense of community through the medium of the Internet is key for virtual activism or electronic advocacy. As the other chapters in this book illustrate, the tools of the Internet are clearly valuable to an advocacy campaign. If electronic community activism is going to succeed, however—if communities of people are going to come together with shared concerns to act for social change—then it must be possible to develop a sense of community on the Internet that may be similar or dissimilar to our current conceptions of community belonging.

COMMUNITY ON THE NET

After seeing the importance of interacting with others as the basis for community and a public sphere, we can ask whether technological advances have caused individuals to become more interconnected or whether these forms of communication have made interpersonal relations superficial and homogenized. Are our interactions over the Internet the building blocks of communities? Discussions of the Internet as a form of community and as an area for political and social involvement are divided, with proponents arguing that the interactivity of online participation makes it a step up from the passivity of television watching, and critics arguing that we are only continuing the trend of more artificial interaction and increasing the risk of declining involvement in the real world.

John Coate (1993) of the Whole Earth 'Lectronic Link (WELL), a popular virtual community site, wrote that you often feel a real sense of place while logged in, though it exists "virtually" in each person's imagination while they stare into a CRT screen. It's old because even if the village is virtual, when it's working right it fulfills for people their need for a commons, a neutral space away from work or home where they can conduct their personal and professional affairs. (n.p.)

The virtual space in which people meet is as neutral a ground as one may find. Theoretically, everyone who logs in starts off on equal footing, and as many people can join in as the bandwidth allows. Access to cyberspace is another matter, of course; there are economic (getting online takes money and time) and educational (communication here is mostly via reading and writing) barriers one must overcome to participate. Once the individual gets there, however, cyberspace is everyone's and no one's (Doheny-Farina 1996).

The primary activity in cyberspace is clearly conversation, but of a sort that favors people good with their words rather than good with their mouths. The Internet provides a neutral ground or place for conversation as an alternative to face-to-face interaction. As with many conversations, online discussions sometimes have lulls, but they definitely have their lively moments as well. Online, the conversation is often much more thought out. It is easier for everyone to have a say without being dominated by one or two loud individuals. This can be particularly important for women, who historically have not spoken out as much as their male counterparts in real-life settings.

The "places" themselves are often taken for granted—as long as the techs on the other end keep the system running without any glitches. These places are definitely open in the off-hours, and one can see by the times when responses were posted that people log in and participate at all hours of the day and night. It does not matter what time one checks in—the conversation is always there and always continuing.

Lapachet (1993) also discusses how time is a critical factor in the building and value of virtual communities. The structure of our society, based as it is around schedules of production and consumption, often leaves little time for outside activities that must be squeezed into the few hours left after work and family. Virtual communities offer not only a multitude of topic areas, but also the ability to participate at a convenient time. There is no weekly meeting to catch after work. The meetings happen whenever the participants have time to log in and read the new postings. This time shifting allows participants time to ponder a particularly serious posting or article, and write a coherent response.

Time shifting also allows individuals from different time zones to participate in a discussion together, making it possible for people located continents away from one another to have conversations or work together without schedule disruption. Time shifting allows people to use their time at their convenience, without restriction to externally imposed schedules that do not work with their lives. This may be particularly important to women, who tend to work a "second shift" at home after a full day at a job outside the home.

Oldenburg (1989) pays a good deal of attention to the notion of convenience and our thoughts of our society as a convenience culture, but argues that "convenience" does not exist in ways that matter. If it did, he argues, more necessities would be within easy walking distance and more easily accessible. Online communities have the benefit of being truly convenient. Wherever one is in the world, as long as a computer is nearby, he or she can instantly be back with friends and community members. Even for those who do not meet or communicate with all the people in the virtual community, it is often reassuring to know that there are others like oneself out there, and that there is the sense of being part of a community, even if only imagined. This is similar to what Benedict (1983) describes in his definition of a nation as an imagined political community: "It is imagined because the members of even the smallest nation will never know most of their fellow-members, meet them, or even hear of them, yet in the minds of each lives the image of their communion" (15). This sense of belonging is part of what Sartelle (1992) meant when he wrote of sharing certain practices that demonstrate commitment to the community.

Lapachet (1993) finds that virtual communities fulfill a need for many, providing unique contacts with like-minded individuals who may be difficult to find in the proximate, physical community. Despite the fact that there are many special interest groups in our real lives, we cannot always find people nearby who are interested in the same topics that we are.

Virtual communities provide a forum for discussions with such people. The participants need never leave home and have some control over how the discussion progresses. Additionally, if no forum is already in place for a certain discussion, almost anyone can set up that forum and create a virtual community of his or her own, although the difficulty varies depending on the network.

In studies of other forms of popular culture, we find that culture can seem to be a *substitute for* politics, a way of posing only imaginary solutions to real problems. Under other circumstances, culture can almost become a *rehearsal for* politics, as we try out values and beliefs that are permissible in art but forbidden in social life. Most often, however, it seems as though culture exists as *a form of* politics, providing us with a means of reshaping how individuals and groups think and operate (Szemere 1992). Will cyberspace serve as the ultimate rehearsal space for real involvement, or will the virtual soak up so much of our time and be so much more fulfilling and malleable to our desires that we cease to bother with participating in and shaping the real world?

MASS CULTURE/CONSUMER CULTURE

In discussing changes to community, it is important to look at the rise of mass media and consumer culture and the historical factors that led to their emergence and acceptance. This century has seen radical shifts in communication, interaction, and recreation which have led to what Erenberg (1981) calls a "public dream," a sense of shared experiences and desires that have found expression in mass media.

The shift from a production-based culture to a consumption-based culture has been inextricably linked to advances in technology, which in turn has allowed mass media and mass audiences to develop. In fact, technological advances and the mass media reflect and encourage each other, allowing for the rapid development of both. How have these developments changed our notions of community?

These changes and developments not only have set the stage for mass media but almost seem to have taken on a life of their own. Following the expansionary principles of the market as shaped by the Industrial Revolution, media corporations emerged and mass media took shape as part of corporate structure. The industry became institutionalized and increasingly oriented toward mass audience and consumption. The controlling forces became the values of consumption and the need to consume more and more.

As our society becomes more dominated by mass media and a consumption culture, these questions of consumption and community become more central to the discussion, forcing the question of whether a market is the same thing as a community (Sartelle 1992). Sartelle (1992) found that "Many people search for an experience of real community through popular culture; but being a part of a particular target market cannot satisfy the desire for membership in a community" (83). He explains that the temporary feeling of community does not last much longer than the act of consumption and then fades away. He argues that this is why we continue to consume these things repeatedly, and that "a substitute gratification always remains a substitute, distracting from the real needs and desires but not satisfying them" (Sartelle & Rubio 1993, 5). Clearly, being part of a market is not the same thing as being part of a community.

The world is a very different place than it was a century ago. The traditional ties that made life at the central square or the corner saloon possible have faded in many countries. It is now virtually impossible to have experiences that are not mediated by the whole consumer system. In many ways, the use of technology to promote a mass consumer culture (i.e., advertising) is destructive of our sense of community. Margaret Crawford (1992) writes that "without familiar neighborhoods and extended-family networks to set social standards, suburban families used their possessions as a mark of belonging. The suburb itself was a product: nature and community packaged and sold" (21). Thus, by using the value system established by the consumer culture, these people were able to set up identities that made them part of a community of people. The Internet may provide a means to escape the consumerism and find an identity as a member of a community.

Poster (1995) argues that the issue of the public sphere must be considered in any evaluation of our democracy. Like Oldenberg and others, Poster stresses the importance of "third places" and explicitly implicates the media in their decline. He finds that although there still exist places like New England town halls, coffee houses, parks, and the like, they no longer serve as organizing centers for political discussion and action. He believes that the media, especially television but also other forms of electronic communication, have substituted themselves for older forms of politics and have isolated citizens from one another (Poster 1995). It is as if these shared public images are more important to us than our shared public spaces. This has radically changed what community looks and feels like and how connected we are to each other.

Putnam (1995) shows how voter turnout, church attendance, and union membership are down, as is the percentage of people who say that they trust the government and who attend community meetings. According to Putnam, the number of Americans who report that they had attended a public meeting on town or school affairs in the prior year had fallen by more than one-third (from 22 percent in 1973 to 13 percent in 1993). Similar or greater declines were evident in responses to questions about attending a political rally or speech, serving on a committee of some local organization, and working for a political party.

Overall, he found that Americans' direct engagement in politics and government has fallen steadily and sharply over the last generation, despite the fact that average levels of education—the best individual-level predictor of political participation—have risen sharply throughout this period (1995). He found that every year for the last decade or two, millions more have withdrawn from the affairs of their communities, a loss he feels will have tremendous ramifications.

One possible explanation that Putnam (1995) gives for this erosion is the technological transformation of leisure:

> Television has made our communities (or, rather, what we experience as our communities) wider and shallower. In the language of economics, electronic technology enables individual tastes to be satisfied more fully, but at the cost of the positive social externalities associated with more primitive forms of entertainment. The same logic applies to the replacement of vaudeville by the movies and now of movies by the VCR. The new "virtual reality" helmets that we will soon don to be entertained in total isolation are merely the latest extension of this trend. Is technology thus driving a wedge between our individual interests and our collective interests? It is a question that seems worth exploring more systematically.

Proponents of virtual communities argue that this medium may be the answer to some of the concerns that Putnam expresses and that it is very much different from the passivity involved in television watching and even the utterly personalized entertainment found in virtual-reality applications. In this way, the technology could serve our collective interest. However, some forsee a future in which we are all linked only to our own virtual-reality pods and not involved at all with other people or our real communities.

Perhaps the traditional forms of civic organization, the decay of which we have been tracing, have been replaced by vibrant new organizations. Putnam (1995) points to the increase in membership in many national environmental organizations (such as the Sierra Club) and feminist groups (such as NOW, the National Organization for Women). Yet he finds that despite the fact that Americans may be members of more organizations, they are less involved in them.

Being a member of NOW (writing a check and getting the newsletter) is very different from being in a consciousness-raising (CR) group, picketing, or doing something similar in which one deals with other people face to face and perhaps has a different level of commitment to the group.

The effect of losing the local, public third spaces has a tremendous effect on our commitment to our community and its affairs. Oldenberg (1989) discusses the great decline in public life over the century, pointing to the loss of many of the casual gathering places that existed at mid-century. He also finds that "the average citizen's interest in public or community affairs [has] been aptly described as 'diluted' and 'superficial.' The individual's present relationship to the collective is as empty as it is equitable: community does nothing for them and they do nothing for community" (285). For Oldenberg (1989), these third places were vital to the formation of community, and "their loss makes the discussion and evaluation of online meeting places all the more important and timely" (265).

Is our development of online communities in part a reaction to the loss he describes of so many of our physical gathering places? (Computer conferencing may be considered an alternative to the third-place settings that have vanished over the past fifty years—although it takes a very different form.) Or is our involvement in technologically contrived communities furthering or even causing this decline in the real world, continuing a trend begun by other forms of mass media and commercialization?

Yet, perhaps some people look to television shows and communities of other fans[1] to recapture some of that sense of belonging to a group—even if these examples do seem to be, in contrast to the richer culture of days past, a pathetic stab at achieving real community. The question remains how virtual communities fit into these comparisons of community. Their interactive nature would seem to rank them much higher than the solitary television-viewer's world. However, even though it may feel as if we are participating in an intense group experience, when we look up we are most likely sitting alone—furthermore, it isn't much fun to sit around watching someone else immersed in an online discussion, so real-life associates may tend to feel pushed away by one's online involvement—if there were any real-life associates to begin with.

ONLINE COMMUNITIES

Community involvement, be it online or off, seems to be an essential part of political activism. Social movements need roots in communities, and, at least to some extent, these roots can be achieved online. It remains to be seen just how effective these online communities will be in the political realm; much of this evaluation will need to wait until the hype over the Internet calms down. It will be interesting to see whether involvement in online activism takes the place of or inspires more real-world involvement. Further study may be able to determine whether real-life involvement draws people onto the Net, or those who are already on the Net are "activated" by what they experienced there. If action online leads to inaction in real life then there is ample reason to be concerned.

Technology should not make us lose sight of the goals of a grassroots organization or social movement. The technology is only a tool—a means one may hope to further the ends, but not the be-all and end-all of the group or of an activity. Computer skills cannot replace people skills in these realms, and computers certainly cannot replace people. That said, we are not making an argument that people should not learn computer skills or be able to program computers and understand how they work. Quite to the contrary, we believe that many more people should be able to use these tools and that a wider variety of people should be involved in designing them.

It is important to remember that, despite the fact that we cannot (for the most part and for the time being) see or touch the other people with whom we are interacting online, they are nonetheless real people. The freedom we may feel when we go online—freedom to be more ourselves or to try out entirely different selves—should not depersonalize others. It is very empowering for people who do not feel that their voices can be heard to feel that they are heard on the Internet. Such people should continue to explore the medium as place to speak up and speak out. The rules of "netiquette" must be respected, however, at least to the point that we treat each other with respect. The number of women who report having been harassed online is a large problem that must be addressed. To overcome this, more women need to use the technology and shape its uses and rules. Only then will this new third space be a safe place for feminist activists and others who seek that elusive sense of community.

It is unlikely that online communities will ever take the place of real-life interactions. People clearly need to interact with others. This is why the Internet has become so hugely popular. Information availability is a main draw for many users, but it is really the ability to connect to other people that seem to draw the bulk of the participants. The most successful virtual communities, such as the WELL in Sausalito or The Meta Network in Washington, D.C., combine their online interactions with face-to-face picnics, dinner parties, and other gatherings. Often people who meet in chat rooms or in conference areas develop relationships independently of the medium. Some exchange phone numbers and communicate in that way; others find ways to meet in person.

Many of us have an idealized view of what communities used to be. We imagine that, back in those "simpler days" of front porches and town centers, people were more connected to each other and felt more of a sense of belonging to something. Much of that idea of community may be myth—and many aspects of that community life were repressive. It was hard for people who did not feel as if they fit in. With the Internet, people are building communities where people who are different can find other people just like themselves and make connections with other understanding people. These online spaces provide a free space to work things through.

CONCLUSION

Technology often receives the blame for increased consumerism in society and the erosion of our sense of community. Perhaps we should look beyond technology and examine how our market economy and the resulting profit motive use technology in particular ways to encourage consumerism. This does not preclude the usefulness of technology in promoting other aims, such as building communities or connecting and empowering people. Clearly, virtual communities or online conversation cannot entirely replace face-to-face communication. It does, however, play a significant role for some in creating a kind of "third space" for connecting with other people in ways previously not possible.

Clearly, there are significant differences between offline and online communities, and each has its strengths and weaknesses. While keyboard communities may be a way to recapture some of the interpersonal bonds that some critics fear our society is losing, those connections are still not as valued as those made face to face. With the technology comes new opportunities to expand the base of people with whom one can interact and the potential to find people who are both like-minded and who can offer new perspectives.

Note

1. "Fan reception cannot and does not exist in isolation, but is always shaped through input from other fans and motivated, at least partially, by a desire for further interaction with a larger social and cultural community" (Oldenberg 1989, 76).

Suggested Readings

Benedict, A. 1983. *Imagine communities.* London: Verso Editions.

Coate, J. 1993. *Cyberspace innkeeping: Building online community.* Available at [http://gopher. well.sf.ca.us:70/0/community/innkeeping].

Crawford, M. 1992. The world in a shopping mall. In *Variations on a theme park,* ed. M. Sorkin, 21. New York: Noonday Press.

Doheny-Farina, D. 1996. *The wired neighborhood.* New Haven, Conn.: Yale University Press.

Erenberg, L. A. 1981. *Steppin' out: New York nightlife and the transformation of culture, 1890–1930.* Westport, Conn.: Greenwood Press.

Lapachet, J. A. 1993. *Virtual communities: The 90's mind-altering drug, or facilitator of human interaction?* Available at [http://bliss.berkeley.edu/impact/students/jaye/jaye_asis.html]. Retrieved on October 21, 2000.

Oldenberg, R. 1989. *The great good place: Cafes, coffee shops, bookstores, bars, hair salons, and other hangouts at the heart of a community.* New York: Paragon House.

Poster, M. 1995. *CyberDemocracy: Internet and the public sphere.* Available at [http://www. hnet.aci.edu/mposter/writings/democ.html]. Retrieved on 10 August 2001.

Putnam, R. D. 1995. Bowling alone: America's declining social capital. *Journal of Democracy* 6 (1): 65–78.

Sartelle, J. 1992. As if we were a community. *Bad Subjects* 1 (September). Available at [http://eserver.org/BS/01/Sartelle.html]. Retrieved on 1 May 1997.

Sartelle, J., & S. Rubio. 1993. A conversation about Bruce Springsteen. *Bad Subjects* 9 (November). Available at [http://eserver.org/BS/09/Sartelle-Rubio.html]. Retrieved on 30 April 2001.

Smith, M. A., & P. Kollock (eds.). 1999. *Communities in cyberspace.* New York: Routledge.

Szemere, A. 1992. The politics of marginality: A rock musical subculture in socialist Hungary in the early 1980s. In *Rocking the boat: Mass music and mass movements,* ed. R. Garofalo, 93. Boston: South End Press.

Chapter 4

Public Policy, Technology, and the Nonprofit Sector

Notes from the Field

Ryan Turner

THE NONPROFIT SECTOR SERVES AS THE MAIN GAUGE FOR AMERICAN PUB-
lic discourse and civic activity. In some instances, associates and charities have
served as the only voice for underrepresented constituencies (Salamon 1999). If it
still holds true that nonprofit organizations are a crucial element of American political participation, we need to look at how they are adapting, reconfiguring, and
changing to meet new challenges. This means looking at the ways in which the capacity of the nonprofit sector is being retooled, increased, and developed to ensure
the continued prominence of the sector in American society.

An exciting area in this regard has been the technology that nonprofits of all
stripes employ to help fulfill their missions and address organizational needs. One
of the most frequently asked questions we have received at OMBWatch is, "Why
should nonprofits use technology for public policy?" Our response: Because they already are! Nonprofits have been using telephones and fax machines for years to
speak out on issues that concern them and to effect change in our society. Newer information and communications technology (ICT) tools, including e-mail and Web
sites, are being used by nonprofits every day to leverage the limited resources and
increase their scope, visibility, and influence. There is also growing ubiquity among
newer technology tools.

There are policy issues surrounding nonprofits' uses of technology in general,
and within the realm of advocacy activities in particular. There are also technology
issues surrounding the policy work of nonprofits. It is at the intersection of technology and public policy considerations within the nonprofit sector that the Nonprofits' Policy and Technology Project at OMBWatch concentrates its efforts.

NONPROFITS' POLICY AND TECHNOLOGY PROJECT

OMBWatch is a nonprofit research, educational, and advocacy organization
that focuses on budget issues, regulatory policy, nonprofit advocacy, access to gov-

ernment information, and the effects of technology on nonprofit organizations. OMBWatch cochairs several coalitions in these issue areas and is a leader in the use of ICT (e.g., e-mail, the World Wide Web, and online databases) for collecting data and disseminating policy information to community groups across the nation.

In late 1997, OMBWatch launched the Nonprofits' Policy and Technology (NPT) Project, a three-year effort to educate the nonprofit sector about using newer information technologies for public policy participation. The NPT Project identifies and provides opportunities for nonprofits to learn about and use newer technologies for public policy activities; to improve communication and coordination between technology and public policy professionals in the nonprofit sector; and to increase the accessibility to—and comfort level with—these tools. The NPT Project functioned through the NPT Working Group on Nonprofits and Technology, which worked to improve communication and coordination among nonprofit infrastructure groups, professionals offering nonprofit ICT services, and organizations engaged in public policy participation.

The Working Group served as a critical role by enabling nonprofits with technology and network expertise and those with public policy experience to build a common base of knowledge. The Working Group also sought (1) to prevent any unnecessary duplication of effort in the provision of advanced technologies to the nonprofit sector, and (2) to provide the opportunity for leveraging investments in these technologies and the training related to them.

The NPT Project has been active in encouraging more interest across the sector with respect to technology and public policy convergence and capacity building. The following are some of the Project's accomplishments.

Demonstrations

The Demonstration Projects Committee advised the NPT Project on the creation and evaluation of new information coordination and dissemination tools. During the course of the project, we have examined a number of different ICT systems, including commercial software products, to see if they might be adaptable to specific nonprofit needs. Our goal was to research and present a number of different models that might work for a sector-wide communications system, and that would allow a broad range of nonprofit organizations to disseminate information across the Internet through state-of-the-art tools. These tools, ideally, would help users to categorize, filter, organize, and deliver that information in a timely manner, and to receive such information selectively, based upon their own personal preferences. We have been fortunate to demonstrate tools based on Web filtering, push, and advanced electronic mailing-list systems, and we are considering a number of other models, including newsgroups and advanced Internet publishing systems. Our work has helped raise the importance of the nonprofit-sector market in the development and beta-testing of software products.

Education and Planning

The Education and Planning Committee provided input on developing (1) an agenda for educating the Working Group about important technology and public policy issues; (2) ideas for improving the education of nonprofits about the uses of technology for public policy needs; and (3) ways to build the technology and public policy capacity of nonprofits. We released two reports that may be of interest to the reader. The first, *Speaking Up in the Internet Age: Use and Value of Constituent E-mail and Congressional Web Sites* (Lemmon & Carter 1998), discusses the value of e-mail sent to Congress and the effectiveness of congressional Web sites for disseminating substantive policy information. The second, *Democracy at Work: Nonprofit Use of Internet Technology for Public Policy Purposes* (Turner 1998), describes the state of nonprofit technology use for public policy work and civic engagement. A third publication (Turner & Carter 2001) reviewed state legislative websites.

A top priority was the creation of online resources that would inform nonprofits about the issues addressed by the NPT Project. Our first such resource, NPTalk, is an electronic forum for professionals, experts, researchers, and advocates who are interested in how nonprofits use information technologies in their public policy activities. A moderated discussion list, NPTalk is distributed in digest form once a day to an average of 800 organizations. NPTalk has enabled us to locate, generate, and disseminate information on resources and issues involving the use of technology in public policy work.

Innovation and Awards

The Innovation and Awards Committee identified and disseminated information on actual innovative uses of technology in public policy contexts and oversaw a process by which selected case examples were recognized through monetary and other types of awards. These awards were meant to highlight existing projects, broaden the base of successful projects by giving recognition to innovative organizations, and build a network of case examples and promising techniques for others to use.

Pilot Projects

The Policy and Technology Applications Committee coordinated the Pilot Project Grants Program, which identified and assisted a limited number of nonprofits that employ ICT strategies to develop or bolster their public policy activities. The Committee gives particular encouragement to regional, state, and local nonprofits to apply ICT (involving, at a minimum, the Internet) to address public policy issues and to involve disadvantaged populations and communities. The NPT Project was conducted by OMBWatch from April 1998 until October 2000, when the Project officially ended. We are no longer conducting the NPT Awards, Pilot Projects, or the demonstration activities. The education and outreach work continues under our nonprofit advocacy work, including NPTalk; and the planning for an online resource center for nonprofit advocacy, policy, and technology resources continues as well.

Other Activities

OMBWatch is doing survey work with the Lincoln Filene Center to determine how nonprofits define lobbying versus advocacy (Arons 1999; Berry & Arons 2000). We are also beginning to cull information on the various types of evaluation research, studies, and sources to gain a better sense of how to define nonprofit effectiveness with respect to technology in public policy.

OMBWatch has also helped to coordinate lobbying activities around the issue of community technology-center funding. We are engaged in this matter because it is an example of leveraging federal resources to empower underserved (low-income, minority, disabled, elderly, immigrant, and rural) constituencies to engage in broader civic participation through educational, job-training, family-building, and technology-access opportunities. This issue underscores the degree to which technology and public policy issues can combine within the nonprofits sector.

WHAT TECHNOLOGY CAN DO

Almost anyone today with access to technology has a potentially powerful advocacy capacity. Enhanced *technological* capacity, however, does not negate the need for *public policy* capacity. The later assumes a base of knowledge that includes such elements as

◆ Communication and message development skills;
◆ Organizational and media contacts;
◆ Distribution networks for messages and advisory alerts;
◆ Volunteer and supporter base; and
◆ Institutional knowledge and credibility around a given set of issues.

A new dynamic is at work in the advocacy landscape: online efforts driven by groups that cannot be categorized according to the rules of traditional advocacy organizations. These newer types of efforts, in some cases, are spurring activity on the part of established organizations.

We know that technology can be helpful to nonprofit organizations. It can break down geographic barriers to communication and increase capacity to receive and disseminate information. It can help attract and engage a wider range of perspectives to specific causes and efforts, which helps to balance insider knowledge with grassroots credibility. It can provide convenient and multifaceted participatory mechanisms for organizational supporters and collaborators. It can help strengthen capacity for coordination and collaboration among partner organizations by providing information on when to engage—and when to restrain—activity. More important, it provides opportunities to address overall organizational effectiveness. There is still considerable debate about which tools are most effective for nonprofits active in public policy roles, particularly the relative advantages of Web-based versus e-mail discussion tools.

The Limits of Technology

Technology will not eliminate the need for personalized communication, phone calls, and face-to-face meetings with elected officials, board members, staff, volunteers, and the nonprofit's constituency. It will not replace solid editorial oversight and quality control with regard to content. It cannot substitute for thoughtful, cogent analysis and research. It is not a substitute for deliberation. It will not, by itself, bring legitimacy to an organization and its activities, regardless of its impact. Although information technologies have come into vogue, it must be remembered they are only tools—albeit tools that can be used strategically.

We must also remember that not all organizations are keeping pace with technology developments, nor do they have the same public policy resources at their disposal. On the technology side, a good number of nonprofits lack the time, money, people, training, skills set, or ability to look beyond their current services and concentrate on innovation. There is also a tendency to focus on technology deployment as a short-term or midrange, project-specific solution in areas like fund raising, membership development, record keeping, and file management. On the public side, we still see 501(c)(3)s that are hesitant to lobby. It may be due to fear of government reprimands, confusion over what they are allowed to do, worries about negative public reaction, mis- or underreporting of their advocacy work, or confusion about how to advocate effectively on issues in the manner that speaks to their organizational strengths.

BUILDING CAPACITY

Successful technology deployment requires an assessment of an organization's current capacity and a clear vision of what it wishes to accomplish. The confidence and comfort levels of infusing technology into the overall activity—not just public policy work—must be addressed if technology is to play a role in advocacy. Once an organization decides to incorporate ICT into its public policy work, it must treat that technology as an ongoing commitment. This means not only investing money in equipment and software, but also training staff.

Nonprofits are concerned about the increasing gulf between organizations on two fronts: (1) between nonprofits and the for-profit and governmental sectors, and (2) between nonprofits who have adequate technology and public policy capacity and nonprofits that do not. Fortunately, we have seen the development of resources to meet both needs. Much of the institutional knowledge within the sector is still shared only via written materials and training that are not widely available to or accessible by nonprofits' sector actors. As a result, there is likely to be a continuing gap on addressing public policy capacity.

WHAT KINDS OF NONPROFITS ARE USING TECHNOLOGY FOR PUBLIC POLICY?

To provide a better initial snapshot of which technology toolsets nonprofits are using—or are building their capacity to use—the NPT Project set up a demonstration Pilot Project Grants Program. Through these grants, we sought to identify and assist nonprofit efforts that employ ICT tools and strategies to bolster their public policy activities. In 1999, the top five categories of policy issues addressed by the 220 project applicants included environment (38), health (37), human needs and services (34), low income (18), and youth (18) (see table 4.1). By comparison, last year, the top five categories of policy issues addressed by the 170 applicants were environmental and conversation issues (34), community activism (20), health and human services (18), children and families (14), and civic participation (13). (Some projects may fit more than one category.)

WHAT TOOLS ARE NONPROFITS USING FOR PUBLIC POLICY?

The Internet has caused a vast sea change in the nonprofit community. Very recently, the Internet has been viewed as a passing fad that had little bearing upon the business of the nonprofit sector; only five or six years ago, in fact, e-mail was seen as a luxury and was hardly used. Yet in 1997, OMBWatch research indicated that nearly three-fourths of surveyed nonprofits had access to e-mail and that nearly half used e-mail on a daily basis. Today, no one questions the importance or vitality of e-mail or the Internet. It is increasingly common for small and large nonprofits alike to have a Web site to draw attentions to their activities.

Conventional wisdom suggests that an e-mail campaign can be the most effective medium for reaching a high volume of potential supporters in a short amount of time, especially if the intent is to educate people and spur activity around an issue. E-mail combines the attributes of telephones, voicemail, fax machines, and regular postal mail—yet an e-mail is less costly than a phone call, fax, or delivery, especially over long distances. The messages are delivered to individual e-mail addresses, and recipients have the option of responding directly to the individual poster or the entire group, or of posting a different message altogether. Electronic mailing lists allow organizations to have ongoing and time-limited group discussions and to share important, time-sensitive information with a huge number of individuals, both cost effectively and efficiently.

Again, using our base of pilot project applicants as a starting point, most of the proposed 1998 projects involved some use of the Web, e-mail, and an electronic mailing or discussion list. The top technology tools among the applicants included Web sites (77), electronic mailing lists (21), chat (19), Web- or video-based conferencing (15), and online databases (15). In 1999, the top tools included Web sites (142), electronic lists (71), e-mail services (68), online databases (48), various other equipment (especially for presentations; 39), fax (23), chat (22), streaming audio/ video and multimedia (22), and geographic information systems (GIS; 19). (See table 4.2; in some instances, a project may fit more than one category.)

Table 4.1: NPT Pilot Project Applicant Themes

Issue Areas Addressed by Applicants	1998 Totals	1999 Totals
Agriculture/food	0	1
Arts and culture	0	2
Budget	1	0
Campaign finance	2	0
Civic education and participation	13	4
Communications and media	5	0
Community development	0	7
Community issues	20	4
Community media and technology	0	9
Community planning and development	0	8
Consumer	0	1
Corporate accountability	1	3
Disability	8	13
Domestic violence	1	4
Economic development	0	10
Education/literacy	6	6
Energy	0	1
Environment	34	38
Families	0	5
General policy	3	2
Government accountability	0	2
Health	0	37
Housing/homelessness	7	8
Human needs and services	18	34
Human rights/peace/tolerance	0	4
Hunger	0	4
Immigrants	0	3
Information access	0	1
Intellectual property	0	1
International	0	4
Juvenile justice	0	2
Labor	0	5
Law enforcement	0	1
Legal reform	0	1
Libraries	0	2
Low income	9	18
Medical research	0	2
Native American	0	5
Natural resources	0	8
Nonprofit sector	9	11
Philanthropy	0	1
Population	0	2
Property rights	0	1
Regulatory	0	1

(continues)

Table 4.1: NPT Pilot Project Applicant Themes (continued)

Issue Areas Addressed by Applicants	1998 Totals	1999 Totals
Rural	3	10
Science policy	0	3
Seniors	1	2
Social Security	1	0
Social justice	0	8
Sustainability	0	6
Volunteerism	0	6
Welfare	5	5
Women	4	11
Youth and families	14	18

HOW DO NONPROFITS USE TECHNOLOGY FOR PUBLIC POLICY?

The focus of the NPT Project has been Internet-based services. The decision was made to limit our scope to newer ICT tools that

◆ Strengthen multidirectional interaction as opposed to a strictly top-down or localized means of communication;
◆ Are being incorporated into the regular activities of nonprofit organizations; and
◆ Can be easily acquired and used by nonprofit organizations and will improve the efficiency and effectiveness of nonprofit public policy activity.

Nonprofits, technology, and public policy intersect in many different areas. Nonprofits that engage in service delivery, for example, are finding ways to use efficiency-improvement technology to respond to an increasingly widespread and diverse audience. There are active engagement activities, such as virtual volunteering, and indirect engagement activities, such as online fund raising, to support organizations in their public policy work. Some nonprofit boards are using e-mail, discussion lists, and online conferencing tools to help facilitate board decisions. Yet these speak only to the administrative and internal activities of nonprofits.

There is another set of activities that reflects the external work of nonprofits in public policy work. We know, for example, that nonprofit organizations

◆ Conduct research and gather information on issues;
◆ Perform educational and advisory roles;
◆ Organize and mobilize constituencies and supporters to initiate activity and respond to issues;
◆ Encourage likeminded stakeholders to gather and make their concerns and voices heard by decisions makers;
◆ Engage targeted audiences through coalition building and strategic outreach campaigns directed at executive/administrative, legislative, and judicial institutions at the federal, state, and local levels; and

Table 4.2: NPT Pilot Project Applicant Technologies Used

Technology Used	1998 Totals	1999 Totals
Bulletin board	11	15
Calendar	0	4
Chat	19	22
Database	15	48
Document archive	3	0
E-mail (hosting, accounts, nonlist)	0	68
Fax (Internet, migrating to Internet)	12	23
Geographical information services (GIS; including community mapping, modeling, and simulations)	3	19
Groupware	2	0
Input and analysis tools (online forms, surveys, statistical applications)	7	12
Interface to elected officials	0	6
Intranet/Extranet/LAN/WAN	0	10
List (Discussion, message, electronic mailing lists, targeted e-mail, newsletters, actions alerts)	34	71
Newsgroup	0	3
Online directory/search engine	2	5
Other tool (barcoding, Web TV, translation, assistive/adaptive technology, instant messaging, personalized news agent)	0	6
Streaming audio/video and multimedia (includes Web cameras and digital video)	5	22
Technology services (includes training and Web hosting)	17	6
Traditional broadcast (video production/television/radio)	4	4
Various other equipment (hardware/software, especially presentation equipment)	0	39
Virtual reality/avatar	2	0
Web-based or video/based conferencing (includes distance learning)	15	7
Web sites	77	142

◆ Work collaboratively with government entities, businesses, and educational and religious institutions to address basic needs and complex problems.

This only scratches the surface, however, of what nonprofits are doing with technology. Two of the more visible forms of nonprofit technology use in public policy work revolve around organizing campaigns and lobbying.

Electronic Organizing

Whereas traditional organizations have used campaigns in times of crises, on-line "flash" campaigns now take advantage of the Web's equalizing potential, and anyone can form a movement around any issue at any time, providing greater opportunity for proactive public policy engagement. There new efforts may lack the veneer of legitimacy or the track record, credibility, institutional knowledge, reputation, or insider relationships within the sector and among potential supporters and the general public.

Electronic Lobbying

To promote greater dialogue with members of Congress, a number of nonprofits have incorporated into their Web sites direct links to congressional members. The most basic of these links a "mail-to" command allowing the user to send e-mail directly from the Web browser to the address of a member of Congress. The most sophisticated of these services allows the user to type in his or her zip code to find the appropriate representatives, bring up a profile of the representatives' views on issues central to the host organization, and edit a letter template to send to the congressional member. The user can send the letter via e-mail or fax.

Despite the growth in these services, there has been little evaluation of their effectiveness or of the value of e-mail being sent to Congress. What research exists raises many questions. E-mail tends to rank the lowest among the most influential forms of communication. The evidence indicates that personalized mail (in whatever format) is significantly better than form mail or unsigned e-mail.

HOW DO WE MEASURE THE EFFECTIVENESS OF NONPROFIT ICT USE IN PUBLIC POLICY?

Many factors determine organizational effectiveness; the NPT Project focuses on the intersection of ICT with public policy capacity and resources as one measure of such effectiveness. To this end, we have developed a working definition of public policy that includes nine activity areas. Organizations are not limited to only one type of activity, and the groupings focus less on what each organization does generally than on the uses to which the organization puts its ICT and public policy capacity, and on the ways the organization uses ICT tools, strategies, and systems to perform various aspects of public policy work.

1. *Education and outreach* includes any activity that aids in the dissemination of perspectives on important public issues. This can include conferences, discussion forums, debates, nonpartisan analyses of legislation or laws, explanation of public policy processes, or increasing public awareness.

2. *Research* encompasses any collection of data or any use of scientific and analytical tools to inform or influence policy, rule making, or advocacy efforts. This includes message development, applied research, and ICT tool development. The distinction between *research* and *access to information* is a fine one. Under the heading "research," the nonprofit uses ICT tools to actually conduct the research; under "access to information," the nonprofit uses ICT tools to obtain the results of research. In many cases, obtaining research findings or data is a form of doing research; in such cases, the two categories are not distinct.

3. *Access to information* describes activity that provides usable information to scholars, practitioners, and lay people. This includes any activity that

shares research findings, data, or key data elements; helps develop missing information; fills in gaps in data collections; disseminates information that informs public policy debates or improves the nonprofit-sector infrastructure; or strengthens the public's right to know, thereby encouraging civic action.

4. *Administrative advocacy* describes attempts to understand and intercede in the rule-making process at the federal, state, or local level. It can include efforts to influence regulatory issues; the shaping of executive branch and agency budgets and grants; teaching or assisting others with the filing of comments on governmental actions and proposed regulations; monitoring program operations; engaging others in the practice of monitoring regulations and guidelines that control implementation of legislation; directing public attention to proposed regulations; or challenging policies or regulations in courts when they are inconsistent with the law.

5. *Judicial advocacy* focuses on the promotion of judicial and correctional systems and law enforcement practices that are both more responsible and more accountable. Efforts include lawsuits, preparing amicus briefs, providing information on court cases, and developing reference and educational tools.

6. *Legislative advocacy and lobbying* refers to attempts to influence the introduction, enactment, or modification of legislation at the local, state, or federal level. Lobbying can also encompass instruction on how to conduct campaigns; the educating of legislators; communications strategies to implement lobbying campaigns; the development of rules regarding lobbying; building legislative networks; and tracking legislation and committee votes. Charitable organizations are permitted to lobby an "insubstantial" amount unless they elect an expenditure test. Electing charities can lobby up to a specified dollar amount depending on the size of the organization. Charities are permitted to engage in direct lobbying (e.g., contacting a legislator directly to support or oppose a bill) and grassroots lobbying (e.g., encouraging others to contact a legislator to support or oppose a bill). Other types of charities, such as 501(c)(4) social welfare groups, do not have limits on lobbying. In other words, lobbying by nonprofits is permissible and encouraged by law. Many nonprofits, however, do not understand that they can lobby or what restrictions are placed upon them. Moreover, many nonprofits do not know how to lobby effectively.

7. *Organizing and mobilizing*—unlike education and outreach activities (item no. 1), which provide a more neutral (nonpartisan) perspective—activities in this category are intended to mobilize with a specific viewpoint, or to inform the public about a particular set of issues. Activities may include voter referenda or resolutions for the public or shareholders to consider, marches, rallies, town meetings, and public recognition campaigns ("soft-sell" approaches, including personal accounts and case studies), as opposed to pure membership recruitment for development purposes. Organizing can also lead to referenda and resolutions that the public or shareholders should consider. For example, nonprofits led the way in encouraging public companies to pass anti-apartheid resolutions. Similarly, nonprofits have helped develop and have

campaigned for referenda that voters are to consider. (Legally, support for or opposition to referenda is considered a lobbying activity for charities).

8. *Public-private collaborations* involve nonprofit organizations addressing local, state, and national problems through negotiated efforts or partnerships with business, government, colleges and universities, or other public or social institutions.

9. *Voter education and participation* includes any activity focused on electoral politics, voter turnout, voter education, or issue advocacy, but not activities designed to increase voter support for a specific candidate. Although charities (501[c][3] tax exempt organizations) cannot legally support or oppose candidates for office, they can, under certain circumstances, engage in issue advocacy, voter education, and voter participation campaigns. Other types of nonprofits, such as unions and social welfare organizations (501[c][4] tax exempt groups), can support or oppose candidates as long as they follow rules established by the IRS and the Federal Election Commission.

What We Have Found

◆ The Internet is not yet a primary policy tool for involving participants. The enormous growth in recent years in the number of nonprofit Web sites and in nonprofits' use of e-mail has not yet translated into widespread use of the Internet or the Web as an important policy tool. Nonprofits that are involved in public policy activities tend to use Web sites as a way to make available documents that they already disseminate through print materials. A growing number of nonprofits are providing the means to inform and engage visitors through e-mail communications, and some provide direct links decision makers. A good many, however, simply ask visitors to register for a mailing list or to join an organization as a member. It is rare that individuals are asked for personal information—including demographic information, professional or personal skills, whether they have contacts with government officials, whether they are willing to write letters, and so on—that may help the nonprofit undertake public policy activities.

◆ There is a gap in knowledge of effective uses of ICT by nonprofits in public policy activities, as opposed to listings of nonprofit best practices in general. Although a growing number of nonprofit use the Internet for policy purposes, they are few in relation to the number of nonprofits with Internet access and the thousands of nonprofits engaged in public policy. As a result, the relatively few examples of nonprofits that use newer ICT in a public policy context really stand out. The few examples that exit are frequently cited as models or indicators of the current state of nonprofit activity, without a rigorous assessment of their actual ability to affect policy.

◆ Web site content is not consistently maintained or kept up-to-date. Even among those nonprofits that are using the Internet and the Web as policy tools, information is often not updated or disseminated on a regular basis.

- The Web is more passive than electronic mailing lists. Anecdotal evidence suggests that the Web, as it is currently viewed and used by nonprofits in general, may be too passive to be considered a powerful advocacy tool.
- Nonprofits are using a narrow set of technologies and applications. Within each of the nine public-policy activity areas covered in this chapter, a fairly narrow set of commonly used techniques emerged. Electronic mailing lists, many of which are distribution lists, are the most common form of policy tool in general.
- Interactivity is narrowly defined by nonprofit activities; although it is a frequently touted concept, the line between the use of technology and its *effective* use is a thin one. While the end goal of nonprofit technology use ostensibly is to engage a potential user's attention and to encourage some level of participation with the organization (as a member or volunteer), the term *interactive* lacks a basic set of definable standards and carries a variety of connotations. In other words, it appears that Internet-based activities are best viewed as supplements to more traditional forms of communication and action.
- Creating a strong identity on the Internet is important for nonprofits, yet nonprofits need a better understanding of how to establish a consistent, sustainable, and easily recognizable presence that integrates and enhances both online and real-world activities.
- Numerous barriers to nonprofits' use of the Internet exist. Lack of knowledge about and access to affordable tools, training, and technical assistance are frequently cited as the main reasons more nonprofits do not engage in online public policy activities.
- Politically conservative and progressive nonprofits use the Internet at different levels and in different ways.
- There appears to be a disconnect between nonprofit interest in using technology for public policy purposes and funding for such activities.
- Nonprofit Internet efforts in general, and Web efforts in particular, appear rarely to provide features that address information coordination and accessibility issues, including access by hearing and visually impaired users, and users who do not speak English.

FURTHER CONSIDERATIONS

In the wake of federal budget cuts, some nonprofits have turned to technology to improve their services; some have gone so far as to charge fees for services delivered via that technology to recoup their costs. The range of issues that have, by necessity, fallen under the purview of the nonprofit sector has increased. In the wake of welfare reform and the increasing trends for devolution, nonprofits are being called upon to deliver products, goods, and services to a client base with a growing number of needs. This, in part, has opened up areas once considered the exclusive domain of nonprofits to for-profit entities. Moreover, the larger number of nonprofits has fueled not only more nonprofit activity, but also competition within the sector for foundation support, memberships, dues revenues, volunteers, and the attention span of the American public. This is not only places economic pressure on nonprofits, it creates a situation in which more nonprofit organizations may be less prepared to step up to the plate when faced with policy issues that affect them as they struggle to meet basic organizational needs.

In some instances, these forces have led to the introduction of innovative or higher-end technology tools, systems, and operational models that have improved the lot of some nonprofits. Others have faced the threat of extinction as they struggle to survive against better-funded and better-equipped efforts.

We see capacity building as one way to protect the nonprofit sector's vital place in our communities and its ability to revitalize our democratic principles. Although nonprofits are making increased use of advanced ICT tools to enhance, complement, and refine their public policy activities, we have found that the Internet's chief values for many nonprofits are still e-mail and access to networking opportunities. "Bleeding-edge" technologies are of less value because most staff members and beneficiaries of nonprofits are not yet fully online. Despite the growing ubiquity of the Internet, access for low-income, minority, and rural groups remains problematic.

A recent study by the U.S. Department of Commerce's National Telecommunications and Information Administration (McConnaughey, Everette, Reynolds, & Lader 1999) points out the disparity in technology access in the United States today. The study found, for example, that Black and Hispanic households are 0.4 times as likely to have home Internet access as White households. Households earning annual incomes of more than $75,000 are more than 20 times more likely to have home Internet access than those at the lowest income levels. Those making less than $20,000 per year who can access the Internet outside the home are twice as likely to gain access through community technology centers. People without home computers are almost 1.5 times as likely as home-computer owners to obtain access to computers and the Internet from library and community technology centers. Currently, 62 percent of those with college degrees now use the Internet, compared to only 6.6 percent of those with an elementary school education or less. At home, those with a college degree or higher are more than 8.0 times as likely to own a computer and almost 16.0 times more likely to have home Internet access than the least educated. At every income level, households in rural areas are significantly less likely—sometimes only half as likely—to have home Internet access than those in urban and central city areas.

If we focus only on the technology tools that prove successful for groups in visible ways, we begin to lose sight of the dynamics that help those groups who lack technology resources to achieve success. This includes outreach to target constituencies, institutional knowledge, and the commitment to doing policy work on an ongoing basis. As more organizations become experienced in building and applying their technology and public policy "muscles," there are questions about the obligations on those organizations to guide, and share, their experience and resources to help raise the efforts and capacities of other sector actors.

In order for nonprofits and the people they serve to benefit from the coming waves of newer technology, we must recognize that technology capacity must be developed in tandem with public policy capacity. For those organizations currently left out of the picture on both fronts, this is an ideal time to consider the benefits of technology, and to position their thresholds for both as high as possible. In addition, the sector must seize upon the opportunity to address the boundaries that will hamper further growth and development for all entities—namely, ideology, turf, and constituency of mission across activities in the wake of outside forces. There will always be inequality within the sector, but by building a base of activity that generates models at all levels, we can begin to infuse technology and public policy resources where they would not otherwise trickle down. Ultimately, we must not lose sight of why we work to develop both technology and public policy capacity for nonprofits: to energize citizen participation in order to ensure a more just, equitable, and accountable government, and a healthier civil society.

Suggested Readings

Arons, D. F. 1999. *Nonprofit management and advocacy: Examining barriers to democracy.* Paper presented at the twenty-eighth annual meeting of the Association for Research on Nonprofit Organizations and Voluntary Action, 4–6 November, Arlington, Va.

Berry, J., & D. Arons. 2000. *Organizational capacity and nonprofit advocacy.* Paper presented at the twenty-ninth Annual Meeting of the Association of Voluntary Action Scholars, 15–18 November, New Orleans, La.

Lemmon, P., & M. Carter. 1998. *Speaking up in the Internet age: Use and value of constituent e-mail and congressional Web sites.* Washington, D.C.: OMBWatch.

McConnaughey, J., D. W. Everette, T. Reynolds, & W. Lader (eds.). 1999. *Falling through the Net: Defining the digital divide.* Washington, D.C.: U.S. Department of Commerce, National Telecommunications and Information Administration.

Salamon, L. M. 1999. The nonprofit sector at a crossroads: The case of America. *Voluntas* 10 (1): 5–23.

Turner, R. 1998. *Democracy at work: Nonprofit use of Internet technology for public policy purposes.* Washington, D.C.: OMBWatch.

Turner, R., & M. Carter. 2001. *Plugged in, tuning up: An assessment of state legislative websites.* Washington, D.C.: OMBWatch.

Chapter 5

The Role of the Internet in Educating Social Work Practitioners as Online Advocates

Stephen P. Wernet

INTRODUCTION

It is the purpose of this chapter to discuss the role of the Internet in educating social work practitioners as online advocates. Practitioners need a full array of skills upon which they can draw to be successful as advocates for social change. The use of the Internet is but one practice skill for the competent social worker, for whom technology skills in general (in conjunction with other skills) are becoming increasingly important. In this chapter, I will discuss advocacy as an area of professional practice; the concept of community; and curricular design for educating advocates.

THE PROFESSIONAL PRACTICE OF ADVOCACY

Defining Practice

Much of the practice of social work advocacy is typically placed in larger arenas known as community and policy practice. Although this chapter will deal primarily with community practice, other areas of social work play an important role. *Community practice* is an array of practices focusing on coalescing individuals into groups concerned with community issues (Checkoway 1995; Gamble & Weil 1995; Stoecker 2000; Weil 1996). This array is predicated on democratic participation and seeks to build the collective power of the citizenry. The goal is a socially just, democratic society in which the plurality participates on an equal footing. The belief is that a socially just society can be attained only if all voices are heard on, and participate in solving, a given issue.

There are several assumptions that underlie the array of community practice approaches. First, citizens have the right to participate directly in decisions that affect them. Second, when provided with the information, citizens will participate in the decision-making process. Third, citizens' not being heard in the democratic process is attributable to either their lack of knowledge about the process or an injustice in the process that disenfranchises them. To achieve a socially just society, outside intervention is sometimes required to assist citizens' participation in the decision-making process. The intervener usually is a person or group of people with skills in community practice, and it is to these skills that we now turn our attention.

Traditional Practice Skills

Suffice to say that the educated practitioner must be solidly capable of assessing a problem or situation. That is, he or she must be able to identify accurately the problem facing a community or citizens' group and then to select the appropriate intervention. (These issues of assessment and intervention planning are beyond the scope of this chapter, and the reader is referred to others who have discussed these issues in greater detail: Checkoway 1995; Rothman 1996; Weil 1996.) My goal is to outline here the array of practice skills used by traditional community practitioners and their counterparts in an electronically based practice.

It is generally recognized that community practitioners must possess two sets of skills: *interactional skills* and *technical skills*. In actual practice, however, one skills set usually dominates. The hallmark of the skilled community practitioner is balancing the use of social and technical skills, knowing when each set is appropriate, and mixing and matching the skills requisite to the problem. Therefore, assessment is a premier skill for the community practitioner.

The knowledge base upon which the community practitioner focuses has two components. The first half of this is *foundation knowledge,* which consists of the theoretical underpinnings of community practice. The practitioner must understand why and how humans gather into social organizations as well as understand the processes of these dyads, groups, organizations, and communities. The practitioner must understand the nature of community power, and the logic of social change and innovation, and must have a host of related skills. The second half of this knowledge base consists of *practice skills.* These are the artful and purposeful use of self to intervene in a human organization.

Three themes apply equally to groups, organizations, and communities. These are *decision-making, leadership,* and *followership.* These themes will inform practitioners not only about functional systems but also about dysfunctional ones and will give explanations for these dysfunctions and the means to correct them. It is this last area, the means for correction—practice skills and intervention—to which we now shift our attention.

Practice skills focus on deliberate human interaction; the goal is to build human infrastructure (McNutt 2000). The skilled community practitioner is interested in building community capacity through the creation of both weak and strong ties. Interventions focus on groups and organizations as well as on creating consortia and community. At the group and organizational level, the practitioner should be skilled in process facilitation, or building capacities from among individuals or interested parties. In contemporary parlance, the practitioner must be able to exert leadership. He or she must be able to engage people while creating a sense of boundedness. The requisite skills include

- Defining issues,
- Defining common ground,
- Clarifying concerns,
- Building consensus,
- Negotiating and mediating, and
- Resolving conflict and obstacles.

At the organizational, consortium, multiorganizational, and community levels, the skilled worker must possess not only group facilitation skills but also the ability to build cohesion across a plethora of interest groups. At the consortium level, the skilled practitioner must know how to connect groups with each other, thereby creating networks, and how to influence public debate while publicizing activities. At the community level, the task of the skilled worker is building a functional community, which may involve working with a geographically or spatially defined community or creating a community of propinquity (Chaskin 1997). In both arenas, the skilled worker must be able to identify and interconnect the common interests of the various individual, group, and organizational actors.

The common skill that links the community practitioner's role across these social units is the ability to assist individuals and units of individuals to change status. The skilled community practitioner must create different intensities of interpersonal connections in the service of solving common social problems. Some have described this work as moving individuals from noninvolvement to a marginal status, to becoming a supporter, to becoming an adherent (McCarthy & Zald 1977). Others have described the work as creating weak ties from no ties, and creating strong ties from weak ties (Stoecker 2000). Still others have described the work as minimizing, reducing, or eliminating the transaction costs for participating while eliminating free-ridership (Bonchek 1995). The common theme is identifying the benefits of participation, thus creating a sense of benefit for participating while eliminating benefits for those abstaining from participation. This is the art of human relationships for the skilled community practitioner. It is understanding the individual's motivators and tapping into these to change people and groups of people.

The second skills set consists of technical skills, a set occasionally subsumed under the practice of social planning. Through sheer presentation of data by the practitioner, people will see the proper solution. Accepting the assumption, albeit flawed, that underscores this philosophy there are important technical skills that the competent community practitioner should command. These include

- Identifying and analyzing issues;
- Evaluating information;
- Analyzing data;
- Developing, evaluating, and measuring outcomes;

◆ Creating access to the decision-making process; and
◆ Influencing policy decisions.

The technical skills set is an amalgamation of three subsets of skills, the predominant subset of which consists of skills in data management. The competent community practitioner needs facility in measurement, instrumentation, and data analysis. This subset includes assessing data integrity—that is, their reliability and validity. The next technological-skill subset is that of translating data into work—knowing how to convert data into action or strategies. The last subset is understanding the policy process—knowing how that process works and how to access it, thereby influencing its outcomes.

A third component or skill for the community practitioner is *balance,* or timing. There are two aspects of balance. The first is balancing task and process; the second is balancing practitioner-group leadership, that is, determining who sets the work agenda and who performs the tasks associated with this decision. Both the group's stage of development and the type of task facing the group determine the choice for leadership.

In summary, competent community practitioners must possess a base in foundation knowledge along with three skills sets: social skills, technical skills, and balance. How these skills sets transfer into community practice in cyberspace is our next focus.

COMMUNITY PRACTICE SKILLS FOR CYBERSPACE

Some of the skills sets for the cyberorganizer will be no different than for the traditional organizer. He or she must still possess social skills, technical skills, and a sense of balance or timing. However, the components of each skills set will be broader than those for the traditional organizer. In addition, technology skills will need to be developed and refined, which can be problematic because of the historically low level of information and communications technology (ICT) expertise among social workers.

The predominant skills set will be that of social skills. As in the traditional setting, the cyberorganizer needs facility in building a community—but what constitutes community in a depersonalized or technology-mediated environment? To answer this question we must both define community and delineate the traditional from the cyber-community.

Many authors have defined and studied community, and many distinguish between genuine and counterfeit community. The common element of communities of all types is a web of relationships (Freier 1998). The overwhelming majority of our community examples are place based. It is argued that community requires a physical environment within which occurs face-to-face interaction. It is further argued that two types of relationships are required for community to occur: first, a relationship between people and the physical environment. Individuals are engaged with and connected to a physical place or space—a bounded area that focuses their attention, such as a neighborhood within which reside people of similarities. The assumption is that people are defined by and share common characteristics with other residents. This community of space creates a platform of connection, a common experience, and consequently the propensity to create a community of relatedness. It is assumed that in such a community, individuals will work through differences and conflicts with neighbors because they are rooted in the physical place, and have nowhere else to go.

For example, the question "Where are you from?" can take on numerous, highly specific meanings. In Chicago, it means "In what parish do you live?"; in Saint Louis, it means "From what high school did you graduate?"; in Boston, "In what neighborhood do you live?" The response, however, provides the questioner with multiple kinds of information—about ethnicity, socioeconomic status, political affiliation, religious orientation, and so on. It prompts both questioner and respondent to assess whether they share enough common experience upon which to build some platform of connection and affinity.

The second relationship that exists as the foundation for community is the web of relationships among individuals. Some describe this as shared or mutual interests. Others have defined it as conscious community (Palloff & Pratt 1999). Community develops because of mutual or common interests that may be independent of the physical environment. The bounded space may be created by a common experience based on something other than physical proximity, that is, affinity. Community is a voluntary experience into which one chooses to enter because of a perceived shared experience. Until discovered to be to the contrary, rootedness is attributable to perceived common norms and common interests.

"What do you do?" can refer to employment, career, hobbies, or extracurricular interests. As with "Where are you from?" the answer to this question can be a platform upon which individuals may build a relationship based on common experience, or from which an individual may dive into a new pool of interpersonal interactions. Professional associations in the United States have reported robust growth in their memberships in recent years, which may be because those who share the same occupational space share similar values.

What is the one most common element that creates community, whether in place or in interest? The answer is *interdependence*. This is based on the intensity of communal involvement, which is, in turn, dependent on barriers, risk, and sacrifice. Community requires boundaries, real or felt. These are by definition based on barriers, which create a sense of limited membership or exclusivity: It is difficult to enter, and it is difficult to exit. These barriers also contribute to the concept of *sacrifice,* because costs are associated with one's membership. To either belong to or leave a community, a member must relinquish something, and it is perceived that this relinquishment will result in a greater gain.

Another component to sacrifice is vital to the concept of interdependence: the idea of reciprocal responsibility. When a member sacrifices, he or she is surrendering some part of his or her individual interests to fellow community members. It is assumed others are doing likewise. Each community member also assumes some part of the common work or agenda of the community. This dynamic of both relinquishing and assuming creates a feeling of connection and solidarity with other members of the community—a sense of mutual obligation. When successful, this dynamic contributes to the creation of effective ties or to a sense of caring for others.

The third aspect of interdependence is *risk*. This is the ratio of unmet expectations to resources committed in sacrifice. Assessing risk is similar to keeping score. At certain, ill-defined points in time, community participants review this *relinquishing-assuming relationship* and compare the ratio to some individual, risk-tolerance assumption. The individual then makes a decision either to continue without change, to rebalance the inequity (whether real or perceived), or to exit the community. The individual's decision will depend on the relationship among the costs associated with each solution, his or her risk tolerance, and the sacrifice made to join the community. Like an algebraic equation, all sides must balance out for a community to maintain its members. When the equation becomes unbalanced, community disequilibrium occurs and conflict ensues.

So, what does this have to do with cyberorganizing and the requisite skills set? Good question! Let's now bring this understanding of community to bear on defining the skills set of the cyberorganizer.

Defining the Skills Set of the Cyberorganizer

Like the more traditional advocate, the cyberorganizer must possess social skills, technical skills, and timing or balancing skills. However, even the social skills are dependent on technology, so that technical skills assume both a social and a data management function for cyberorganizing. Within the social skills area, the practitioner must be proficient in building or creating a bounded community. Unlike the community built on spatial boundaries, the cybercommunity is non–place-based and totally voluntary, built upon mutual, shared interests; it may be a conscious community (Palloff & Pratt 1999) or a community of propinquity (Chaskin 1997). The boundaries are attributable to mutual or shared interests. People may join the cybercommunity because of an interest in and commitment to the focal issue. Socially, the practitioner must facilitate group formation and participant connection and commitment. Trust, cohesion, and group development are promoted by the interaction among the group members.

As with traditionally organized groups, cyberorganized groups are built on group interaction; unlike with traditional groups, however, this interaction occurs through a mediated or weakly connected medium that is frequently delayed and archived. Group conversations usually occur through discussion lists that can be either moderated or unmoderated as well as being asynchronous. In some situations, interaction may occur in real time through chat rooms. Because the written word rather than face-to-face interaction is the medium of communication, cyberpractitioners must possess compositional skills. They must know how to use and assess written communication for emotional content and meaning and must be adept at creating a common experience through written discourse. They must be able to help others develop their voices through written communication. The challenge for the cyberpractitioner is to create a community with a traditional sense of benefit for participating through interaction, negotiation, and conflict resolution, but in a novel environment with weak ties, low exit barriers, and a lack of personalized, physical interaction. Therefore, the cyberpractitioner must be skilled not only in facilitating group interaction and processes but also in both written communication and in the use of the ICT used for list services, chat, and electronic mail.

The term *technical skills* has an expanded meaning in cyberorganizing. Practitioners must have competency with the usual and customary data analytic tools. In this brave new world, there are two sets of technical tools available for the cyberpractitioner, and an expanding array of data sources for citizens. The first set includes online databases, geographic information systems (GISs), and mapping resources, and an increasingly important skill is the ability to evaluate the utility and validity of databases.

The second set of tools contains analytic tools or applications, the numbers of which have been increasing exponentially. These include both desktop and Internet-based tools. Among the older desktop tools are word processors, spreadsheets, database management programs, presentation software, and statistical packages; newer tools include publishing (including Web page production) and mapping tools. The Internet-based tools include Web server operations, push technologies, videoconferencing, whiteboards, teleconferencing, virtual offices, searching, and peer-to-peer computing. Rather than focusing on technical expertise alone, the cyberpractitioner is a master of pairing the best technical application to the task at hand. His or her job is not to be a technology developer but rather to be a high-end user of these applications in the service of organizing constituencies for problem resolution.

The final skills set is the art of balancing or timing—uncharted territory because of the novelty of cyberorganizing. We possess two pieces of information that have implications for cyberpractice. First, from distributed or distance learning, we know that building a conscious, voluntary community requires more time and effort than in the brick-and-mortar environment. Community building in the cyber-classroom or online course requires great patience, structure, and luck. This knowledge should serve as a warning for aficionados of cyberpractice.

Second, we know that cyberspace tends to be a homogeneous environment, if only a little less so than in the past, when it tended to include only males and those who were well off. With respect to gender, the environment has changed; but with respect to the marginalized, the disenfranchised, and the disempowered, things are much the same, with such individuals being less likely to seek involvement in technology and cyberorganizing. The digital divide is a very real issue here—yet another warning to aficionados.

For the cyberorganizer, the skills discussed here are well used in the face of such challenges in a Web-based or -enhanced environment. In the Web-enhanced environment, the practitioner works in both the usual face-to-face environment and a complementary, mediated environment that is considered an add-on to his or her mainstream efforts. As is seen in the educational environment, however, Web enhancement is likely to assume a role of growing importance. The Web-based cyberorganizing environment is the practice arena to which most discussions refer when delineating this topic. It is unlikely that a totally mediated organizing environment will become the mainstay of community practice. However, it is not unusual for some organizing ventures to begin in the "ether," or mediated, realm and then later to include some direct, unmediated, interpersonal interaction. Therefore, it is most likely that all community practice will eventually contain some type of mediated communication.

EDUCATING FOR CYBERORGANIZING

Addressing the education of cyberorganizers requires that we address two final issues: curricular content and delivery formats. Curricula should cover three areas to prepare the cyberorganizer of the future: human behavior or theory, practice methods, and technical methods.

◆ *Human behavior* or *theory* must include organization theory, community theory, policy process, and group dynamics. Covering both social organization and the theory of interpersonal processes, these four areas provide the range of theoretical content required for knowledgeable community practice.

◆ *Practice methods* must cover an array of intervention techniques, including communication, interviewing, group facilitation, mediation and negotiation, and planning. Public speaking or communication has always been a requisite skill of the organizer; given the growth in mediated formats, however, writing skills are now equally important. Interviewing and group facilitation skills continue to be as important as ever, but reading the individual's or group's emotional undertones in the Web-mediated environment requires something new. Physical, nonverbal cues are missing. Emotional tone is frequently absent. Being able to understand and intuit the tone of written communication has become a new, requisite skill for the cyberorganizer. As for mediation and negotiation, these continue to be necessary skills for organizing, although these efforts are, again, untried in the ether and remain a frontier to explore. Finally, planning is a technical skill that will continue to be built upon in contemporary community practice. Evaluation is another critical skill.

◆ *Technical methods* will become increasingly important for organizing in the mediated environment. Traditional data management—collection, validation, and analysis—will still be needed for accurate planning practice, but mastery of newer software for these tasks—such as spreadsheets, relational databases, and mapping/GIS software—will become more important tools of the planner and organizer. Another cluster of new software tools with which the organizer must become comfortable is the communication software tools—it is increasingly important for organizers to use alternative means of drawing and communicating with people, these tools will provide the avenues. Push technology will enable organizers to reach out to others while also enabling others to reach back preemptively to communities of interest. Video and audio conferencing will enable people to meet in real time without having to convene in the same place. These technologies will augment, and in some cases replace, traditional face-to-face meetings. Publishing will continue to decentralize and move to both the desktop as well as the screen and electronic formats, and delivery will increasingly replace the hardcopy or paper format. The community organizer will need familiarity with and a modicum of skill in digital tools in order to be successful in the future.

As for the formats for delivering curricula to student cyberorganizers, there are three available: traditional face-to-face, fully Web-mediated, and Web-enhanced (a hybrid of traditional and mediated formats). Face-to-face instruction is the hallmark of traditional education. The assumption has been, and in many venues continues to be, that the best learning occurs when a novice receives instruction by direct tutelage from a master. These two can at first engage in personal discourse, so that the novice observes and learns the nuances of the master's field. The novice is then able to engage in practice under the direct supervision of the master, thereby receiving expert responses and immediate correction and refinement. Although this method is time intensive, the usual and customary wisdom is that face-to-face learning is the most effective means for educating professionals.

In the contemporary debate on education and technology, traditional students (whether undergraduate or graduate) and faculty prefer the traditional format (Wernet, Delicath, & Olliges 2000a,b). They expect to be engaged in a face-to-face system to which they have become fully acclimated, and are somewhat reluctant to abandon it. Social work students in particular seem to prefer the traditional format (Wernet, Berg-Weger, et al. 2000). This is not unexpected given the nature of social work.

At the other extreme is a fully Web-mediated learning experience. Contact between student and educator is always indirect, never face to face, and technology is the delivery medium for the content of interest to the student. Discussions may occur either in real time, which requires all participants to be involved simultaneously in the activity, or in a relay or delayed fashion, which enables all students as well as the educator to participate in the activity on an idiosyncratic schedule. Course content is delivered through a combination of tools, including online lecture notes, whiteboards, wave or audio files, and mpeg or video files. In lieu of classroom discussion, bulletin board, listserv, and chat room tools are the places of debate and exchange of ideas. E-mail takes the place of office hours and appointments, and of pre- and postclass discussion between student and teacher and among students. In the contemporary debate on education and technology, nontraditional students prefer the mediated format (Wernet, Delicath, & Olliges 2000a,b), which allows flexibility in balancing competing life demands. Nontraditional, graduate social-work students who return to school with work experience and pursue the degree on a part-time basis also appear to prefer the mediated format. This is not unexpected, given their attempts to balance work, family life, and school. The actual experience of the mediated environment, however, can be unexpectedly demanding for some students, especially those who are unable to maintain focus or who are less well self-directed (Wernet & Delicath 1998).

The final solution is a hybrid that mixes the traditional with the mediated formats. This solution is referred to as Web-enhanced education. In this format, teacher and student mix and match mediated and traditional education for a time-convenient or content-relevant format. Web enhancement mixes the best of both extreme formats. It uses traditional formatting to engage students through the familiar method, and mediation to facilitate students balancing competing demands. The classroom is used to retain the human contact in an increasingly depersonalized world and to help students apply course content to problem situations. The Web-based format is used for depositing course materials and facilitating out-of-class discussion. In the contemporary debate on education and technology, students and educators appreciate the hybrid, or Web-enhanced, format (Wernet, Delicath, & Olliges 2000a,b; Wernet & Olliges 1999). It provides students and faculty alike with personal contact and flexibility in balancing competing life demands, mixing the best of both approaches while compensating for the weaknesses of each.

What Would a Cyberorganizing Curriculum Look Like?

As one might expect from what has been discussed thus far, many of the current elements in social work education would stay reasonably the same. Both accreditation requirements and the expectations of stakeholders will prevent serious changes from taking pace. Also, much of what we know about social change is directly applicable in this regard. There are, however, some new materials that should be added.

Technology Skills

Every social work student needs technology skills. The ability to use common office, communications, and similar software programs is essential for any future practitioner. McNutt (1999) argues that students need the competencies shown in table 5.1; these areas can be addressed in a set of courses within a standard social work curriculum.

Electronic Advocacy Skills

As practice develops, students will need a set of skills in designing and developing e-mail–based advocacy campaigns. These skills will involve knowledge from a number of areas, including political science, organizational computing, and social informatics.

CONCLUSION

Preparing social workers for the future of advocacy practice in cyberspace is a daunting task. Much of what we have learned through years of training people for traditional careers in promoting social change is directly applicable. On balance, we

Table 5.1: Competencies Necessary to the Social Worker of the Future That Can Be Addressed in a Standard Social Work Curriculum

Internet Use	Web Site Design
Networking	Setting up an Internet site
Basic programming	Use of common office applications
Database design	Telephony and videoconferencing
Client-server systems	Security
Project managers	Innovation techniques
Program development	GIS techniques

need to develop more completely the technology side of the equation. As the practice evolves, new roles will develop and additional training requirements will emerge. Social work educators must be aware of these developments and create a learning environment that is both current and complete.

Suggested Readings

Bonchek, M. 1995. *Grassroots in cyberspace: Using computer networks to facilitate political participation.* Available at [http://www.ai.mit.edu/people/msb/publs/grassroots.html]. Retrieved on 22 January 1997.

Chaskin, R. 1997. Perspectives on neighborhood and community: A review of the literature. *Social Service Review* 71 (4): 522–547.

Checkoway, B. 1995. Six strategies of community change. *Community Development Journal* 30 (1): 2–20.

Freier, J. F. 1998. *Counterfeit community: The exploitation of our longings for connectedness.* New York: Rowman and Littlefield.

Gamble, D., & M. O. Weil. 1995. Citizen participation. In *Encyclopedia of social work,* ed. R. L. Edwards, 483–494. Washington, D.C.: NASW Press.

McCarthy, J., & M. Zald. 1977. Resource mobilization and social movements: A partial theory. *American Journal of Sociology* 82: 1212–1241.

McNutt, J. 1999. *Building social work knowledge for policy practice and the Internet: A design and development approach.* Unpublished paper, Chestnut Hill, Graduate School of Social Work, Boston College.

————. 2000. Organizing cyberspace: Strategies for teaching about community practice and technology. *Journal of Community Practice* 7 (1): 95–109.

Palloff, R., & K. Pratt. 1999. *Building learning communities in cyberspace: Effective strategies for the online classroom.* San Francisco: Jossey-Bass.

Rothman, J. 1996. The interweaving of community intervention approaches. *Journal of Community Practice* 3 (3/4): 69–99.

Stoecker, R. 2000. *Cyberspace vs. face to face: Community organizing in the new millennium.* Available at [http://comm-org.utoledo.edu/papers2000/cyberorganize.htm]. Retrieved on 28 June 2000.

Weil, M. 1996. Model development in community practice: An historical perspective. *Journal of Community Practice* 3 (3/4): 5–67.

Wernet, S., M. Berg-Weger, J. Birkenmaier, R. Banks, R. J. Wilson, & R. Olliges. 2000. *The use of Web-based education in social work field education.* Paper presented at the annual program meeting of the Council on Social Work Education, 26–29 February, New York, N.Y.

Wernet, S., & T. Delicath. 1998. *The application of WebCT (Web Course Tools) in social work education.* Paper presented at National Technology Conference, "Information technologies for social work education and practice," 16–23 August, College of Social Work, University of South Carolina.

———. 2001. Distributed learning: Does it make a difference? Working paper, School of Social Service, Saint Louis University.

Wernet, S., T. Delicath, & R. Olliges. 2000a. *What works, what doesn't: Modeling instructional tools to enhance student satisfaction with Web-based instruction.* Paper presented at WebCT2000 conference. University of Georgia, Athens. Available at [http://www. webct2000.org/conferencepapers.html].

———. 2000b. Post-course evaluations of WebCT (Web Course Tools) classes by social work students. *Research on Social Work Practice* 10 (4): 487–504.

Wernet, S., & R. Olliges. 1999. Using WebCT for educating practice professionals. *Proceedings of the First Annual WebCT Conference on Learning Technologies,* 17–19 June, University of British Columbia, Vancouver.

Part II

Organizing for Social Change

Chapter 6

Organizing for Social Change

Online and Traditional Community Practice

John McNutt
Steven Hick

COMMUNITIES DO NOT SIMPLY ORGANIZE THEMSELVES, EITHER WITH OR
without new technology. Organizing requires people. Someone must build strong
enough relationships between individuals that they can support each other through
long struggles for social change—and if the community already exists, someone
must help transform it to support social action. In all cases, communities need both
strong leaders and someone on board with the appropriate organizing skills and
knowledge. Community organization or community practice represents a central
method of traditional social work practice (Rothman 2001). Under this label falls a
variety of submethods that range from community development and consensus organizing, through social planning, to social action. This vast collection of orientations, methods, and techniques provides a rich arsenal of ways to address a wide
range of issues and problems, ranging from homelessness to globalization
(Meenaghan & Gibbons 2000).

    In recent years, the extension of community practice to cyberspace has become
more and more evident (McNutt 2000). In much the same way that organizing physical communities has led to a variety of approaches and methodologies, the emergent practice in cyberspace has spawned some new and interesting approaches
(Hick, Halpin, & Hoskins 2000). Even with these new approaches and methods, the
tie between online and traditional organizing remains strong. This chapter will discuss traditional social work community organizing and the development of online
organizing, and will discuss the integration of the two in social work practice.

ORGANIZING FOR SOCIAL CHANGE

    Organizing for social change has always been a part of social work's mission
(Fisher 1984; Garvin & Cox 2001; Trattner 1994;). This tradition has included or-

ganizing communities and neighborhoods for social and economic justice, organizing new services, promoting progressive legislation, and creating new programs and agencies. Community organizing is a change strategy that is rooted in an ethos of solidarity and social justice. With the emergence of economic globalization, which is, in part, facilitated by new technologies, community workers need to think about "globalizing from below," or connecting people around the world. The same technologies that have helped large corporations organize globally can also help people organize globally and ensure that individuals' issues and human rights are part of the global agenda.

Community practice covers many methodologies and addresses many issues. Several major attempts have been made to deal with this diversity. Although a complete discussion of these issues goes beyond the scope of this chapter, we will review some of the major ideas here. Rothman (2001) divided community practice into three models: locality development, social planning, and social action. *Locality development* is designed to increase community participation and enable democratic decision making. It represents attempts by definable localities, such as neighborhood associations or ratepayer associations, to identify and solve problems cooperatively (Wharf & Clague 1997). *Social planning* is a research-and-rationale problem-solving approach to community decision making, and it takes a neutral position relative to power. *Social action* deals more with empowerment of oppressed communities. Its practitioners believe that positive change will occur when power and resources are redistributed. Rothman (2001) also provides for using the approaches together either in sequence (*phasing*) or in concert (*mixing*). Warren (1978) presented a similar approach.

Weil and Gamble (1995) build on Rothman but add a variety of additional approaches to the mix. These approaches include neighborhood and community organizing, organizing functional communities, community social and economic development, social planning, program development and community liaison, political and social action, coalitions, and social movements. Each of these represents a different approach to community change, although they all share some similarities. Based on their analysis of community-organizing case studies in Canada, Wharf and Clague (1997) concluded that community organizing and social movements are largely similar, except that the former is generally grounded in communities of place, whereas the latter tends to transcend local issues and tends to be national and even international in scope. With the advent of new communications technology this distinction is fading even further. The Internet is enabling communities to link together, allowing individuals located far from one another to join struggles and forge new global movements. The success of the anti–free trade movement is an example of Internet use by a variety of communities and organizations joining together to work toward a common purpose.

Given the different strategies, it is not surprising that a huge variety of tactics and techniques are used (Meenaghan & Gibbons 2000). These include door-to-door membership recruiting, holding meetings, power research, issue research, fund raising, using the media, public education on issues, negotiation, and so forth. A common core of the methods and approaches is the centrality of communications.

ORGANIZING ONLINE

Organizing online is a relatively recent development. Within social work, community organizers were probably the first to use the Internet extensively (some may argue that social policy analysts were also at the forefront). For a variety of reasons the Internet was seen as an appropriate and useful tool for community organizers. The motivation for traditional community practitioners to use the Internet include the following:

- ◆ *Economics*. As Boncheck (1995) notes, organizing activities incurs significant transaction costs. These include time and resources needed to contact people and coordinate their activities in an action program. In addition to transaction costs, the shrinking resource base makes it imperative that the economies provided by these new tools be used.
- ◆ *Distance and devolution*. The continued dispersal of the power structure and the geographic scale present in some social problem areas makes the Internet a needed ally. As globalization promises to aggravate these problems, groups will need this worldwide reach as well.
- ◆ *New capacities*. Technology adds to the tool base of community practice and makes many previously unheard-of things possible. Technologies such as groupware, geographic information systems (GIS), and even desktop publishing can add much to traditional community practice.
- ◆ *The realization that cyberspace is a new constituency*. People and problems are moving into the cyberspace arena. The growth of both a high-technology workforce and a population that has turned toward the Internet means that organizers who are attuned to meeting people where they live will have to go online.

Approaches to Online Organizing

Online organizing is so new that theoretical approaches are still being developed. In chapter 1 we used a rough categorization to delineate the extent of technology use in organizing and advocacy work: technology-assisted and technology-based. *Technology-assisted* practice is the use of the Internet to support traditional practice, whereas *technology-based* practice is practice that takes place primarily with technology.

Technology-Assisted Traditional Practice
Information and communications technology (ICT) can assist the traditional community organization process by automating certain parts of it. The major components remain as they always were.

A number of organizations have added technology to their efforts without major changes in their ways of working. In many cases, this means adding tools that will work with the traditional processes. Examples include

◆ Desktop publishing for newsletters and flyers,
◆ Databases for membership,
◆ GIS for constituency and problem analysis,
◆ Fund-raising software, and
◆ Spreadsheets and statistical analysis programs for assessing issues.

Many of the office-type applications have excellent applications to community organization. As in any other organization, technology can add to productivity if used correctly.

Technology-Based Practice

These new practice techniques are based on technology and cannot exist without it, although they still have strong ties to traditional practice. Some examples are

◆ Community computer networks or FreeNets (Schuler 1994, 1996),
◆ Virtual communities and community economic development organizations,
◆ E-mail campaigns, and
◆ Efforts at organizing virtual communities (Wittig & Schmitz 1996).

As might be expected, the dividing line between technology-assisted and technology-based constructs is never completely clear. As indicated in chapter 1, they represent points on a continuum between traditional community practice using no technology, and organizing accomplished totally in cyberspace.

Commonalties and Differences

Both online organizing and traditional community practice have substantial areas of conformity. All community practice efforts have a similar value base and share many processes and techniques. All place substantial weight on coordination, communication, information sharing, and education.

At a substantive level there is little difference between technology-assisted approaches and traditional approaches. The technology acts as a facilitator of the traditional methods. For example, mass e-mailing of an event announcement simply replaces the past use of fax, telephone tree, or postal mailing. Community organizers have always been quick to integrate new technologies into existing methods, as the prevalence of e-mail listservs indicates.

Use of the Internet is different from past incorporations of new technology into organizing. The capabilities of the Internet extend beyond that of a communications device such as the fax or telephone, and beyond a broadcast device such as television or radio. The Internet is a comprehensive and integrated communications, information, and broadcast tool with a global reach. As we reposition our practice toward the technology-based approaches, the differences become more apparent. The link to the local community becomes less an issue, or else the community becomes defined differently. We have always discussed nonplace communities in the community literature (Lyons 1987), but organizing within them was rarely mentioned. With the communications capabilities of the Internet, practitioners are increasingly finding that organizing individuals separated by space and time is readily enabled. This is a major issue as social problems become more global in nature.

The advent of the Internet has spawned two developments: First, people are working at a distance from one another and occasionally (or in some cases more frequently) joining in face-to-face meetings or events. The organizing of local committees for the protest against the Free Trade Agreement of the Americas (FTAA) in Quebec City used the Internet to coordinate the coming together of people and groups, and Wittig and Schmitz (1996) describe a successful effort to organize online to protect the homeless.

The second development is the organization of virtual communities or organizations. Individuals, usually disconnected by distance and having limited resources, connect online and undertake online protest and advocacy actions. For example, the connecting of a variety of people, groups, and organizations to fight "third world" debt formed a virtual coalition called the Jubilee 2000.

Even with these new capabilities, the tie between traditional community practice and online community practice remains important. Even those efforts that are conducted largely in cyberspace still need a connection in the physical world. As Chomsky notes in the preface, prior organization is needed for any communications medium to work. This means that in order to do any meaningful organization, we will need first to do the work of traditional methods. It is, of course, possible to do some or all of that work via the Internet, but much of the work of activists is within the traditional arena.

In addition, the newness of Internet-based techniques means that their acceptance by political decision makers is still questionable (for a review of this literature, see chapter 2). This can be expected to change as the technology becomes more widespread.

A third question is whether virtuality will damage the real-world community (Doheny-Farina 1996). There have been reports of Internet addictions whereby people's personal and family relationships have been strained by excessive Internet use. Young (1998) found that of those defined as dependent Internet users, 90 percent said they suffered "moderate" or "severe" impairment in their academic, interpersonal, or financial lives. In contrast, none of the nondependent users reported any impairment. Clearly, for the small number of people who become addicted to using it, the Internet is a problem. For the majority of users, the Internet is a useful communication and information tool. A survey (Patrick 1997) of 1,073 National Capital FreeNet (NCF) users found that 95 percent of users reported positive impacts on their lives (Patrick 1997). Many reported that they spent more time socializing beyond the Internet, and that they found the Internet beneficial for meeting people and engaging in discussion. Some users (62.8 percent) stated that the NCF has been an important aid to community action for them. A similar percentage responded that the NCF encouraged them to get more involved in community life

(Patrick 1997). These studies indicate that the Internet is a problem for a select segment of the population, but that, overall, it provides new opportunities and can be beneficial to community life.

* * *

The chapters in Part 2 provide a rich discussion of these issues. In chapter 7, Joseph Clarke discusses an electronic collaboration between a faith-based organization in Philadelphia and its local community through electronic means. This is very much in the vein of traditional community organizing. A critical issue in his chapter is community ownership of its information.

Chapter 8 takes a very different tack: organizing in the virtual world as a discussion group with members from around the globe takes on a local power structure. Gouthan Menon describes the efforts of the organizers to free a mentally challenged person jailed for stealing a cup of coffee. Ed Schwartz discusses his experiences as an online organizer in Philadelphia and presents his vision of a new online organizing system with Congressnet.org. Irene Queiro-Tajalli and Craig Campbell examine how women of color are using the Internet for advocacy. They discuss both local and international efforts and hash out the implications for feminist organizing. Nick Buxton investigates organizing around North-South issues, particularly the issue of "third world" debt. He explores how the Internet became central to the strategy of the Jubilee 2000 campaign—beginning as a vehicle for communicating campaign ideas, to becoming the central locus of information in a global movement and coordinating key decision-making events. He concludes that although future campaigns will be unable to ignore the Internet, it is essential that they do not rely too heavily on it. Finally, David Barnhizer tells us about the state of environmental organizing over the Internet. Again, the play between local activists and real communities is compared to that between virtual activists and virtual communities. He concludes that the Internet is an enabling mechanism that allows development and application of the powerful tools required to deal with ever larger, increasingly unaccountable public and private institutions. Without the Internet, such institutions would be uncontrollable.

CONCLUSION

Whether we communicate online or face to face, the skill and knowledge of community work is required. The emergence of Internet tools and even virtual spaces has not negated the need for traditional skills and the building of strong communities and relationships. To date, the use of the Internet in organizing has facilitated the building of a broad coalition of people who may be separated by space and time and has enabled new efficiencies in communication. In a few instances individuals have connected in a virtual community without ever meeting face to face. As all the chapters in Part 2 indicate, however, problems and pitfalls remain. The Internet is a useful tool, and as the following case examples indicate, organizers and activists will be wise to make use of the benefits and advantages it confers. At the same time, it is perhaps foolhardy to ignore the limitations and dangers that the Internet poses for community organizing.

Suggested Readings

Bonchek, M. S. 1995. *Grassroots in cyberspace: Using computer networks to facilitate political participation.* Paper presented at the fifty-third annual meeting of the Midwest Political Science Association, 6 April, Chicago, Ill. Available at [http://www.ai.mit.edu/people/msb/pubs/grassroots.html]. Retrieved on 8 January 1997.

Doheny-Farina, D. 1996. *The wired neighborhood.* New Haven, Conn.: Yale University Press.

Fisher, R. 1984. *Let the people decide: Neighborhood organizing in America.* New York: Twayne.

Garvin, C., & F. Cox. 2001. A history of community organization since the Civil War with special reference to oppressed communities. In *Strategies of community intervention* (6th ed.), ed. J. Rothman, J. L. Erlich, & J. E. Tropman, 65–100. Itasca, Ill.: F. E. Peacock.

Hick, S., E. F. Halpin, & E. Hoskins. 2000. *Human rights and the Internet.* London: Macmillan.

Lyons, L. 1987. *The community in urban society.* Philadelphia: Temple University Press.

McNutt, J. G. 2000. Coming perspectives in the development of electronic advocacy for social policy practice. *Critical Social Work* 1 (1). Available at [http://core.ecu.edu/socw/csw/]. Retrieved on 15 May 2001.

Meenaghan, T. M., & W. E. Gibbons. 2000. *Generalist practice in larger settings.* Chicago: Lyceum.

Patrick, A. S. 1997. *Personal and social impacts of going online: Lessons from the National Capital FeeNet.* Ottawa, Ontario: Industry Canada. Available at [http://debra.dgbt.doc.ca/services-research/survey/impacts]. Retrieved on 13 April 2001.

Rothman, J. 2001. Approaches to community intervention. In *Strategies of community intervention,* ed. J. Rothman, J. L. Erlich, & J. E. Tropman, 27–64. Itasca, Ill.: F. E. Peacock.

Schuler, D. 1994. Community networks: Building a new participatory medium. *Communications of the ACM* 37 (1): 39–51.

———. 1996. *New community networks: Wired for change.* Reading, Mass.: Addison-Wesley.

Trattner, W. 1994. *From poor law to welfare state* (5th ed.). New York: Free Press.

Warren, R. 1978. *The community in America* (3rd ed.). Chicago: Rand McNally.

Weil, M., & D. Gamble. 1995. Community practice models. In *Encyclopedia of social work* (19th ed.), ed. R. Edwards, 577–594. Washington, D.C.: NASW Press.

Wharf, B., & M. Clague (eds.). 1997. *Community organizing: Canadian experiences.* Don Mills, Ontario: Oxford University Press.

Wittig, M. A., & J. Schmitz. 1996. Electronic grassroots organizing. *Journal of Social Issues* 52 (1): 53–69.

Young, K. 1998. *Caught in the Net: How to recognize the signs of Internet addiction.* New York: Wiley.

Chapter 7

NetActivism 2001

How Citizens Use the Internet

Edward Schwartz

ON *NETACTIVISM: HOW CITIZENS USE THE INTERNET*

In June of 1995, Andy Oram—an editor at O'Reilly and Associates, already well known for its publication of *The Whole Internet Book* by Kiersten-Connor Sax and Ed Krol—sent me an e-mail asking whether I would be interested in writing a book on the growing use of the Internet in politics. It was the Internet itself that had brought me to the attention of O'Reilly, through a political listserv called "civic values" that I had been managing for less than a year. We ended up negotiating the book contract and editing drafts of each chapter via e-mail—again, a process that was now possible through the Internet.

Once *NetActivism: How Citizens Use the Internet* was published in mid-September 1996, a few months before the Presidential election, most of the book's promotion was also conducted through the Internet—including online interviews with the *Boston Globe,* the *Christian Science Monitor,* and *Wired.* In effect, the medium that I was describing had made it possible for me to develop, write, and now market this book on a timetable that would have been impossible in the past. This was in itself a testimonial to the power that this new medium was making available to ordinary citizens all over the country.

Unfortunately, the fate of *NetActivism* was as ephemeral as much of what appears on the Internet itself. Within a short period the book had generated enormous attention, but limited sales. There was a launch at the National Press Club, copies sent to every member of Congress, feature stories in *USA Today* and local papers like the *Dallas Morning News* and the *Philadelphia Inquirer.* By January, however, there was too little to demand to justify keeping it on O'Reilly's list. They did offer the Institute for the Study of Civic Values the opportunity to purchase the remaining copies, and we have become the distributor for *NetActivism* ever since.

Fortunately, the impact of *NetActivism: How Citizens Use the Internet* went far beyond its sales. Political and civic organizations at every level have sought copies of the book as an introductory guide on how to benefit from using the Internet in the course of their work. I became a featured speaker on the role of the Internet in numerous conferences, starting with a "Politics: USA" conference in Washington just after the 1996 election. Since then, groups such as the American Library Association, Americans for Democratic Action, the Food Research Action Council, and Amnesty International: USA have asked me to make similar presentations.

A few weeks prior to the 2000 election, I appeared on a New Jersey Public Television show exploring how the Internet was now being used to reshape politics in America. The trends that I had predicted in 1996 were now well underway—and when journalists submitted the term *NetActivism* to various search engines, such as Google, reviews and interviews that had remained online emerged among the first few responses. The Internet had brought *NetActivism* into existence; now it was keeping the book alive.

A great deal has happened in America since 1996, however, that has further defined and strengthened the Internet's role in citizen politics. To be sure, it was clear even then that e-mail and the World Wide Web would enable grassroots organizations and activists at every level to communicate with one another, share information, and advocate for change in ways that had been available only to well-financed interest groups in the past. Conservatives were already becoming well versed in these technologies through organizations such as the Christian Coalition and the National Rifle Association (NRA)—but the Left was catching up. Environmentalists, especially, had begun to use the Internet, and the Children's Defense Fund had begun to disseminate public policy alerts related to the federal budget via e-mail to thousands of online activists all over the country. The widespread use of the Internet in politics was no longer a question of "whether," but of "when." Although my book did put a spotlight on these developments, it ultimately served to speed up the process.

Where are we today? Obviously, e-mail and the Web have become indispensable political resources for groups throughout the country—but what have we learned about the effective use of the Internet in the process? What, for example, are the strengths and weaknesses of e-mail as a medium of political communication? What have turned out to be the best uses of the Web in calling attention to organizations and causes? Where has advocacy online been most successful, and what sorts of organizing might we expect through the Internet in the future? What, finally, are we learning about the real and potential impacts of the Internet on the broad effort to strengthen democracy in America by involving citizens more effectively in the decision-making process?

Exploring these issues can help us better understand what has happened with NetActivism since 1996 and what we have learned in the process. As I originally argued in the book, this technology merely provides us with a new set of tools. Whether they end up helping or hurting us depends on how we choose to use them.

Within this framework, then, let me address each of these questions in turn.

COMMUNICATIONS: FROM DEBATE TO DELIBERATION

The E-mail Revolution

In *NetActivism* I argued that,

> as an activist, the most important Internet system you need to understand remains e-mail. For all the hoopla surrounding Web sites, it is e-mail that you will be using most. The heart of our work as advocates and organizers is communicating with other people...E-mail is now creating entirely new ways for people maintain contact with one another." (Schwartz 1996, 39)

The point remains as pertinent in 2001 as it was in the mid-1990s: E-mail, not the Web, is *still* the most powerful online tool for activism. A Web site can introduce people to an organization or cause, help people obtain information, and even be used to solicit contributions or sell products as part of an ongoing fund-raising campaign. Even with all these benefits, e-mail continues to be the most widely used activist tool.

Yet it is e mail that we use to communicate with one another, and it is communication that makes collective action—the essence of organizing and effective advocacy—more possible.

Indeed, for all the hoopla surrounding the Web, most people still spend far more time sending and receiving e-mail on the Internet than they do surfing the Web, because what we want most is to connect with one another. Calculate how you spend most of your own time on the Internet, and you will likely come to the same conclusion.

So, what has happened with e-mail over the past five years, especially in relation to civic and political activism? Here, in my judgment, are a few of the major developments.

E-mail has become an essential instrument of our work. Whatever digital divide may exist among American citizens at different economic levels, e-mail is now as important to our offices as phones and fax machines have been in the past. This is almost as true now for grassroots organizations as it has been for large corporations. Once an organization purchases a computer today, e-mail is not far behind. Indeed, a primary reason for groups to buy computers today is to be able to access the Internet; the more organizations go online, the more pressure is placed on every other group to join them. This has certainly been the case in Philadelphia, even for groups in our poorest neighborhoods. Low-income residents may not be able to access the Internet yet, but groups representing them can—and they all use e-mail.

E-mail and the Web now connect effortlessly with one another. In 1996, it was not easy to link to a Web site from an e-mail or to send e-mail via the Web. We take both for granted now. The result is that we now use e-mail to disseminate complex information and data to one another, well beyond the notes that we started exchanging with one another a few years ago. Organizations, in turn, can now urge visitors to their Web sites to subscribe to an e-mail list that will keep them connected to the group once they leave the Web.

Anyone can create an e-mail list now—for nothing. In *NetActivism,* I devoted an entire chapter to the virtues of e-mail lists or listservs that were making it possible for groups of people to communicate with one another via e-mail without having to be in the same place at the same time.

Managing a listserv in 1996, however, meant finding a college or university or Internet service provider with ListProc or Majordomo software to support the list, and then learning the complex commands that were needed to manage it over time. Moreover, although it was possible to create a list-archives file on the Web to retrieve past messages, it was a complicated process. Not much else could be done to support an e-mail list on the World Wide Web. Even within these limitations, however, listservs remained the Internet's most powerful tool for communications, but it took considerable time to learn how to use them.

This is no longer the case. Online services such as Yahoo! Groups (formerly E-Groups) and Topica make it possible for anyone to create their own lists within minutes after signing up for the service. At this writing, at least, these services are free. Moreover, we can participate in and manage these lists from both our e-mail accounts and the Web as well. People can join the list, post messages to it, and leave it from either online location. If the list is visible to the public (managers have the option of creating either public or private lists) anyone can read past messages on the Web—now easily searched by topic—and retrieve the e-mail addresses of its members. Yahoo! Groups [http://groups.yahoo.com] even provides each member with a calendar that sends reminders of events to the list, a chat room, a polling mechanism, and various databases for files and Web links.

In *NetActivism,* I noted that "We need substantial improvement in the software now used to manage e-mail lists," including search engines for list archives, a way to vote on lists, and new ways to block disruptive members (Schwartz 1996, 179). All of these features are now readily available online, either in these free services—where we put up with ads—or in listserv software such as Lyris and Mailman. Managing an e-mail list is literally just a phone call away.

Managing the E-mail Glut

As is often the case, however, these new opportunities for the use of e-mail and listservs present a new set of challenges. Having managed or participated in dozens of lists over the past five years—in part, with support from the Surdna Foundation, OMBWatch, and the William Penn Foundation in Philadelphia—I can speak from considerable experience on several points that are now abundantly clear.

Activists, especially, are now far more interested in connecting with people who agree with them—not in debating with advocates from the other side. In 1996, encouraging activists to join e-mail lists was relatively easy. Since e-mail was not widely used, lists had little competition. In fact, joining listservs was often the main way that people involved in communities and causes found one another online.

Today, that has all changed. Now we connect with coworkers, associates, and friends online as part of our daily routine. We send articles and proposals to one another via e-mail as if we had been doing this for years. Those of us with computers in both our offices and homes have now extended the workday well into the night—and with the advent of wireless personal data assistants (PDAs) that receive and send messages from our pockets, we are beginning to be connected to the Internet throughout the day. As a result, within just a few years we have gone from receiving no e-mail at all to dealing with an e-mail glut that is a major challenge for us to manage.

This has changed significantly the reasons activists agree to participate in a listserv. In the 1990s, e-mail lists were an interesting diversion, and people often were willing to devote much of their time to them. It was fascinating to reach people all over the world with similar interests and concerns. Using the Internet to debate issues proved interesting as well. In the autumn of 1994, for example—as the Republican Party was in the process of taking over Congress—a spirited debate on "civic values" developed between a number of community activists and a few members of the Christian Coalition who had joined the list. The religious Right is not well represented in Philadelphia, and the online debate gave me invaluable insight into what they thought and why they have such an impact around the country. The debate with these conservatives stands among the most interesting exchanges on the civic-values listservs in 1994—and it was totally spontaneous.

Today, however, as we are now being bombarded with e-mail from every direction, most activists no longer need or even want to engage in extended debates online, especially with people who simply do not agree with us. At this point, most of us feel the need to connect with our allies and to use e-mail to develop common goals and strategies. Whatever our exact ideology, we have moved from debate to deliberation via e-mail, and anyone creating a listserv needs to develop it on that basis.

This leads us to several points relevant to managing listservs today: First of all, whatever the goals, e-mail lists do not just happen—we need to make them happen. This principle is self-evident in relation to other kinds of groups, but somehow it eludes many of us online. The directories of services such as Yahoo! Groups are filled with five-member list entries that were created and then abandoned when the list failed to attract hundreds of members right away. It may take only a few minutes to create a listserv online today, but the real challenge lies in persuading people to join it and use it in pursuit of common goals. Why should organizing people online be any less challenging than organizing within our communities?

Second, the goals of an e-mail list membership must be clear, and the list manager should have no qualms about unsubscribing people who do not share them. The goals should be set forth clearly in the stated purpose of the list, and subscribers should meet certain criteria to be allowed to join. That way, it becomes possible to remove people from the list who clearly should not be there. If some unsubscribed participants complain that their freedom of speech has been violated, you can point to the list objectives as the basis for the decision. If the purpose is clear, the great majority of subscribers will not only agree with that purpose, they will welcome your efforts to keep the group focused on its goals.

Third, most lists should be moderated. By that I mean that the manager should screen every posting. This was not so necessary in the 1990s, when the volume of e-mail was relatively low. Today, however, even a list whose participants are simpatico can generate too many messages in a day for subscribers to handle. By moderating the list, the manager can spread the postings over two or three days, or send them out in a cluster—like a list digest—so participants can focus on them all at once.

Fourth, the list should be connected to a Web site. This becomes indispensable to building a strong online support system for the list. People should be able to join the list from the Web and use the Web to provide easy access to past messages. Older Web software (e.g., Majordomo) makes this difficult. Newer packages, such as Mailman and Lyris—along with Yahoo! Groups and Topica—are far easier to use. Newer does not always mean better, but in this case it does, and these programs are now readily available online.

Finally, one should always keep the real-world purpose of the list in mind. An online exchange can develop a life of its own, even on a list with specific objectives for organizing or advocacy within the community. The result is that members may end up engaging in extensive discussion on issues that bear little relationship to our daily work, which is fine as long as the members of the list find the exchanges interesting and useful. If the list volume gets out of hand, however, many of the most active subscribers will leave. That is when a list manager needs to urge participants to "go private" with their discussion—just as a chairperson of a live meeting would "call the question" after an extended debate. If the list was created to build NetActivism, then its participants will even insist that the manager make a real effort to control the process.

The e-mail glut that faces us now has developed because e-mail *is* extraordinarily useful, both in broadening person-to-person communication and in enabling us to share information and ideas with entire groups. However, if we are strategic in our use of the telephone and the fax machine—and for that matter, in planning meetings—then we must be equally as disciplined in creating and managing e-mail lists. The most successful lists are already being managed on this basis.

INFORMATION: FROM SURFING TO SHARING

The Ever-Widening Web

Remember the World Wide Web in 1996? One needed to know hypertext markup language (html) to design a Web site, and the number of people who could do so remained relatively small. Corporate America had yet to catch on to the Internet's potential for marketing and sales, so we were spared the enticement—and intrusion—of e-commerce into every aspect of our lives. Most politicians had not even heard of the Internet, and most governments outside Washington, D.C., had no clue how they might use it. Conservative groups were developing Web sites, but the Left still had quite a bit of catching up to do—a point that I made rather strongly in *NetActivism*. Even then, however, more was happening than was evident on the surface. An "Internet in Politics" conference held shortly after the 1996 election produced a survey showing that 11 percent of the voters had used the Internet to obtain political information—as many as had used magazines. This came as quite a surprise. The webmaster of the Dole campaign reported to the conference that thousands of volunteers had signed up from their Web site. Pat Buchanan, we learned, used an e-mail list to connect campaign volunteers with each other throughout the winter and spring primaries. These developments were shades of things to come.

Now, however, so much of what we see and hear about includes its own Web site that it is difficult to imagine how a person can function without one. Needless to say, however, there are new challenges here as well; three are especially important in relation to NetActivism.

◆ As Web sites proliferate, it becomes increasingly difficult to find specific ones.
◆ Conversely, as Web sites grow more professional, many small groups now conclude that they must spend a lot of money to develop one.
◆ As Web sites take advantage of new broadband technologies for audio and video, many activists have begun to think of the Net more as a broadcasting system than as a tool to share information with one another about who we are and what we do.

Under the circumstances, if organizations conclude that whatever they develop on the Web will go unnoticed and underused, they will not take advantage of it. This would be a mistake. It is important to recognize, then, what a great many nations have learned about being on the World Wide Web.

Web Insights

Although several basic principles of Web site design apply to all sites, others relate specifically to the use of the Web to support campaigns and causes. These are the points we shall address here. They can help us focus on how to use the Web to our best advantage.

A Web site is just another outpost for your organization—nothing more, nothing less. Remember this whenever you think that unless your Web site features the latest in high-level graphics, animation, and Java, you will disgrace yourself. You would not expect your newsletter to compete with *The New York Times,* and people interested in your organization would not hold you to this sort of standard, either. What matters is using your Web site to present who you are, what you do, and how people can help you in a clear and simple way. The rest will take care of itself.

Getting your own Web domain is easy—and cheap. Even activists who have been online for some time but have never developed a Web site are surprised at how easy it is. Just go to Network Solutions [http://www.networksolutions.com], use their search engine to determine whether your preferred domain is available (often it is), and then spend no more than $55.00 to register it for two years. The Internet service provider (ISP) or Web hosting service that will be working with you can tell you what to enter in the "technical host" section of the form. Even I was astonished at how easy this was after five years of designing my own Web sites while letting a Web hosting service handle the registrations.

Moreover, once you begin registering domains, you begin to think of new ones that your group might want to have. Civic and political activism are still relatively low-level priorities in America (as opposed to sex, money, and entertainment), and you may be surprised how many domains are still available. This is by far the easiest part of the process—much simpler than writing a fund-raising proposal, for example.

A group's Web site needs to present its purposes, its location, and its main activities, and then provide a way that visitors and members can use e-mail to connect with it on a regular basis. Note that I did not include a calendar and a monthly newsletter on this list, even though these are standard features of services such as Neighborhood Link [http://www.neighborhoodlink.com]. (Such services offer prefabricated, community-group Web sites in every zip code in a metropolitan area if a group or groups can raise the funds to support them.) In my experience, both upcoming events and newsletters are better distributed via e-mail—where recipients must either read or delete them—than on a Web site that even group members may visit only occasionally.

Outside your own promotional efforts, most people will reach your Web site via one or more search engines and the Yahoo! Directory. Thus, becoming listed on these search engines should be a major priority—which, in turn, will depend on how the Web developer describes the site in the MetaTags associated with it. This should offer some reassurance that there are ways to reach your Web site through the clutter of the millions of sites that now coexist on the Web.

Your Web site should link to a form that enables interested visitors either to receive e-mail from your organization or to subscribe to an interactive list of its members, or both. Services such as Yahoo! Groups provide a prefabricated "submit" form that you can use simply by cutting and pasting the appropriate code into your site. Again, just as you want people who come into your office to join your organization and receive its newsletter, so you should aim to have people who visit your Web site subscribe to your list before they leave.

If your organization is devoted to a particular cause or causes, then its Web site should aim at becoming a portal for the major groups and online information centers related to the cause. By using your Web page to link to the sites that you find useful, you increase the value of the site to your members and give them added reasons to return. Moreover, if you regularly inform participants on your e-mail list of new links on the site, then you encourage them to use the site again and again. This in itself builds support for your organization.

If your organization does attempt to influence elected officials, be sure to include links to their e-mail addresses on your site. Project Vote Smart [http://www.vote-smart.org] and other sites provide this information. Because many of these seem to go out of business, however, it would be best to submit "write elected officials" forms to a search engine such as Google and pick out the service that works best at the time.

In short, in the five short years since the publication of *NetActivism,* the Internet has changed from a place where only a few people could even produce a Web site to one where almost anybody can. From America Online [http://hometown. aol.com] and Geocities, now managed by Yahoo! [http://geocities.yahoo.com], to Microsoft's Front Page, now included in the Microsoft Office Suite; to more complicated packages such as NetObjects Fusion and Dreamweaver, a wide range of Web development packages are available. If these do not work for you, you can often find college or even high school students who have real talent in this area and who would welcome the opportunity to do something useful for the community.

Indeed, at this point there is really no excuse for a strong community organization *not* to have a Web site, given how easy it has become to develop one.

NET ADVOCACY: FROM ONLINE PETITIONS TO POLITICS

No Longer Whether, but How

Much of *NetActivism: How Citizens Use the Internet* was aimed at persuading activists that the Internet could be useful to them. In the introduction, I observed that

> if you haven't started using the Internet yet, you probably think of it as an additional burden—another set of "things" you'll have to attend to in an already overcrowded day. Once you get into it, however, you'll see it as an invaluable resource, enabling you to communicate rapidly with thousands of people all over the country and retrieve information that you now have to spend hours trying to get, if you can find it at all. (Schwartz 1996, 17)

This case no longer needs to be made. Every kind of organization, from volunteer civic groups in small towns to such major national associations as the American Association of Retired Persons (AARP) and the AFL-CIO, are now aware of the enormous power of the Internet in mobilizing people to support causes and campaigns of mutual concern.

The defining moment, I suspect, came in September 1998, when Joan Blades and Wes Boyd—two Silicon Valley software developers with little prior political experience—propelled a well-written petition throughout the Internet urging Congress to "censure" President Clinton for his indiscretions and "move on." As now reported on the MoveOn.Org Web site [http://www.moveon.org], the group grew to 500,000 members within a matter of weeks, delivering more than 2,000,000 e-mails to Congress and generating more than 250,000 phone calls.

MoveOn failed to dissuade the House from impeaching the President, but the online outcry that its petition generated was a likely reason the Senate failed to convict him. Moreover, MoveOn soon moved on to politics, becoming a significant online fund raiser for candidates running against representatives who voted for impeachment in defiance of their constituents' views. Today, the organization has become a more or less permanent online advocacy group, with petitions supporting campaign finance reform and other causes related to democratic reform among its ongoing activities and concerns.

However we measure the impact of MoveOn's petition on the impeachment debate in Congress, it stands as the undisputed watershed in the use of the Internet to empower citizens in the political process. Before MoveOn, activists would ask whether it made sense to use the Internet, as opposed to mass mailings and the telephone, to mobilize citizens. After MoveOn, the answer was obvious.

NetAdvocacy in the New Millennium

At this point, a growing number of organizations are using the Internet effectively to advance the causes and campaigns they support. These include a little group called Barking Dogs in Lower Greenville, Dallas, Texas [http://www.barking-dogs.org], which uses the Web to demand tougher code enforcement from the Dallas city government; N.A.I.L.E.M. (Neighborhood Activists Inter-Linked Empowerment Movement), based in Phoenix, Arizona, which bombards the Arizona state legislature with e-mails on issues related to law enforcement and insurance reform; and Doctors Without Borders and ACT-UP (both based in Philadelphia), whose online petition generated 250,000 signatures demanding that pharmaceutical companies permit the South African government to make affordable AIDS medicines available to their people. Thirty-nine pharmaceutical companies dropped a lawsuit against the South African government in response to this online petition.

In short, the number of causes and movements that are now being mobilized via the Internet grows every day. Here, too, we are learning a great deal about how to organize these campaigns effectively. Several important elements are common to all of them:

- ◆ Online campaigns around specific issues—"flash campaigns," as they are called—must aim at specific targets. People will respond only if a specific law, regulation, or decision is at stake for which public pressure can make a difference. Merely calling attention to a problem (drugs, global warming, child poverty) or demanding a generalized solution (drug treatment, environmental protection, a better health care system) will not do the job. There is no effective way to measure the success of abstract public-education campaigns, but it is suspected that people are less likely to participate. If, however, we are asked to lobby for or against a specific bill, we will know soon enough whether we won or lost. The bill either passes or it does not. This kind of clarity is often enough to persuade people that their participation can really make a difference.
- ◆ Online petitions are emerging as the most common vehicle for advocacy on the Internet. Petitions are easy to generate and to circulate online. Even if the originating organization does not have a huge e-mail list of its own, the Internet is now a chain with so many links that well-conceived appeals can be spread quite a distance within a matter of hours. MoveOn showed how easy it is to do this—and a number of groups have learned well from its example.
- ◆ There must be a common Web site from which all participants can gain additional information on the cause and what more they can do to support it. Beyond the obvious organizational benefits that the Web site provides, it

may also be needed to reassure potential supporters that the cause and the people organizing it are legitimate.

♦ Petitions sent to Congress or state and local legislatures and councils must be targeted to the elected officials who are appropriate to receive them. It is especially important for senators and sepresentatives to hear from *only* their own constituents. Congressional staffers have for some time been bothered by having to screen out unwanted e-mails, a process that makes it much more difficult to assess what the sentiments in their own districts really are.

♦ People who support an advocacy campaign need to receive periodic reports on how well it is going. This is not just common courtesy; it is essential if the sponsoring organization hopes to mobilize these online allies in the future. The MoveOn group has been especially skilled at maintaining contact with its original supporters—just often enough to keep us informed, without barraging us with appeals every few days. Indeed, groups or concerned citizens planning to undertake similar flash campaigns would do well to study MoveOn, whose managers have shown real understanding not only of the Internet, but of the political process itself.

♦ If you can afford it, hire an online campaign consultant—if only to get help in building an e-mail database. Two of the best of agencies in this area are TechRocks, supported by the Rockefeller Brothers Foundation [http://www.techrocks.org], and e-advocates [http://www.e-advocates.com], affiliated with Capital Advantage based in Washington, D.C. Each is staffed with activists who learned how to use the Internet as extensions of their own political work. The value of these agencies, then, lies not simply in their activists' knowledge of the technology, but in their recognizing how it can be used to best advantage. Furthermore, their rates are reasonable—generally shaped to what a potential client can afford.

To be sure, even though we have come a long way in a short time in using the Internet for civic and political advocacy, we remain at the dawn of this era. Online advocacy groups still need to develop strength within individual congressional and state legislative districts, strength of the sort that the labor movement and groups such as the NRA have built over many years.

If we have learned anything at all about the Internet over the past five years, it is that time online really does fly. The advice that I offered activists in 1996 is relevant today, even though it is being put into practice by many. I have little doubt that the trends I am describing in this chapter will be well established by the next presidential election in 2004.

THE DEMOCRATIC CHALLENGE: NETACTIVISM AND POLITICAL REFORM

Where, then, do these new online initiatives fit into the broader effort to strengthen American democracy by making elected officials more accountable to the people?

Unfortunately, there appears to be little public understanding of how citizen action on the Internet is already bringing about political reform, beyond occasional references to Web sites that enable us to track where candidates receive their funds.

In contrast with the projects that I have described here—all involving collective action—the Web sites developed around the presidential campaigns (e.g., Web White & Blue, the Democracy Project, and even Project Vote Smart) aim primarily to make it easy for individual voters to obtain information about individual candidates, without helping any of these voters connect with one another. The low-key debate over the merits of online voting does relate to political reform, but it is unlikely that on election day we will be showing up on the Internet—not at the polls—for many years to come.

I would contend, however, that when organizations and advocates use the Internet to bring citizens together, to share political information and ideas with thousands of people online, and to send powerful collective messages to Congress, they are contributing just as much—if not more—to democratizing the political process as any of the campaign finance and election reform bills pending in Congress right now.

It is one thing to reduce the role of money in politics; it is quite another to insure that an active citizenry will fill the vacuum. That effort—like NetActivism itself—must be organized on a block-by-block, district-by-district basis. All the tools of the Internet I have described here can contribute to this process, but again, only if we *make* it happen. This is the ultimate challenge facing champions of democracy online today, and it will involve a considerable amount of work.

One initiative undertaken by the Institute for the Study of Civic Values in Philadelphia during the 2000 presidential campaign gives us grounds for hope. We called it the NonVoters Campaign, and it was designed to use the Internet directly to build a grassroots, get-out-the-vote campaign among unlikely voters—an effort such as I urged in the last chapter of *NetActivism* in 1996. The key here was to mobilize an army of nonvoter volunteers who would go door to door in their voting divisions, encouraging people to show up at the polls as an expression of neighborhood empowerment.

Although many of the nonvoter volunteers did not have Internet access, those who did were added to an e-mail list and directed to a Web site with information on past voting patterns in every ward in the city. We also included links to the major Web sites devoted to candidates and campaign issues. The Web site remains online [http://www.nonvoters.org] and includes a report on the 2000 campaign along with information on how we intend to build this campaign in the future.

The NonVoters Campaign itself was a big success. The 160 divisions (roughly 10 percent of the voting divisions in Philadelphia) in which we fielded volunteers increased participation by 10 percent—as opposed to only 3.7 percent in the city as a whole. This held true throughout the city, regardless of the racial and ethnic composition of each division. We proved once again that if get-out-the vote organizers are prepared to knock on doors and talk personally with the voters, the voters will respond.

We also demonstrated how effective the Internet could be in helping campaign volunteers keep in touch with one another and make good use of the information about candidates and issues that we obtained online. Our mailings to campaign volunteers reprinted much of what we found on the Web, since this was generally the best information available to us. Thus, even those without access to the Internet benefited from what we found there.

The Institute for the Study of Civic Values most certainly will be reviving the NonVoters Campaign during the gubernatorial, congressional, and state legislative elections of 2002, and in every major election thereafter. We will be using our Web sites and national e-mail lists to encourage voters throughout the country to join us. If MoveOn has demonstrated how a national campaign can affect local politics, we aim to demonstrate how sustained get-out-the-vote campaigns in local districts throughout the country can affect national politics.

Before the Internet became available, only a strong national organization like the AFL-CIO could even contemplate a major national effort of this kind. Through the Internet, however, even a relatively small local group like the Institute for the Study of Civic Values can build this sort of campaign in local districts all over the United States.

There are many ways, to be sure, that the Internet may ultimately undermine democracy in America. It still is largely a medium for the "haves" who can afford computers and who know how to use them. By mobilizing support for national causes without strengthening local organizations in the process, Internet organizers are merely amassing power for themselves without sharing it with anyone else. Furthermore, the more we become enthralled with audio and video on the Internet, the less we communicate with one another, and the closer the Internet comes to being just another top-down broadcasting system like television. The Internet posed these threats to democracy in 1996; they remain no less threatening today.

Yet despite these risks, the major trends in online politics all move in the opposite direction. The Internet continues to help us connect with one another and to focus our collective concerns as citizens on influencing the people in power. Digital divide notwithstanding, the power really can reside with the people on the Internet, and we are learning how to use it.

From at least this activist's perspective—just a few blocks away from Independence Hall in Philadelphia—that is what Jefferson had in mind when he called for a revolution every twenty-five years. It is still about "we the people," shaping both the vision and the fundamental values of America so that our future will continue to be better than the past.

Suggested Reading

Schwartz, E. 1996. *NetActivism: How citizens use the Internet.* Sebastopol, Calif.: O'Reilly.

Chapter 8

Environmental Activism on the Internet

David Barnhizer

INTRODUCTION

This chapter demonstrates ways environmental activists are using the Internet to enhance their effectiveness. In less than ten years, the Internet has infiltrated our economic, social, and political processes and caused the creation of new public and private institutions on all levels (Wertheim 1999). The Internet has become a vital part of environmental activism. This holds true whether the environmental organization is a large national or international organization, such as the Natural Resources Defense Council (NRDC), World Wildlife Fund, or Greenpeace; or a smaller organization with a more local focus. The Internet is important whether the activists are based in the United States or in a developing country. Environmentalists are using the Internet to increase dramatically their power to mobilize forces, publicize their own activities, expose their opponents, and protest harm to the environment. This new set of capabilities is of significance to activists in general—but even more particularly to environmental and human rights activists, who are uniquely communication dependent. This relates to the fact that many of the activities they undertake to attack the problems they challenge and to identify and implement the solutions they seek are both caused and related to transboundary, global-commons, and other global phenomena. In such a context it is essential that low-cost communications networks exist because the activists are typically operating on very limited budgets, with severe staffing limitations, and without the financial ability or time to engage in frequent international travel.

Simultaneously, the chapter analyzes some of the dangers inherent in becoming too dependent on the Internet. Although the Internet offers expanded capabilities, and there is no question that many organizations are more effective because of its existence, the Internet has limits and dangers. The negative side effects of Internet use and dependency are subtle and incremental rather than obvious (Rochlin 1997). Some of the consequences flow from activities that initially appear desirable but that quickly consume the organization in a flood of minutiae or information overload. Others divert energy, talent, and focus from the organization's central mission. The Internet is only an enhancement tool—not a substitute for action. It is easy to become enamored with technology and to attribute nonexistent magical capabilities to it. The dangers of Internet dependence also include the inhumanity of the Internet, and our forgetting of the continuing need for face-to-face human communications and relationships. Furthermore, the Internet is highly vulnerable to infiltration by opponents and virus attacks (see, e.g., Freedman & Mann 1997).[1]

Commerce and its ability to produce environmental degradation on a massive scale are truly global phenomena. As the scale of economic activity expands it creates an ever-greater potential for environmental harm. There is no way of reversing the changes wrought by the Internet. Information technology has transformed business and governments—compressing time, accelerating action, magnifying impact, and enlarging scale. The structure of economic activity and its regulation has shifted in what might be best thought of as the Fourth Kondratiev Wave—a transformation in the nature of the entire economic system and not just a linear extension of the system that existed prior to the 1990s (see also Sennett 1998).

The Internet is perhaps best understood as the mechanism through which the Information Age is enabling the development and application of the powerful tools required to deal with ever-larger, increasingly unaccountable public and private institutions. Without the Internet, such institutions would be uncontrollable; with the Internet there is at least some potential for balanced opposition. The power and scale of institutional structures is part of the economic technique that Jacques Ellul (1965) described as shaping modern society, often through the use of propaganda. Ellul (1965) writes that "propaganda seeks to induce action, adherence, and participation—with as little thought as possible" (180). The Internet can, of course, be used for the purposes of propaganda as well—but its very newness, diversity of access, and ability to bypass traditional communications media have so far made it a creative instrument with which to challenge power structures and transmit information that would otherwise be suppressed. What will occur as special interests become more sophisticated in imposing limitations on Internet use is an important question.

Much of the rhetoric used to justify the creation of market-driven institutions and governmental policies that favor economics and trade over all else is only propaganda and espoused ideology. As is so with all effective propaganda, there are seeds of truth beneath the lies and distortions. Of course there is a need for economic growth, trade, alleviation of poverty, and new jobs and opportunity. Those themes, however, are being used cynically to trump virtually all other considerations and to gloss over the many harms of the processes and the fundamental shift in power that is occurring. Martin Buber (1965) warned four decades ago that

> Our age has experienced . . . [a] paralysis and failure of the human soul successively in three realms. The first was the realm of technique. Machines . . . invented to serve men in their work, impressed him into their service. They were no longer, like tools, an extension of man's arm, but man became their extension, an adjunct on their periphery, doing their bidding. (158) [Note that Buber's second realm was the economic, and his third, the political.]

Technology—and the Internet is one of history's most powerful examples—creates capabilities but also alters us, collapses existing systems, and constructs new barriers between us. A central element of the change is the reorganization of human activity and systems according to the new capabilities. Amazingly complex information and data management systems have, for example, allowed us to track and subdivide things into ever more discrete bundles, and we have learned how to package these bundles and charge fees for them. Health care has, for example, been turned into an extremely profitable but morally bankrupt set of institutions. Information is power and because we *can* do it, we do it because there is no countervailing value. In a system whose sole guiding principle is money, only "fools" give things away or charge less than the market will bear. This antiprinciple has a dehumanizing impact on many cultures, just as assembly lines and the breaking down of manufacturing into precise units of specific activity to occur within a constrained time period have had dehumanizing effects on workers with the rise of mass production.

Without the free Internet the environmental movement would in many ways be deaf, dumb, and blind compared to the power and capabilities of the institutions that environmentalists challenge. Tools, values, and processes must be developed that are sufficient to allow for protective actions to match the scale of the destructive activities and to deal with the more powerful institutions whose actions are creating the undesirable effects. Tools are needed that allow concerned citizens of all kinds to improve the quality and scale of their ability to communicate, network, track, and monitor (see, e.g., Bergeson 1998; Mannan and O'Connor 1999; Stimson 1999; Webb, David, and Paterson 1998 for examples of monitoring). The enhanced tools offered to ordinary citizens by the Internet include those of information management and synthesis; monitoring for the purposes of keeping organizations' processes transparent and imposing greater accountability on decision makers; increased democratic organization and citizen participation; and more quickly organized and focused protest activities.

ENVIRONMENTALISTS' APPROACHES TO INTERNET USE

The best way to show the pros and cons of this powerful tool is through real-life examples that show not only which approaches work most effectively, but also how to organize activities to take advantage of the Internet's capabilities while avoiding its negative aspects.

Consider the case of the wealthy owner of a consumer-oriented company who must feel he inadvertently entered an environmental activist's version of *The Twilight Zone*. This individual was a major initial contributor to George Bush's presidential campaign. Bush's questionable environmental record raised red flags with environmental activists who threatened to launch an Internet campaign aimed at convincing consumers to boycott the wealthy contributor's company. The contributor stated publicly that he was out of politics and would no longer contribute to the Bush campaign ("Bush Backer" 2000). One person's activism is another's digital terrorism. Anticorporate activism is increasing through groups of hackers trying to inundate particular corporate Web sites using an extremely high volume of messages. The *Plain Dealer* reported an even more aggressive strategy in a recent news article relating that so-called electrohippies were planning a massive attack by hackers to protest the development and sale of genetically altered food products. The targets of the Internet attacks were to be companies that sell or produce genetically modified food products. The attacks would send the companies tens of thousands of e-mails to overload the businesses' computer systems ("'Electrohippies' 2000).

The organization, Environmental Defense, has created an action alert network—the names of 10,000 individuals reachable by e-mail who have indicated they are willing to respond to selected Environmental Defense requests for action messages directed to specific targets on hot issues. Such a network offers immediate, numerous, and focused responses and communication free of charge. As such networks become more common, however, they can be expected to lose both effectiveness and novelty in the eyes of those targeted. Environmental Defense has also created a searchable version of the Environmental Protection Agency's Toxic Waste Inventory, which allows anyone concerned about toxic and hazardous chemicals in his or her neighborhood to determine the condition of the specific local situation. The Mangrove Action Project (MAP) has created a wide, international contact network of activists, researchers, academics, and environmentalists. The MAP has been an effective user of the Internet and has operated through newsletters, workshops, and the linking of its extensive network across many countries. The Industrial Shrimp Action Network (ISA Net) is truly global, made up of environmental and community organizations from Latin America, North America, Africa, Asia, and Europe. It emerged from concerns about irresponsible shrimp aquaculture voiced by groups such as MAP, NRDC, Greenpeace, Accion Ecologica, PREPARE, and others. Communications and cooperative action among the far-flung ISA Net members would be impossible without the Internet. It allows the frequent communications needed to sustain the network, facilitates strategic cooperation, permits the sharing of research findings and other information, and helps focus and improve fund raising.

Virtually no organization is without a Web site. Such electronic bulletin boards are useful for focusing public relations messages, fund raising, membership recruiting, and updating existing memberships. They can provide hot-issue reports with links to other key sites or full-text offerings of their own. As recently as 1997, organizational Web sites were relatively unique. The NRDC's Shrimp Tribunal was an early example. Lately there has been such a proliferation of Web sites, however, that they are no longer novel, although they remain very useful. The Internet is also extremely helpful in organizing—including the identification of potential allies. Those interested in a particular issue can create listservs and similar mechanisms that save significant communication time and disseminate messages widely.

One of the most important powers of the Internet is that it creates real-time communications capability. The Internet is a multiplier: It enables both the public-interest activist and the business decision maker to overcome the global time barrier, and communicate anywhere in the world with very little lag time. Along with the ability to communicate is the ability to transfer files and data, and to interact on collaborative projects. In an era in which large commercial interests have taken control of traditional media and publishing systems, the Internet offers a low-cost alternative by which an environmental organization can ensure that its message reaches interested parties. The Internet offers the ability to bypass traditional media by disseminating information that does not find its way into the popular media.

In some countries the media are controlled and news suppressed. In Malaysia, enterprising activists with digital cameras took pictures of the presiding judge in the Anwar case meeting socially with the prosecutors. The pictures went up on the Internet within hours, giving the impression that Anwar could not get a fair trial. There is likely to be an expansion of that kind of activism, particularly in countries with controlled media. *The New York Times* Electronic reported on 20 May 2000, in an article titled "China Suspends Web Site for 'Spreading Rumors,'" that China had shut down an organization's Internet access because it had reported a news story the Chinese government claimed was false. In other nations, including the United States, the media have become so selective or sensationalized that a great deal of information does not pass the commercial-interest filters that have been created to appease a mass audience.

The Internet is an equalizing mechanism that allows an approximate balance of strategic power.[2] Consider some examples. The Mitsubishi Corporation recently joined with the Government of Mexico in a plan to build a very large salt processing plant in an area of the Gulf of California that environmentalists regard as an important breeding ground for whales. A wide array of environmental organizations organized to oppose the project, successfully using a combination of electronic networking, publicity, and face-to-face negotiations. This reminds us that although the Internet is a powerful tool, activists still require other approaches to be successful.

The Shrimp Tribunal was founded in 1996 by the NRDC to focus attention on the serious environmental and social dilemmas inherent in the explosive expansion of shrimp aquaculture in developing countries. Funded by the Rockefeller Brothers Fund and located at NRDC, the Tribunal combined a Shrimp Tribunal Web site with a provocative forum as part of its nongovernmental organization (NGO) activities at the 1996, 1997, and 1999 sessions of the United Nations Commission on Sustainable Development (UNCSD). This combined, direct challenge of the UNCSD, along with the building of an accessible electronic record of abuses, served numerous functions: It gained the attention of the opposition; it served as a research and investigative tool, and as a means of creating and disseminating information; and it created both face-to-face and electronic links throughout the Internet among actors in the field seeking to protest the spread of irresponsible aquaculture. The detailed information posted on the Tribunal Web site was regularly monitored by both friend and foe. A high-ranking Ecuadorian business leader admitted that the challenges had caused the industry in Ecuador to take notice of the environmental complaints and begin changing their behaviors to those more environmentally sustainable much sooner than would otherwise have occurred.

In Ecuador, the world's third largest producer of farmed shrimp for export, Ecuadorian environmental organizations such as Accion Ecologica and Fundecol have become part of a global network of environmental organizations that are using the Internet as an important part of their communications and strategy development. Environmentalists, traditional farmers, and local communities opposed to the widespread destruction of mangrove forests in coastal areas and to the dislocation of local economies have protested the rapid expansion of shrimp aquaculture. The Internet is only one part of a complex process, but it has enhanced the ability of Ecuadorian NGOs and their external partners to network, obtain information, mobilize international pressure, seek and obtain funding, protect activists who have been arrested, and press for legal reform.

These activities only touch the surface of what is made possible by the Internet. The NRDC, for example, negotiated a settlement with the U.S. Department of Energy (DOE) in which the DOE has agreed to pay $6.25 million into a privately managed fund from which environmentalists concerned with nuclear waste issues can obtain project financing. As part of the settlement, the DOE also agreed to establish a comprehensive database, searchable by NGOs, that contains most of the DOE's information. The NRDC's physicists also work with Russian environmentalists to obtain information about nuclear waste disposal in that country. The NRDC scientists then create data displays, graphics, and maps that are posted to the Internet for public access. The NRDC also served in the capacity of consultant to the government of Mongolia in the creation of Mongolia's Agenda 21 strategy for sustainable development. Several site visits were required, but the Internet made possible the frequent transfer of information and work product that allowed successful completion of the project.

THE INTERNET'S ECONOMY OF SCALE

Environmental activism using the Internet as a key tool cannot be understood outside the context of *globalization*—a compression of time, space, and action that is altering all institutions and cultures. Globalization is a consequence of the availability of information—availability that allows the management of enormous quantities and complexities of information, the better to alter fundamentally the economies of scale that have previously constrained the activities of private and public institutions (Kumar, Desai, & Kumar, 1998; Paget-Brown 1998; Quinn 1998). Because it has altered the rules of political, economic, and social activities, globalization has increased our ability both to benefit and to harm on a larger scale. Much has been made of the transformational shift to an information-based economy and to a global scale of economic competitiveness. Some see the changes as almost completely positive; others consider the shift a virtually unmitigated disaster. Yet, although some people quite understandably want the effects of globalization to go away, it is a reality with which we must deal. The processes being generated by globalization cannot be reversed; they can only be mitigated or re-envisioned as transforming opportunities.

Regardless of one's opinion of globalization, there can be no question that it has created a tier of invisible economic actors who are endowed with powers beyond those possessed by many national governments. Through technologies of information acquisition and management and the resulting economies of scale, there has been a quantum shift in the ability of vast and powerful institutions to concentrate and mobilize resources. Private-sector actors are using their global power to manipulate national policy making; to influence both corrupt and honest political leaders; and to move their resources and bases of activity freely from one country to another if they see better deals elsewhere or are resisted in their efforts to gain concessions.[3]

These changes in the scale, speed, and mobility of private capital activity have transformed economic actors to such a degree that they have become largely unaccountable for their actions (see Spiro 2000).[4] Using their ability to influence governmental action, these interest groups have successfully lobbied to create or expand mechanisms such as the North American Free Trade Agreement (NAFTA) and the World Trade Organization (WTO). Through a very clever dynamic, this has transferred power from national governments and the internal constituencies of nations such as the United States to smaller groups. We have irresponsibly allowed the construction of smaller but disproportionately more powerful institutions—resulting in an increasingly limited segment of our population possessing an increasingly large amount of the power. Power is transferred through "privatization" on a global scale to "small" (relative to government) enterprises. These "smaller" entities, in their own global networks, then effectively control power that once belonged to the much larger states, which now find themselves severely disempowered. The transfer of power from democratic nations to private hybrid institutions (such as the WTO), which strive to maintain the illusion that they are public institutions, is a profound and undesirable shift in the fundamental nature of modern democracy and the Rule of Law. If the WTO and similar diversions of public power were perceived more accurately—that is, as coalitions of powerful private enterprises that have convinced decision makers that "what's good for General Motors is good for everyone"—the legitimacy of the resulting transfer of public power would assume a very different cast. At the very least, the public-private distinction central to our governmental system has become increasingly blurred as a result of this power transfer.

With governmental and multilateral policy and institutional structures driven by the rhetoric of trade, development, and globalization, the ability of private-sector actors to use their new capabilities to even greater advantage has grown. All this has led to transfers of power to increasingly larger and more consolidated private sector institutions and to the bypassing and transcendence of democratic political processes. The expansion of the powers of ostensibly public institutions such as the

WTO has masked the nature of what is occurring and has further blurred the lines of decision-making legitimacy and accountability. This reduced accountability—combined with greatly increased power—has emerged at the very point at which the potential consequences of the behavior of such institutions have increased exponentially. One result of this transmutation of private economic institutions through information systems and the mobility of capital is that, for those countries desiring to participate fully in the global marketplace, the traditional forms of national sovereignty have become quaint artifacts. Even powerful nations such as the United States are finding that the new system is resulting in a transfer of power to invisible transnational and multilateral institutions and in a corresponding reduction in the political power of ordinary citizens.

It does not overstate to say that the very concept of democracy is threatened by the scale on which enormously powerful and unaccountable private economic institutions operate and by the actions of organizations such as the World Bank, the International Monetary Fund (IMF), and the WTO.[5] Such institutions depend—like the Wizard of Oz—on convincing people they are all-powerful and absolutely essential. Their power rests not in their physical scale, but on the basis of nations' having transferred a vital part of policy making and regulatory authority to the particular institution. In each instance, if the linchpin on which the delegated authority is pulled or newly forged, the institution's legitimacy either disappears or changes to something more democratically valid than can be said for the system that has been allowed to emerge. The institutions themselves are vulnerable to challenge for their antidemocratic behavior, but it will require a concerted and strategic effort.

These institutions operate outside the ability of any single nation's citizens to control, making decisions, creating policies, and implementing actions that have never been directly agreed to by the citizens of a particular nation. Even the elected representatives of a powerful country such as the United States have little voice in the decisions of international institutions, other than through the formalistic and tenuous threads legally spun through past legislative consent to the terms of the particular treaty by which the entity is established and empowered.[6] The result is that the mechanisms of citizen participation and political control in regard to decisions that impact their lives in fundamental ways are becoming increasingly remote. This is not a phenomenon only of the Internet. Paul Tournier (1957) concludes: "One effect of the increasing uniformity of life and of the crowding of people together in huge populations has been to mould vast numbers of them to a standard pattern" (40). He continues: "They have become merely cogs in the machine of production, tools, functions. All that matters is what they do, not what they think or feel. In any case their thoughts and feelings are similarly moulded by propaganda, press, cinema and radio. They read the same newspaper each day, hear the same slogans, see the same advertisements" (40).

An economic system fully committed to convincing individuals of the desirability of consumer society engages in various forms of propaganda to achieve the required value system. Mitch Albom (1997) captured what is happening in these words:

"We've got a form of brainwashing going on in our country," Morrie sighed. "Do you know how they brainwash people? They repeat something over and over. And that's what we do in this country. Owning things is good. More money is good. More property is good. More commercialism is good. More is good. More is good. We repeat it— and have it repeated to us—over and over until nobody bothers to even think otherwise. The average person is so fogged up by all this, he has no perspective on what's really important anymore." (124–125)

THE FREE INTERNET AS A COUNTERBALANCE TO MASSIVE INSTITUTIONS

Albert Schweitzer (in Fromm 1955) described the rise of institutional control over our lives as one of the most critical challenges humans have faced, suggesting that, while institutions have always played such controlling and defining roles, the sheer magnitude of what we are now experiencing has resulted in a unique change:

> About the struggle which must needs ensue no historical analogy can tell us much. The past has, no doubt, seen the struggle of the free-thinking individual against the fettered spirit of a whole society, but the problem has never presented itself on the scale on which it does to-day, because the fettering of the collective spirit as it is fettered to-day by modern organizations, modern unreflectiveness, and modern popular passions, is a phenomenon without precedent in history. (201–202).

If public and private institutions are molding people to fit into their desired patterns, no equivalent set of public and regulatory organizations has arisen to balance these massive private and public forces. The Internet has the potential to facilitate the rapid evolution of such a device, but if it serves this connective and interactive function, it must do so through the efforts of NGOs and individual citizens rather than governments and multilateral bodies.[7] The activists' newly acquired capabilities have led to attempts by some to impose charges on Internet use. If such proposals were accepted, the result would be to mute the new voices and reduce or even eliminate pressures on the institutions that are finding themselves the targets of focused public criticism (as in the case of "China Suspends Web Site," mentioned earlier).

Information is power. This is obviously not an original observation, but rarely has it been more true. The Internet provides an intelligence-gathering system far beyond what has historically been possessed by virtually any government, not to mention by ordinary citizens. It provides a means of real-time communication, free publicity and information dissemination, and both intra- and interorganizational networking. The enhanced capabilities of intelligence gathering, information dissemination, and networking have created an enlarged scale of action for the public interest community. A result is that the competitive game between environmentalists and those they challenge has changed immeasurably. The Internet has greatly expanded the ability of NGOs to monitor the proposed activities of such institutions as the World Bank, the Asian Development Bank, the IMF, the U.S. Environmental Protection Agency (EPA), the United Nations Food and Agricultural Organization, the U.S. Congress, and the like.

The importance of keeping information in the hands of NGOs is that institutions such as those just mentioned are accustomed to behaving without transparent processes. As with many national governments, they reach their desired decisions behind closed doors or through decision-making processes that allow only very carefully chosen interests to participate.[8] They have long expected their goodwill and expertise to be taken as a given. The Internet has allowed NGOs to strip much of the "smoke and mirrors" away from such decision makers. It has increasingly allowed activists to make early interventions into the institutions' planning and decision-making processes in ways that challenge their assumptions and force other concerns onto their agendas.

A TYPICAL DAY ON THE INTERNET

Perhaps the best way to understand how the Internet works as a productivity-multiplying system is to go through a reasonably normal day of Internet communications in my own professional life. One of my e-mail messages was from a university instructor who teaches in Leeds, England, who spoke recently at a human rights conference I coordinated. He sent ideas for a conference follow-up and a draft of a paper for the conference proceedings. I initially identified this individual as a conference speaker by disseminating the working concepts for the conference on a human rights listserv five or six months before the April 2000 meeting and asking for ideas.

A second message was from the director of the Mangrove Action Project, who sent an article on shrimp aquaculture and protection of mangrove forests and coastal communities. An activist filmmaker in New York, with whom I am developing a manual on the abuses of cost-benefit analysis by multilateral institutions done in connection with the environmental impacts of their projects, sent me a draft of a questionnaire she designed to send to environmentalists in an effort to obtain relevant information. When completed, the questionnaire will be sent over the Internet and responses received through that medium.

A participant on an international environment and human rights listserv sent some thoughts in response to another participant's request, stating,

> In response to your post this morning for new ideas to study and apply environmental law, I would like to offer the subject of environmental refugees. This concerns millions of people not yet recognized as *bona fide* refugees by international law but who nonetheless suffer in a similar fashion and have a great need for asylum and resettlement in safe countries. However, distinct from conventionally-recognized ethnic, political and religious refugees who often are able to return home after a change in repressive government, environmental refugees may never be able to return if their environment has been destroyed, contaminated, eroded, deforested, flooded or made uninhabitable in a number of other ways.

The Executive Director of ISA Net offered a message to the organization's steering committee on which I serve, suggesting: "One of the tools we can use in our work is [research into] how certain shrimp aquaculture projects are financed. We . . . need to work on the financing side of shrimp farming projects." She adds, "Here is an article from the *Bangkok Post* regarding the presence of tetracycline in farmed shrimp that is exported from Thiland."

The Mangrove Action Project also transmitted *The MAP Late Friday News, 61st Edition*. This is the latest edition in a long-running newsletter distributed by MAP to more than a thousand environmental activists, conservationists, and academics in nearly sixty countries. The Chinese Ministry of Fisheries sent me an invitation to participate in the Third World Fisheries Congress in November 2000 in Beijing, based on a meeting at which I spoke in Bangkok several months prior. Noam Chomsky responded to some information I had sent at his request. This information was related to the WTO's shrimp/turtle decision that found the U.S. ban on imports of trawled shrimp from countries that do not require the installation of turtle excluder devices (TEDs) on shrimp nets to be in violation of trade rules. Mutuso Dhliwayo of the Students for Environmental Action at the University of Zimbabwe sought help from participants on a special list concerning the role of law and custom in environment and resource management.

This very limited sampling of daily communications shows the rich promise, potential pitfalls, and labor-shifting nature of the Internet. It allows communication from a Zimbabwean student group to a wide network of lawyers and other activists. In the form of MAP's newsletter, it allows free and instantaneous global distribution of information to a diverse network of concerned activists and academics. It enhances the ability of a widely dispersed environmental and community-based activist network such as ISA Net. With members in more than twenty countries on five continents, it would be virtually impossible to link, update, and connect ISA Net's diverse membership in any other way. The Internet allows individuals to share great amounts of detailed information instantaneously. It allows the exchange of files, concepts, planning, and strategy between individuals and organizations. It provides the means by which activists in regions distant from one another can make counterparts aware of developments of which they might otherwise never learn, as in the sharing of a story from the *Bangkok Post*. It even permits the distribution of targeted "action alerts" designed to focus pressure of those planning to engage in actions contrary to the environmental agendas.

Dangers of the Internet

All is not beautiful in Internet Heaven. If information is power, it can also lead to paralysis. Much of economic theory assumes rational decision makers with perfect knowledge, making presumably perfect decisions. This is an exceedingly powerful ideal. In a perfect world with the ability to process, sort, and prioritize total information flow, the Internet seems an almost magical mechanism bordering on omniscience. Environmental activists, however, must by definition be active and take action. Paradoxically, at least from the perspective of the activist, too much information can paralyze the ability to take effective action. We must therefore seek to develop information screens and management systems or risk being overwhelmed by a flood of both relevant and irrelevant information.

As with the computer concept of GIGO ("garbage in, garbage out"), it is very easy to become infatuated with the Internet, communicating and receiving so much information that the time required to sift through the chaff to find the grain creates a barrier. I receive numerous action alerts about environmental hotspots or human rights situations that sound convincing. Many times they are, but in too many instances the claims are either false or at least significantly overstated or one sided. Considerable time must be spent determining the validity of the situation prior to having a knee-jerk reaction that would prove embarrassing and lead to a loss of credibility.

Many activists with whom I work, for example, particularly those in developing countries, seem to understand intuitively the Internet's information trap. They communicate as infrequently as possible through the Internet because they see it as a diversion from real work with real people in real communities. Others, particularly those in the United States, increasingly seem to live in front of their computer screens. As the contacts and networks expand and the number of voices on various Internet communicating systems grows, it is easy to spend many hours each day writing and responding to e-mail messages or researching relevant news and technical information.[9] There is an equivalent danger in submerging oneself in the absolutely incredible array of resources the Internet offers.

A consequence of this expansion of power and capability is that many of us have become, as Gene Rochlin wrote, "trapped in the net." The Internet is changing those who use it. Marshall McLuhan once observed that the printing press altered us profoundly, making us into something he called "typographic man."[10] Less than a decade into our use of the Internet it is obvious that Internet users have become something different. This difference is not automatically or inevitably bad—it is simply a *difference*. One element of this difference is that we are extending our consciousness and capabilities through the linkages and incredible range of information the Internet offers us. Yet dependence on the Internet is changing us.

One of the main challenges environmental activists face in using the Internet is that its power must be harnessed and focused; otherwise, the Internet can become a source of inefficiency, diversion, and even loss of organizational credibility. It is also in many ways an inefficient information system because it vastly increases the inflow and outflow of information. This information must be sifted, managed, evaluated, prioritized, and often shared. As many people certainly experience, an increasingly significant part of the day (or night) is spent dealing with communications through the Internet.

Similarly, in any system that becomes dependent on specialized technology, the users have made a sort of Faustian bargain in which a price must be paid for the power that is offered.[11] In the case of the Internet, several elements of the human cost have become clear. One is that the Internet is not a labor-*saving* device but a labor-*shifting* device. Economists have referred to technological changes such as the cotton gin, telephone, and printing press as labor-*saving* devices. Another way to think about fundamental technological changes is to conceive of them as labor-*shifting* devices and productivity-multiplying systems. Certainly the Internet and associated technologies such as the computer have combined to create one of the most profound productivity-multiplying systems we have seen.

As is so with many of my colleagues, I have probably never worked as hard in my life as I do now. This near total immersion in work is created by the fact that the Internet has compressed and stripped time from the work equation, and in many ways made the location of work irrelevant. There used to be some downtime in communications that allowed for a more reflective pace. Letters were sent that would take several days to reach their destination. Files had to be sent through mail systems. Information was not at our fingertips, so we would have to schedule some time to obtain what we needed. Now time has become an almost irrelevant factor because our communications are instantaneous. There is virtually no interstitial space remaining in our work lives, and the clear break between work and nonwork has become blurred or even nonexistent. The Internet and mobile communications technology create the opportunity (or curse) of always being reachable. We therefore have no downtime for of regeneration and spirituality.

DEVELOPING AN INTERNET STRATEGY

It is imperative for organizations and individual activists to have a strategy for using the Internet. Although it is impossible to cover these strategic issues in detail in one chapter, the following is at least an outline of issues to consider in creating an organization's Internet strategy. These categories reflect, first of all, the enhanced capabilities afforded by the Internet; second, the kinds of needs of environmental organizations and individual activists that can potentially be served by the Internet tool; third, the dangers of the Internet; and fourth, difficulties or obstacles to the effective use of this tool. These categories should be analyzed in the context of specific examples. The members of a specific organization should focus on that organization's mission, goals, and capabilities and then develop a strategy that harnesses the Internet's power rather than overloads, diverts, or weakens the organization's efforts.

I. Capabilities created by the Internet
   1. Real-time communications
   2. "Democracy"
   3. Exponential communications
   4. Targeted communications
   5. "Free" communications
   6. Networking
   7. Conferencing
   8. Chat rooms
   9. Organizational Web sites
   10. Fund raising
   11. Rapid outreach
   12. Protests to targets

13. Exposure
14. Access to data
15. Joint research
16. Research
17. Investigation
18. Tracking
19. Investor organizations and financial tracking (social investment, etc.)
20. Enhanced economies of scale

II. Needs to be served in environmental activism
1. Informal networking/interorganizational communications and linkages
2. Formal operations/intraorganizational communications and linkages
3. Brainstorming
4. Research
5. Fund raising (populist)
6. Fund raising (foundations)
7. Fund raising (governmental)
8. Early warning systems
9. Action alerts
10. Real-time communication
11. Transborder communication (general)
12. Transborder communication (strategic)
13. Travel efficiency
14. Transborder exposure ("The whole world is watching")
15. Newsletter
16. Planning and strategy
17. Research into opposition
18. Mobilization of public will
19. Research into supporters
20. Research into potential allies
21. Maintaining relationships

III. Dangers created by the Internet
1. Overreliance on remote communications technology
2. Becoming trapped in or addicted to the Net
3. Vulnerability and security breaches regarding strategy
4. Inhumanity/flatness of Internet communications
5. Rumors spread rapidly and grow exponentially
6. "SPAM"/overload and diversion from real work
7. Illusion of action created by words (smoke and mirrors)
8. Assumptions (security/actually read, etc.)
9. Marginalization of non–English-speaking advocates in multilingual global networks
10. Excessive egalitarianism and process often give the impression that "no one is in charge"

IV. Difficulties
1. Being realistic about organizational needs
2. Focusing on priorities
3. Web site maintenance (cost and expertise)
4. Web site quality issues
5. Diversion from organizational mission
6. Self-deception as to effectiveness
7. Spies? ("Loose lips sink ships")
8. Invisibility of pass-on distribution once a message is sent ("rumor mongers")
9. Listserv tap-ins/hackers
10. Encryption
11. Viruses

Notes

1. A colleague who specializes in intellectual property issues responded to this point as follows: "I find this interesting as we have the same problem in so-called Intellectual Property Law. It is not unusual to find large corporate IP owners—or their unidentified individual representatives (a kind word for spies) sitting on the boards or steering committees of supposedly consumer or activist organizations" (Michael Davis, Cleveland State University College of Law, e-mail to author, 1 June 2000).

2. Michael Davis remarks: "Even reading your following examples I find this impossible to believe. Why would these corporations give up this tool? Is it credible to believe that consumers somehow are able to use this resource in ways equal to that of enterprises with funds far outstripping their own? Is money less important when using the Internet? I think that would be an important analysis" (Michael Davis, e-mail to author, 1 June 2000).

3. Economics is taking over everywhere. See, for example, Ted Solotaroff's "Free-Market Writing" in *The Nation,* 16 October 1995, page 439, in which the author comments on the changes he perceives within the publishing industry in terms of a decline in professionalism caused by the "takeover of the arts and other professions by the market economy." Although I am generally in favor of the market approach to much of economic activity, the system is inherently predatory. Business schools have attempted to develop curricula to improve the situation, but their efforts are really too little, too late. Increasing attention has been paid in business schools to the development of business ethics. A sampling of articles that provide useful insights includes Edward Schumacher's "49% of Americans Polled Say Businessmen Less Ethical," in *The Washington Post* (12 March 1977); John Wilcox's "The Ethics of Business Face Challenge," in *The New York Times* (31 January 1982, sec. 11, p. 18, c. 5; and William Bole's "Excesses Shame Business," in the *St. Petersburg Times* (10 August 1991).

4. "Shalmali Guttal, picking up a theme earlier explored by Wendy Espeland, described how the language used by development experts, including cost-benefit analysts and those influenced by them, puts into shadow rural communities' knowledge and ways of life and functions to disempower them and exclude their thinking and experiences. It is, she said, like questionnaires which give a choice of a, b, c and 'other,' where 'other' encompasses nearly everything important to the respondent" (Lohmann 1999, p. 13).

5. "Peter Soderbaum stated that CBA was 'not compatible with dominant ideas of democracy' in that it denied, falsely, its own value-laden nature" (Lohmann 1999, p. 5).

6. "In particular, CBA denied that its view of humans as consumers, social organizations as producers, and ecosystems as commodifiable, fungible and tradable, was only one ideology among many. This can be seen in, for example, the way that the cost-benefit analyst's engagement with interested parties in a complex conflict is limited to questionnaires without 'open'questions. Unlike 'good science,' Soderbaum said, CBA was thus 'ideologically closed'" (Lohmann 1999).

7. The power and scale of institutional structures is part of the economic technique, which Jacques Ellul describes as shaping modern society (see Ellul 1969).

8. See, for example, the summary of a recent conference at Yale dealing with the behaviors of organizations such as the World Bank, and its use of cost-benefit analysis techniques to do what was desired. The Yale CBA Conference Summary includes the following: "James Scott underlined one of the contradictions when he remarked that a technique such as CBA which is 'opaque to 99.9 per cent of the population' has limited claims to transparency. This point was supported by Alex Wilks, who related the tribulations of non-government organizations (NGOs) in Chad who recently had to come to terms with 19 volumes of impact assessment in English, with no effort at translation or discussion. Mishka Zaman noted that the extreme difficulty of helping ordinary people in Pakistan who don't speak English to understand such assessments and the institutions which produce them, lobby for their rights, and get access to information posed a strategic problem for activists. Other participants suggested that a claim by (say) the World Bank that CBA is 'transparent' can be used to lure activists down the risky path of clamoring uncritically for 'inclusion' in Bank processes." (Lohmann 1999)

9. Several examples of databases are discussed in Hun (1998), Job (1999), Johnson (1999), and Louis (1999).

10. Ellul describes the shift toward specialization and what it costs us. "Techniques is of necessity, and as compensation, our universal language. It is the fruit of specialization. But this very specialization prevents mutual understanding. Everyone today has his own professional jargon, modes of thought, and peculiar perception of the world.... The man of today is no longer able to understand his neighbor because his profession is his whole life, and the technical specialization of this life has bound him to live in a closed universe." (1969, 132)

11. For insights into the unanticipated consequences of the information society, see Rochlin (1997).

Suggested Readings

Albom, M. 1997. *Tuesdays with Morrie.* New York: Doubleday.

Bergeson, L. L. 1998. Environmental databases: Online and ready to roll. *Pollution Engineering* 30 (6): 41–43.

Bole, W. 1991, August 10. Excesses shame business. *St. Petersburg Times.*

Buber, M. 1965. *Between man and man.* New York: Macmillan.

Bush Backer Quits Presidential Politics. 2000, April 5. *USA Today,* pp. 00.

Dyson, F. J. 1999. *The sun, the genome, and the Internet: Tools of scientific revolutions.* New York: Oxford University Press.

Electrohippies' planning hack attack to protest genetically altered food. 2000, April 9. *Plain Dealer,* n.p.

Ellul, J. 1965. *Propaganda: The formation of men's attitudes.* New York: Vintage.

———. 1969. *The technological society.* New York: Knopf.

Freedman, D. H., & C. C. Mann. 1997. *At large: The strange case of the world's biggest Internet invasion.* New York: Simon & Schuster.

Fromm, E. 1955. *The sane society.* New York: Rinehart.

Hun, T. 1998. EPA project provides compliance data for industrial sectors online. *Water Environment and Technology* 10 (9): 46–48.

Job, C. 1999. EPA establishes National Drinking Water Contaminant Occurrence database. *Ground Water Monitoring and Remediation* 19 (3): 51–53.

Johnson, J. 1999. Chemical accident plans go on the Web. *Chemical and Engineering News* 77 (28): 23–24.

Kumar, A., R. Desai, & R. Kumar. 1998. The environmental professionals' World Wide Web nontechnical directory. *Environmental Progress* 17 (2): S11–S17.

Lohmann, L. 1999. CBA Conference Summary. Cost-Benefit Analysis Conference, 7–10 October, New Haven, Conn., Yale University.

Louis, M. 1999. Been there, done that: Learning from others' environmental successes. *Waste Age* 30 (9): 20–21.

Mannan, M. S., & T. M. O'Connor. 1999. Accident history database: An opportunity. *Environmental Progress* 18 (1): 1–6.

McLuhan, M. 1962. *The Gutenberg galaxy: The making of typographic man.* Toronto: University of Toronto Press.

Pagel-Brown, N. 1998. The European Environment Agency Web site. *Database* 21 (2): 47–49.

Quinn, B. 1998. Web sites open the doors of EPA and DOE research. *Pollution Engineering* 30 (8): 25–26.

Rochlin, G. 1997. *Trapped in the Net: The unanticipated consequences of computerization.* Princeton, N.J.: Princeton University Press.

Schumacher, E. 1977, 12 March. 49% of Americans polled say businessmen less ethical. *The Washington Post,* n.p.

Sennett, R. 1998. *The corrosion of character: The personal consequences of work in the New Capitalism.* New York: Norton.

Solotaroff, T. 1995, October 16. Free-market writing. *The Nation,* p. 439.

Spiro, P. J. 2000. Globalization, international law, and the academy. *New York University Journal of International Law and Politics* 32 (2): 567.

Stimson, J. 1999. Montana's Natural Resources Information System (NRIS): Streamlining access to important information. *Surveying and Land Information Systems* 59 (3): 174–178.

Tournier, P. 1957. *The meaning of persons.* Translated by E. Hudson. New York: Harper.

Webb, C. J., A. David, & C. J. Paterson. 1998. Comprehensive inventory of known abandoned mine lands in the Black Hills of South Dakota. *Mining Engineering* 50 (7): 84–86.

Wertheim, M. 1999. *The pearly gates of cyberspace: A history of space from Dante to the Internet.* New York: Norton.

Wilcox, J. 1982, 31 January. The ethics of business face challenge. *The New York Times,* Sec. 11, p. 18, c. 5.

Chapter 9

Organizing Women of Color Online

Irene Queiro-Tajalli
Craig Campbell

THIS CHAPTER PRESENTS AN ORGANIZING FRAMEWORK FOR USING THE Internet as a tool to fight human rights violations against women of color and bring about social change. We condemn violence against women within the international environment and review organizing through a feminist perspective. We discuss the presence of women on the Internet and present a framework for online organizing based on existing practices and theoretical concepts that include the ecological perspective (Germain & Gitterman 1996); the empowerment perspective (Lee 1994; Miley, O'Melia, & DuBois 1998); current models of community practice (Rothman 2001); feminist organizing (Gutierrez & Lewis 1998, 1999); and technological advancements and inequalities (McConnaughey, Everette, Reynolds, & Lader 1999; Slater 2000). Intrinsic to this chapter is a search for the construction of the meaning of organizing in an information society. In sum, we propose that postmodern community organizing embraces both our organizing roots and new contexts of this social work practice. Organizing in the twenty-first century calls for the development of analytic skills that translate theoretical concepts to praxis and that support innovative methods of collaboration among women to promote social change. Additionally, organizing efforts must facilitate opportunities for online access to those with limited voices in the mainstream media.

VIOLENCE AGAINST WOMEN: A WORLDWIDE PHENOMENON NEEDING A GLOBAL RESPONSE

We cannot talk about community organizing online by women of color without first dissecting their situation of oppression and unfair treatment around the world. Women of all races suffer personal and legal discrimination and marginalization (Corrin 1996; Nagengast 1997) in spite of explicit international declarations

We would like to thank Marguerite Grabarek, former faculty member of the Indiana University School of Social Work, for her suggestions on an earlier version of the organizing framework.

calling for women's rights (Okin 1998). Women are the direct objects of sexual assault, unlawful incarceration, bride burning, and exposure to violence brought about by poverty, political dictatorships, and discrimination.

Nagengast (1997) reports on the harsh conditions that Afghan women are experiencing under the rule of Taliban party policies including banning women from employment and public service, forbidding them to be seen in public unless completely shrouded and accompanied by a male relative, and closing schools for females. This treatment of women is not surprising in a world replete with widespread sexual abuse of women and girls, sexual enslavement of female political prisoners, and multinational trafficking in sex (Bunster 1993; Wetzel 1993), and where women and children are the primary targets of regional wars (Sivard 1993).

In 1948 the United Nations issued the Universal Declaration of Human Rights, which calls for "faith in fundamental human rights, in the dignity and worth of the human person and in the equal rights of men and women" (United Nations 1948). In spite of this specific declaration regarding women's rights, the deplorable treatment of women continued. Therefore, the United Nations, in an attempt to bring international focus to the conditions of women, declared 1975 the International Year of the Woman and immediately proclaimed 1975–1985 the U. N. Decade of Women (Wetzel 1996). The United Nations Fourth World Conference on Women, held in Beijing, China, in 1995, set an agenda to empower women worldwide. Among the twelve topics at the Beijing Women's conference were the denunciations of the heavy burden of poverty on women, violence against women, and economic inequality. United Nations delegates emphasized that shared power between men and women would be possible only when the rights of women were recognized as human rights (Reichert 1998).

Long gone is the anticipation and expectations initially brought about by the U. N. Decade of Women with conferences in Mexico City (1975), Copenhagen (1980), and Nairobi (1985), and subsequent international conferences in Beijing and Huairou in 1995. As the recommendations from those conferences have begun to fade from society's collective memory, assaults against women have remained daily occurrences all over the world. Amnesty International (2001) argues that abuse against women in U.S. prisons includes the use of restraints on sick or pregnant prisoners, sexual abuse, and punitive isolation of women. Mass and systematic rape of women in war situations is common. Well-documented sexual atrocities were commonplace in the military conflicts in the state of Bosnia and Herzegovina, where thousands of women of all ages were registered as victims of genocidal rape and many were killed or listed as missing (Scapcanin 1995). Furthermore, female activists find themselves in jail as political prisoners for speaking out against gender-based violence (Van Soest & Crosby 1997). We believe that government-backed violence against women is also a way to keep men oppressed. During Khomeini's regime in Iran, women were subjected to a great many restrictions in the name of religion. One can hypothesize that this process also subdued men, because they experienced the overwhelming power of the government through the limitations imposed on and treatment of the women in their lives.

If we refer back to the role of women in the precolonial Americas, we see a parallel to that of men. In those societies, women were partners in securing the well-being of their communities. During the colonial period, and as the European invaders asserted their culture, women were assigned more private roles, and their sphere of power was reduced to domestic roles, such as housewife and mother. Briles (1996) depicts the historical roots of sexism with a quote from Wilma Mankiller, Cherokee principal chief:

> Sexism is not a native concept. When the Europeans arrived in America, Cherokee women living in the Southeast were consulted on major issues, attended councils and had an equal vote. The tribe's creator was called the *Mother-of-All-Nations,* and men and women lived in harmony. With the arrival of the Europeans, Indian women began marrying white settlers. Where they had been participants in councils in the past, their new spouses expected them to be quiet. The tribe's creation story was altered, and acculturation assigned women to secondary roles. (32)

The role transformation was so intense that after a long period of time, the assigned roles were seen as innate characteristics of women. That is, after more than three centuries of colonization, the invaders were successful in institutionalizing their patriarchal system based on gender differences. This process of integrating oppressive patriarchal practices within the precepts of the culture is well stated by Rich (1977) as being

> a familial-social, ideological, political system in which men by force, direct pressure, or through ritual, tradition, law, language, customs, etiquette, education, and the division of labor, determine what part women shall or shall not play, and in which the female is everywhere subsumed under the male. (57)

Vitale (1986) makes an excellent point as it relates to the Spanish Conquistadors and the liberation movements: "The people became independent of Spain, but this event did not resolve the issues of economic dependency nor did it solve the oppression of the ethnic groups, and the problems of half of the population: that is the women" (68).

In spite of such oppressive and unlawful treatment, women are keeping their social cause alive by organizing around issues intrinsic to their well-being. One cannot have a healthy family, community, or society when large portions of its women are besieged by violence. Finally, while we recognize that the oppression of women is universal and take into account the commonalties shared by all women, we must emphasize that women of color around the world may experience human rights violations differently based on regional wars, racism, marginalization, discrimination, neoliberal policies, and colonialism, among others.

WOMEN ORGANIZING AROUND THE WORLD

Throughout history, one of the approaches used by women to address violence in their lives has been community organizing and networking. Feminist activism can be traced to early advocates such as Mary Wollstonecraft (1759–1797), who pointed out the oppression of women as a group in her classic work *The Vindication of Women,* and who believed that "women deserve social equality with men and should be given the education necessary to achieve it" (Zeitlin 1990, 40). Elizabeth Cady Stanton believed that the religious institutions and the belief that men should have sexual rights over women were primary sources of the oppression of women (Flynn-Saulnier 1996). Chicana activists such as Manuela Solis Sager, Emma Tenayuca, and Luisa Moreno mobilized the Latinas against oppressive labor conditions and police brutality during the 1930s (*Profiles of Chicana Activists,* 2000). Contemporary feminist organizing is at all societal levels, from the grassroots organizing of women in the rural communities of Appalachia to nationwide organizing by groups such as the National Organization for Women (NOW) and the National Institute for Women of Color (NIWC). Furthermore, there exists global organizing that aims at unifying women under the premise that women's oppression is a worldwide assault on humanity.

Women have used different means of communication to denounce the mechanisms of oppression and repression and bring about change. Some groups have used "homemade" publications such as *Mujeres de Barrios,* printed by SUM (Servicio Universitario Mundial [Global University Service]) in Buenos Aires, Argentina; others have used public spaces to denounce violations of human rights. For example, in 1977, the *Madres de Plaza de Mayo* (also in Buenos Aires) began to march weekly in front of the government house to raise public awareness of the military government's atrocities against their children—"*nuestros hijos*"—and demand the return of the "*desaparecidos*" (the disappeared) alive. Argentina returned to democracy in 1983, but *Madres de Plaza de Mayo* have continued their peaceful marches to denounce the devastating effects of neoliberal policies on vulnerable populations, the privatization of social services, and human rights violations. Knowing that their loved ones will not return, they continue the symbolic demand for their return alive in an effort that the atrocities committed by the military government against those seeking just social conditions will not be forgotten by younger generations.

The most recent efforts at reaching a wider audience to advocate for the rights of women are the numerous women's groups on the World Wide Web, such as

- ◆ Women of Color Resource Center [http//www.coloredgirls.org/]
- ◆ Ethnic Women International [http://www.thefuturesite.com/ethnic/thelma.html]
- ◆ Women of Color Web [http://www.hsph.harvard.edu/grhf/WoC/]
- ◆ Native American Women's Health Education Center [http//www.nativeshop.org/nawherc.html]
- ◆ Hispanas Organized for Political Equality [http://www.latinas@latinas.org/]
- ◆ Women's Environmental and Developmental Organization (WEDO) [http://www.wedo.org/]

These and other Web sites serve to educate, achieve political parity, advocate, promote social and economic development, and share information. The issues they address include women's health, education, human rights, violence against women, women's accomplishments, reproductive health, and others.

In an information age, women organizers must use new technologies to continue their organizing efforts. Although community organizing has traditionally taken place within a geographic setting, it is now imperative that it also take place in nonspatial or "virtual" communities. Organizers must rethink organizing within the new global context, and to consider the possible inequalities that an international society brings to women of color. Electronic activism has many positive possibilities; but the digital divide is still with us due to race, ethnicity, income (McConnaughey et al. 1999), and geographic region (Organization for Economic Cooperation and Development 2000).

When one thinks of community organizing, more often than not it is the traditional community work done in a given geographic setting that comes to mind. This conventional model has served social work and communities in bringing people together for a common good. A new model is emerging in which women are organized in nonspatial, virtual communities based on public access to technology. This has not, however, displaced the importance of traditional organizing in today's society. An example of traditional organizing that has a global flavor and involves substantial technology use is that of certain ongoing demonstrations in the United States and other parts of the world. These demonstrations take place to denounce the concentration of capital in the northern hemisphere—a concentration resulting from disastrous policies imposed by the World Trade Organization (WTO), the International Monetary Fund (IMF), and the World Bank—and to promote a democratized global economy (Danaher and Burbach 2000). Clearly, organizers must understand the elements of traditional community organizing and then move forward to online organizing.

Understanding Community Organizing

The models of community organizing are as varied as the communities and issues they serve. Common to all basic community-organizing blueprints is the act of helping individuals build community structures so that community members own their decision-making processes and destinies, and thus building on individual and communal strengths (Queiro-Tajalli & Campbell in press). Furthermore, organizers help create an atmosphere in which people are willing to challenge government with a sustained, long-term, and collective plan (Rubin & Rubin 2001), by using coalition building and establishing political savvy, knowledge, and understanding.

It is essential for the community to come together as a whole if it expects to be heard by those in power. According to Kahn (1991), an empowered, unified voice is the key to access to local politicians: "If you have power, then you can get something done" (6).

Another approach to organizing is social action rooted in the premise that society is divided between the "haves" and the "have nots." Rothman (2001) observes that the existence of disadvantaged or disenfranchised populations calls for interventions that aim at "making fundamental changes in the community, including the redistribution of power and resources and gaining access to decision making for marginal groups" (33).

Finally, Weil (1996) defines organizing as "bringing people together for the betterment of social conditions and for social justice in neighborhoods, communities, regions, nations and the world" (5). She stresses four integral parts of the process: organizing, planning, development, and change. Tasks attributed to these four groups include joining individuals together for a common cause, planning for integration of new services and resources, long-term development efforts to improve and protect the community, and "social action and social change" (5).

Organizations of women of color are beginning to use newer technologies for more than office management. Using computers to generate quick and easy phone lists, mailing lists, letters, flyers, and information Web sites, members of these organizations are producing both paper and electronic versions of these products. Cordero (1991) argues that "Computerized production of community newsletters can help organizers to reach a wider audience more easily and effectively" (91). The obvious advantage of this technology is its ease of use. Information Web sites allow Internet users quick access to news, statistics, research information, chat rooms, and online sources that are of help to groups in their organizing efforts. A good example is the Web site of COMM-ORG, an online resource for community organizers, which hosts both a Web-based presence [http://uac.rdp.utoledo.edu/comm-org] and a listserv format [comm-org@uac.rdp.utoledo.edu] to allow the free flow of ideas on organizing. This site began as an online seminar on the history of community organizing and has grown to be a site for conversation on and references about organizing for scholars, community organizers, community developers, workers, and others.

Women Leaders Online: Women Organizing for Change [http://www.wlo.org/] claims to be the "first and largest women's activist group on the Internet—empowering women in politics, media, society, the economy and cyberspace." The site provides links to action alerts, voter education, e-mail addresses of U.S. senators and representatives, international links to sites concerned with women's issues, and other links and resources.

Many advocacy groups are determined to eradicate the existing stereotypes concerning minority groups by reaching a large audience on the Internet with positive images and accomplishments of those groups. They also mobilize themselves when they perceive "attacks" on their people. Some long-standing grassroots organizations such as the League of United Latino American Citizens (LULAC) [http://www.lulac.org] are using the Internet to take their message to a larger audience.

Toward a Framework for Organizing Women of Color Online

Organizing on the Web is an attractive option. The number of people who can be reached by online organizing is unheard of in traditional organizing efforts. The speed and efficiencies in targeting specific people for specific issues far surpasses that available with traditional methods (Schwartz 1996).

A framework is required to address online organizing based on theoretical concepts, rapid technological changes, established ways of organizing, and current approaches of advocacy by women of color online. The framework for organizing women of color online needs to use those dimensions from current organizing models that are consistent with the goals and philosophies of feminist organizing and that are appropriate to online organizing. By interconnecting relevant theories, concepts, and praxis, we provide a systematic approach to guide organizing on the Internet, and in doing so, assist women of color to advance their cause. Organizers must seize the momentum of discovery felt by others who are exploring the dimensions of new technologies to engage their participation in the change process. Figure 9.1 presents the main components of this framework.

The framework proposed here includes a number of components: knowledge base, praxis, technological advancements, professional stance, evaluation, and challenges and opportunities. The premise of this framework is that organizing women of color online must embrace both the long history of women's organizing and the approaches already existing on the Web.

KNOWLEDGE BASE

The knowledge base is composed of theories, models of practice, and community-related concepts. The theoretical underpinnings of this framework are the ecological perspective, empowerment perspective, feminist theories, and constructivist perspective. From the knowledge base we derive the key components and approach to the framework. In this way, we view the person as a responsible member of society who enriches the change process with the uniqueness of her or his own realities. At the same time, it is understood that society has an obligation to consider and respond to the needs of all its subpopulations. Therefore, organizing based on these theoretical concepts aims at embracing all voices, at connecting the disconnected, and at creating just conditions among disenfranchised communities.

Ecological Perspective

The ecological perspective calls attention to the interaction between the person and her or his environment, and views individuals as "living in constant reciprocity with the community" (Compton & Gallaway 1994, 4). Conflicts may occur between the individual and the physical/social environment, creating an "unsafe fit" between the two systems (Germain & Gitterman 1996). Within the parameters of this framework and based on the ecological perspective, conflict occurs between patriarchal oppressive practices and women of color as they are negatively impacted by such practices. It is the organizer's role to recognize that these unhealthy practices threaten the ability of women of color to function in a safe environment and enjoy basic human rights.

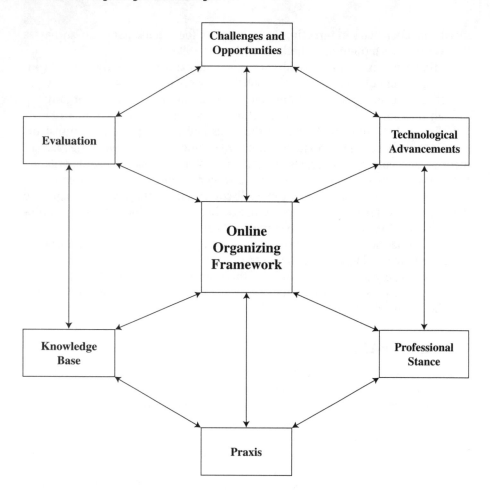

Figure 9.1 Framework for organizing women of color online

The next three theoretical conceptualizations chosen for this framework are closely interrelated. They complement each other and provide a holistic view of the person and society.

Empowerment Perspective

According to DuBois and Miley (1996), "Empowerment implies exercising psychological control over personal affairs, as well as exerting influence over the course of events in the sociopolitical arena" (26). A conceptualization of empowerment as a process that can take place at all societal levels provides a rich vision for the way organizing among women of color must be constructed and implemented.

Feminist Theories

Although there are numerous perspectives on feminist theories, including liberal feminism, radical feminism, global feminism, and cultural feminism (Flynn-Saulnier 1996), they all have in common a particular way of defining the problem at hand. That is, centuries of patriarchal domination, devastating colonization, and misuse of power have deprived women of essential human rights. Problem resolution seen through a feminist perspective leads the organizer to consider the use of power carefully. From a feminist perspective, power is both a patriarchal institution and a result of consciousness raising to liberate oneself and others from oppressive conditions (Freire 1970). Therefore, it helps the organizer understand the issues involved in organizing the disenfranchised in an information society. In our assessment, a feminist perspective helps to conceptualize the target of change as those processes and entities that sponsor human rights violations, and the change objective as the mobilization of community assets to promote fair and equal treatment of those historically oppressed by a patriarchal system.

Gutierrez and Lewis (1998) identify a number of values and practice principles that guide feminist organizing; these include the recognition that organizing is an empowering process; the need for consciousness raising to impact the social order; the importance of the well-accepted stance that the personal is political; the quest for bridging differences based on personal and societal attributes while being respectful of different ways of organizing; and the belief that organizing takes into consideration all dimensions of human experience.

Closely related to empowerment and feminist theories is "conscientization," or consciousness raising, as eloquently described by Pablo Freire (1970) when he proposes that the

> great humanistic and historical tasks of the oppressed [is] to liberate themselves and
> their oppressors as well. The oppressors, who oppress, exploit and rape by virtue of
> their power, cannot find in this power the strength to liberate either the oppressed or
> themselves. Only power that springs from the weakness of the oppressed will be suffi-
> ciently strong to free both. (28)

Although Freire's conceptualization presents a challenge to women organizers, given the physical and emotional distance between the oppressed and the oppressors in a global society, women are closing that distance by using the World Wide Web.

Constructivist Perspective

Central to this organizing framework are the concepts of diversity and difference that can be explained by a constructivist perspective. In the proposed framework, diversity and differences are respected and welcomed in the organizing process. Concepts from a constructivist approach are useful to community organizing in that they alert organizers to the devastating effects of socially defined stereotypes of societal groups. Society often assigns to groups, especially minority groups, attributes that are divisive, incorrect, or idealized (Gilmartin 1997; Vidal de Haymes 1997). Therefore, this framework supports the idea that both the organizer and the community members must coconstruct the meaning of the community change process. This coconstruction of change empowers the members of the community to do the work necessary to bring about change in their environment.

PRAXIS

Praxis in this framework refers to the process by which the organizer partners with communities of women of color in their struggles for creating just conditions. Participants are to be thoughtful about each step taken as part of the online organizing effort. The underlying assumption of this framework is that oppression experienced by women of color is created by cultural, socioeconomic, and political institutions, and that organizing is a process of denunciation by women of both the nature and the agents of oppression. This process includes the *what, why, who, where,* and *how* of organizing.

What are the goals of organizing? To work toward the enhancement of a participatory democracy and the elimination of oppressive conditions. One method of doing this is to work with communities to access and develop alternative information sources. Much of this may well occur through the use of Web-based technologies, as well as access to Usenets and electronic mailing lists. If knowledge is power, then one means of keeping groups on the margins is the erecting of barriers to information needed to challenge the status quo. Technology can be such a barrier, if not available to vulnerable populations; but when available, it can also be an incredible resource. Web sites such as Community Voices Heard [http://www.cvhaction.org] and others are excellent examples. Another aspect of *what* is the development of adequate public access to technology for those women with limited financial means. Although many communities are providing Internet services in their libraries and other public places, this clearly is not enough for either urban or rural populations. Locations for the provision of even a few computers are limited only by the imagination. Senior citizen housing locations, social service agencies, youth recreation clubs, community centers, job training sites, and religious institutions are but a few of the possibilities for access points.

Why bother with organizing? Traditionally, disenfranchised women of color have not shared the wealth of society despite their hard work and rich contributions to business, institutions, and organizations. This trend will continue as society demands highly skilled knowledge workers and as it develops new technologies that eliminate existing jobs (Bridges 1994). This situation is compounded not only by the many human rights violations against women, but also by their status as indirect targets of oppression brought about by globalization. Therefore, more innovative approaches to advocacy are needed. Although geographic organizing is still relevant to women's struggles toward a just society, advocating on the Internet may prove more efficient and less costly.

Who does the organizing? This framework proposes that the organizer needs to be a dreamer as well as a doer. A dreamer takes the giant step of thinking outside the traditional "organizing box" and a doer leads the change process to completion. The organizer should be knowledgeable of the strategies and techniques of organizing in both geographical and online communities. At the same time, she or he should also be a learner to understand sincerely the diverse voices of the community. In this framework, the community members are cocreators of a praxis that is meaningful and useful to their realities. They bring to this process many strengths, skills, and strategies, often in spite of oppressive situations and environments.

Where does organizing take place? The development of diverse means of communication has radically enhanced the interconnection of women across nations and around the world. As Web sites become more sophisticated, they may function as the connection source for organizers and group members.

How is organizing done? This framework calls for the conscientization of constituency groups, the development of a power base, and the sustaining of cohesion. At the same time that organizers are strengthening the organization, they must build alliances with other grassroots and human rights groups. We propose a collaborative approach rather than a competitive one. In doing so, the online community does not ignore the opposition, but rather becomes savvy in its dealings with all societal factions.

A number of factors must be considered when organizing in cyberspace. As much as oratory eloquence has been important in motivating individuals to organize and achieve community goals, written eloquence is a necessary tool in an online community. This communication must be clear, succinct, grammatically correct, and representative of all women of color. Perhaps most important, it must be denunciative and educative. It must raise the collective consciousness of women and those who support women in their struggle for justice.

TECHNOLOGICAL ADVANCEMENTS

The pace of innovation has been and continues to be quite rapid. Although technology is becoming ever more sophisticated, it is also becoming more user friendly. Within the past few years, developments such as speech-recognition and text-to-speech software are greatly expanding the possibilities for people who are visually or physically challenged. Given the dominance of the English-speaking world in the development of computers and the Internet, language translation applications are an invaluable resource for global organizing among those whose primary language is not English.

Some advocacy organizations use their Web sites for fund raising, selling cause-related products, and providing information to their constituencies. More important is their capacity to bypass the corporate media to present their cause. Interactive forms can enable the submission of comments or requests to decision makers, and the increase in Web conferencing technology can bring groups together from around the world. Many human rights organizations have adopted such information communications technology (ICT) systems to enhance their missions (Metzl 1996).

PROFESSIONAL STANCE

Although the Internet is helpful to women's organizations as a low-cost means of denouncing their oppression and of organizing to achieve just conditions, there are some ethical and professional considerations to take into account. The safety of population groups with little legal protection, such as women of color, as they strive for the recognition of their rights can be severely compromised if the oppressors know their identities. Community members must understand that complete anonymity is, for the most part, impossible, and that advocacy on the Web carries many of the same risks as advocacy in geographical areas. We must notify participants that even though security measures will be taken, organizing efforts could be linked to them individually. In addition, databases, like other organizational records, must be as secure as possible. For some hackers, personal information on individuals can be just as valuable as credit cards or banking information. We must not forget that organizing against violence, specifically violence against women of color, means to confront and challenge those in power and the offices they represent. Just as the demonstrators at the opening of the World Trade Organization summit in Seattle in 1999 encountered harassment and physical assault by the police (Danaher and Burbach 2000), those using virtual boycotts and other organizing tactics on the Internet may also put their lives on the line.

EVALUATION

The organizing framework calls for an evaluative component to analyze the process and the results of the organizing efforts. This is not an easy task and not much clarity exists on the subject. We propose that evaluation approaches should indicate not only whether the Web site is user friendly and whether it recognizes the unique characteristics of the women in that group, but also the extent to which the word about the cause is widely heard—and most important, the extent to which the organizing efforts are reaching the desired goals.

CHALLENGES AND OPPORTUNITIES

Organizing online creates a number of challenges, yet these are not insurmountable. This framework design is one of organizing women of color who have little power and quite often have distanced themselves from or have been distanced by society. One of the challenges is that of providing these groups with access to technology and empowering them with the necessary knowledge required in an information society. While technology is reaching more and more people, there are still those with no concept of the current technologies, or of the advantages these modern marvels can offer. An additional challenge is the lack of clarity in defining what constitutes online organizing, and a faulty definition could have serious implications for the advancement of best practices. The opportunities are many and promising. The vision is that women of color, to advance their struggle for a just society, will use sit-ins, public forums, peaceful demonstrations, and other organizing techniques online.

CONCLUSION

Human rights violations against women of color are prevalent throughout the world. Social work advocates and activists require a systematic framework to assist their efforts. We need innovative types of community-organizing leaders who have the vision, knowledge, and skills to foresee the host of new challenges and opportunities created by the advent of technology, and who can challenge the old and new forms of violations against women in a globalize society. Technology clearly has a role in community practice, and the Internet can open a host of new possibilities for successful social work activism. Organizing in the twenty-first century requires women of color to take a central place in the organizing efforts on the Internet. We expect other frameworks to emerge in the future that will further capture the transformation of technology and its potential application to the ongoing struggle of women of color.

Suggested Readings

Amnesty International. 2001. *Annual Report 2000*. Available at [http//www.webamnesty.org/web/ar2000web.nsf/countries/]. Retrieved on 2 March 2001.

Bridges, W. 1994. The end of the job. *Fortune* 129: 62–74.

Briles, J. 1996. *Gendertraps: Conquering confrontophobia, toxic bosses, and other land mines at work*. New York: McGraw-Hill.

Bunster, X. 1993. Surviving beyond fear: Women and torture in Latin America. In *Surviving beyond fear: Women, children and human rights in Latin America,* ed. M. Agosin, 98–125. New York: White Pine Press.

Compton, B. R., & B. Gallaway. 1994. *Social work process*. Pacific Grove, Calif.: Brooks/Cole.

Cordero, A. 1991. Computers and community organizing: Issues and examples from New York City. *Computers in Human Services* 8 (1): 89–103.

Corrin, C. (ed.). 1996. *Women in a violent world: Feminist analyses and resistance across "Europe."* Edinburgh, Scotland: Edinburgh University Press.

Danaher, K., & R. Burbach (eds.). 2000. *Globalize this! The battle against the World Trade Organization and corporate rule*. Monroe, Me.: Common Courage Press.

DuBois, B., & K. K. Miley. 1996. *Social work: An empowering profession*. Needham Heights, Mass.: Allyn and Bacon.

Flynn-Saulnier, C. 1996. *Feminist theories and social work: Approaches and applications*. New York: Haworth Press.

Freire, P. 1970. *The pedagogy of the oppressed*. New York: Seabury Selections.

Germain, C. B., & A. Gitterman. 1996. *The life model of social work practice*. New York: Columbia University Press.

Gilmartin, R. M. 1997. Personal narrative and the social reconstruction of the lives of former psychiatric patients. *Journal of Sociology and Social Welfare* 24 (2): 77–102.

Gutierrez, L. M., & E. A. Lewis. 1998. A feminist perspective on organizing with women of color. In *Community organizing in a diverse society* (3rd ed.), ed. F. G. Rivera & J. L. Erlich, 97–116. Boston: Allyn and Bacon.

———. 1999. *Empowering women of color.* New York: Columbia University Press.

Kahn, S. 1991. *Organizing: A guide for grassroots leaders.* Silver Spring, Md.: NASW Press.

Lee, J. 1994. *The empowerment approach to social work practice.* New York: Columbia University Press.

McConnaughey, J., D. W. Everette, T. Reynolds, & W. Lader (eds.). 1999. *Falling through the Net: Defining the digital divide.* Washington, D.C.: U.S. Department of Commerce, National Telecommunications and Information Administration.

Metzl, J. F. 1996. Information technology and human rights. *Human Rights Quarterly* 18: 705–746.

Miley, K. K., M. O'Melia, & B. L. DuBois. 1998. *Generalist social work practice.* Needham Heights, Mass.: Allyn and Bacon.

Nagengast, C. 1997. Women, minorities, and indigenous peoples: Universalism and cultural relativity. *Journal of Anthropological Research* 53: 349–369.

Okin, S. M. 1998. Feminism, women's human rights, and cultural differences. *Hypatia* 13 (2): 32–52.

Organization for Economic Cooperation and Development. 2000. *Learning to bridge the digital divide.* Paris, France: Author.

Profiles of Chicana activists: Texas labor history. 2000. Available at [http://www.utexas.edu/ftp/student/subtex/.web/Groups/crossborder/wia.html]. Retrieved on 24 May 2000.

Queiro-Tajalli, I., & C. Campbell. In press. Resilience in macro social work practice. In *Resilience theory and research for social work practice,* ed. R. R. Greene. Washington, D.C.: NASW Press.

Reichert, E. 1998. Women's rights are human rights: Platform for action. *International Social Work* 41 (3): 371–384.

Rich, A. 1977. *Of woman born: Motherhood as experience and institution.* London: Virago Press.

Rothman, J. 2001. Approaches to community intervention. In *Strategies of community intervention* (6th ed.), ed. J. Rothman, J. L. Erlich, & J. E. Tropman, 27–64. Itasca, Ill.: F. E. Peacock.

Rubin, H. J., & I. Rubin. 2001. *Community organizing and development* (3rd ed.). Needham, Mass.: Allyn and Bacon.

Scapcanin, A. 1995. Violence against women in armed conflicts: Genocide in Bosnia. In *The emergence of women into the 21st century,* ed. P. M. L. Munhall & V. M. Fitzsimons, 93–99. New York: NLN Press.

Schwartz, E. 1996. *NetActivism: How citizens use the Internet.* Sebastopol, Calif.: O'Reilly.

Sivard, R. L. 1993. *World military and social expenditures 1993.* Washington, D.C.: World Priorities.

Slater, D. 2000. Low-income grassroots organizations work to close the digital divide. Available at [http//comm-org.utoledo.edu/papers.htm]. Retrieved on 13 March 2001.

United Nations. 1948. Preamble to the universal declaration of human rights. New York: Author.

Van Soest, D., & J. Crosby. 1997. *Challenges of violence worldwide: A curriculum module.* Washington, D.C.: NASW Press.

Vidal de Haymes, M. 1997. The golden exile: The social construction of the Cuban success story. *Journal of Poverty* 1 (1): 65–79.

Vitale, L. 1986. *La mitad invisible de la historia: El protagonismo social de la mujer latinoamericana.* Buenos Aires, Argentina: Sudamericana/Planeta.

Weil, M. 1996. *Community practice: Conceptual models.* New York: Hawthorne Press.

Wetzel, J. W. 1993. *The world of women: In pursuit of human rights.* New York: New York University Press.

———. 1996. On the road to Beijing: The evolution of the international women's movement. *Affilia: Journal of Women and Social Work* 11 (2): 221–232.

Zeitlin, I. M. 1990). *Ideology and the development of sociological theory.* Englewood Cliffs, N.J.: Prentice Hall.

Chapter 10

Dial-Up Networking for Debt Cancellation and Development

A Case Study of Jubilee 2000

Nick Buxton

> Jubilee 2000 has pioneered a new form of global net activism in which thousands of activists and communities are in regular contact, unleashing a form of solidarity which flexed its new political muscle during the WTO meeting in Seattle. In all of that lies a hope for the new millennium that the decisions which affect millions of lives will not all be made in board and committee rooms, but also on the street and increasingly at the computer terminal.
>
> Editorial in British newspaper *The Guardian,* 30 December 1999

INTRODUCTION

When Jubilee 2000, the campaign for cancellation of the unpayable debts of the poorest countries in the world, was launched in February 1996, those involved knew that the only way to challenge the obtuse and secretive world of international finance was to mobilize public opinion on an unprecedented international scale. Taking the issue of debt to people on the street was not new. Ever since 1985—when Tanzanian president Julius Nyerere made an impassioned speech to the Organization of African Unity (OAU) in which he appealed to creditors, "Must we starve our children to pay our debts?"[1]—groups had worked to raise awareness of the impact of the crushing debt burden on the world's poor. Their efforts, however, had sadly failed to dent the ever-increasing mountain of debt. The visionary founders of Jubilee 2000 hoped that their "big idea" of linking debt cancellation to the celebration of the millennium would be a catalyst, uniting disparate efforts against debt bondage with the potential to capture the imagination of people worldwide. What

The author wishes to thank the staff of Jubilee 2000 campaigns around the world, especially in Germany, Haiti, Norway, Uganda, Spain, and Zambia as well as to partners in the United Kingdom Coalition for their valuable contributions to this case study. Thanks also to staff in the U.K. Secretariat, especially Marlene Barrett, Angela Travis, and Lucy Matthew, for their helpful and constructive comments.

no one fully appreciated was that Jubilee 2000's launch would coincide with an explosion in Internet use that would provide an essential vehicle for communicating that big idea. For the first time, the computer terminal would play a central role in carrying global issues onto the street. Caught almost unknowingly on the rising crest of a new media wave, Jubilee 2000's direction was, inevitably, also shaped by the Internet, providing valuable lessons for future international campaigns.[2]

This chapter explores both how and why the Internet became central to the strategy of the Jubilee 2000 campaign—from beginning as a vehicle for the initial communication of campaign ideas, to becoming the locus for information sharing in a global movement and for coordinating key decision-making events. The chapter analyzes only the time until the end of the year 2000, when the Jubilee 2000 UK campaign officially dissolved, even though campaigning has continued around the world on the debt issue since then.[3] The chapter also examines the limitations of the Internet as a medium for both campaigning and mass communication, and in particular in working closely with partners from indebted countries where Internet use is highly restricted. The chapter concludes by highlighting some of the lessons that can be drawn from Jubilee 2000's experience and pointing to likely future developments in the world of global campaigning and the Internet.

VIRTUAL TAKEOFF

It was not a coincidence that Jubilee 2000's takeoff from a bold and big idea to an international movement mirrored the explosion in Internet use. In 1996, Jubilee 2000 had the backing of three U.K. church aid agencies and about 180 individual supporters. The Internet had a global online population of 44 million (mostly based in the United States) at the end of 1995. Four years later, the number of people online had gone up by 700 percent, dot.com fever had broken out, and the Internet had become part of everyday life for many people (*Computer Industry Almanac* 1999). Jubilee 2000's growth was similarly dramatic. In less than four years' time, Jubilee 2000 was set up in more than sixty countries, had won the backing of tens of thousands of organizations, and had handed more than 24 million petition signatures to the leading creditor nations (see fig. 10.1 for statistics). Its collective impact forced the Group of Seven (G7) leaders to put debt at the top of the agenda at their summits in Cologne, Germany, in 1999 and Okinawa, Japan, in 2000, and to begin a process of debt relief for the poorest nations. In the words of the U.K. Secretary of State for Development, Jubilee 2000 was "a broad coalition which has moved the earth" (Short 1999).

Jubilee 2000's use of the Internet evolved as both the technology and the number of people online expanded. Jubilee 2000's online work centered around e-mail, the only Internet activity in which some campaigns in indebted countries could participate. As soon as Jubilee 2000 UK opened an office in April 1996, e-mail was used to circulate the campaign charter and a petition to e-mail contacts from international meetings, as well to networks interested in international development issues.

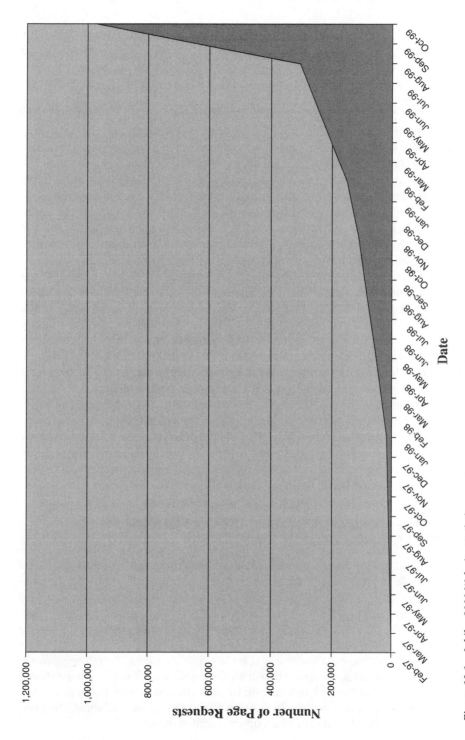

Figure 10.1   Jubilee 2000 Web site statistics

In November 1998, the first conference of nascent Jubilee 2000 national campaigns decided against establishing an international secretariat in favor of maximizing communication. Consequently, organizers established an e-mail listserv of more than 300 key campaigners, which became the linchpin of the international movement's communication and coordination.

Jubilee 2000 UK campaign's Web site [http://www.jubilee2000uk.org] was launched in February 1997 to provide background information on the debt crisis and the campaign. In October 1998, it was relaunched in a lively newspaper format with weekly updates, actions, features and policy research and received 8,000 to 15,000 international visitors each week, mainly from the United States and Europe. Since the passing of the millennium mark, the Web site has been taken over by Jubilee Plus, with the same Web address. Alongside the U.K. Web site were the popular "Drop the Debt" site [http://www.dropthedebt.org] and a growing number of Web sites of Jubilee 2000 campaigns at both the national level (including indebted countries) and the regional level.[4]

These developments put the Internet at the heart of Jubilee 2000's coordination work. Both national secretariats and active national organizations used the Internet for at least half of their debt-campaign work. Nearly all material produced in the United Kingdom was relayed onto the Web site, and e-mail became the primary means for transmitting information, setting up meetings, and discussing developments and strategy. As more communication, even within an organization, took place on the Internet, the ability to dial in to the computer server also enabled leading activists to travel yet stay in touch with campaign developments.

Voluntary organizers at the regional level spent much less time on the Internet, using it to gather information but relying on more traditional methods to establish liaison with their networks. Increasingly, however, local activists used the Internet to develop new relationships worldwide—for example, the Birmingham coalition in the United Kingdom was in regular e-mail contact with activists in the United States, South Africa, Japan, Malawi, and Germany.

DIAL-UP NETWORKING: SPREADING THE CAMPAIGN WITH INTERNET TECHNOLOGY

Jubilee 2000's success was predicated on communicating a large idea to as many people as possible, and dramatic changes in information and communications technology (ICT)inevitably brought major benefits to the campaign. The first reason the Internet played such a crucial role is that its structure as a system of networked computers fitted closely with Jubilee 2000's central strategy of reaching networks and individuals who could pass the campaign message on to larger networks. *Dial-up networking* (networking by telephoning into a computer network) provided the perfect tool to realize this goal. E-mail allows information to be shared to large networks at the click of a button; this information can be multiplied to potentially millions more networks. In this way, the campaign idea of Jubilee 2000 was shared on an international scale at an unprecedented pace.

Second, the Internet allows cheap, fast, and efficient communication on a global scale, which was vital for a movement with limited resources and a very tight deadline of the end of (at the time) the year 2000. Petter Hveem, the Norwegian campaign's only full-time paid staff member, calls the Internet his "best colleague" because it helped multiply his campaign efforts. E-mail was essential in responding to campaign developments. On 13 April 2000, sixty-three campaigners were arrested in Kenya during a debt march. News of their arrest was circulated via the Internet, prompting letters of protest from around the world, and the eventual dropping of the charges on 22 May 2000. Andre Hotchkiss, one of the arrested marchers, said, "Without the avalanche of e-mail, fax, and letters that poured into Kenya, this thing may have pushed on for a longer time." The Kenyan campaigners' experience of international solidarity mobilized via the Internet reinvigorated the campaign in Kenya.

Third, the Internet enables the accessing and sharing of high-quality information. The maxim that "information is power" is particularly true in the world of international debt. Secretive deals between Northern-Hemisphere creditor governments and elites in the poorest countries (which tend to be in the Southern Hemisphere) are at the root of the debt crisis. Ordinary people in indebted nations have been excluded from knowledge of corrupt loans but have paid all the costs as resources have been diverted from schools and hospitals to servicing debts to the rich North. The Internet has the potential to reverse the information poverty in the South. The ease of uploading and downloading information on the Internet has rapidly increased the volume of up-to-the-minute information, crucial for any campaign. In indebted countries, activists used the Internet to access information from Jubilee 2000 and World Bank sites about their countries' debt situations and the state of play among the creditors. This strengthened their respective hands locally. In Britain, Jubilee 2000 earned a reputation for having extremely well-informed supporters. Russell Price, a member of the U.K. coalition who worked with church groups, says that "providing high quality information through the Internet to busy people has given them confidence to articulate support for debt at church policy meetings."

Fourth, and perhaps most important, the Internet became central to Jubilee 2000 because it is a flexible medium that can be controlled by campaigners. This is particularly crucial when other forms of media and communication are increasingly concentrated in the hands of a few, with news agendas and analyses determined by criteria that often exclude intelligent examination of seemingly complex issues such as national debt. On the four British terrestrial television channels, the total output of factual programs on developing countries has dropped by almost 50 percent since 1989 (Stone 2000). The Internet gave supporters control because they could access information almost instantly and at any time. Dynamic local supporters in Seattle used information from the Jubilee 2000 UK Web site to build a powerful local coalition that brought together a human chain some 30,000 strong for debt cancellation on 29 November 1999, the first day of the World Trade Organization (WTO) summit. At the G7 leaders' summit in Cologne in 1999 (see sidebar, "On the Road to Cologne") Jubilee 2000 was able to use the Web site to provide detailed

On the Road to Cologne

On 19 June 1999, 40,000 people from around the world gathered in a human chain to circle the summit of the G7 leaders in Cologne, Germany. Joining the demonstration were more than sixty buses from Britain, two trains of supporters from Sweden, and a ship from the Netherlands. On the same day, 15,000 people in Stuttgart formed a parallel human chain. Friedel Hutz-Adams, communications director for Erlassjahr 2000 in Germany said, "Organizing the international aspects of the Cologne summit would have been impossible without the Internet." Through regular international e-newsletters and the posting of detailed information (including maps, travel guidelines, and contact details of bus and travel organizers) on its Web site [http://www.erlassjahr2000.de], Erlassjahr 2000 was able to organize and coordinate an international demonstration on an unprecedented scale. Through this immense mobilization, the G7 leaders were put under serious scrutiny by the world and were forced to make the first steps toward debt relief through the Cologne Debt Initiative. Erlassjahr 2000 had also set a precedent for future international meetings that would be dramatically followed up by demonstrations at the Seattle WTO conference in November later that year.

analysis and warn supporters not to believe the spin given by government press spokespersons.

CELEBRITY.COM: CELEBRITIES, INTERNET, AND CAMPAIGNING

Dial-up networking was at the heart of Jubilee 2000's work, but in a world where membership organizations are generally on the decline it was clear that building a mass popular campaign would also mean securing coverage in the mass media, on television in particular. The concentrated ownership of these media leaves outsiders at a distinct disadvantage by limiting diversity of views. Conversely, however, for those who are able to get coverage there is the potential to reach a massive global audience. Jubilee 2000 therefore invested considerable time in courting mass media's favorite partner: the global entertainment industry. The work paid off as celebrities, particularly from the music industry, began to give public backing to the campaign. The fact that Live Aid's $200 million was being paid back by Africa every *week* in debt repayments shocked many in the music industry and propelled ex–Live Aid stars like Bob Geldof and U2's Bono into active support.

Television coverage is still by far the most important medium for reaching a mass audience, particularly in the North. When the *Brits* music awards decided in 1999 to back the campaign after both Muhammad Ali and Bono said they would attend, the *Brits* onstage promotion of the campaign reached a global television audience of more than 100 million viewers in 130 countries, along with massive coverage in popular tabloid media. This immediately raised awareness of the debt crisis to a significant new international audience and prompted political leaders to begin

Bringing Pop and Politics Together?

Netaid, the global concerts on 1 October (linked to the Web site [http://www.Netaid.org]) was the largest attempt to date to bring the global worlds of music and Internet together to tackle causes of poverty. One of the five "pillars" of action identified as essential for reducing poverty was debt, and the Jubilee 2000 campaign was a leading partner in Netaid. The format of the Web site highlighted the issues behind the concert and allowed individuals to discover for themselves development issues at their own comfort levels. It channeled some new people into campaigning—in fact, the event tripled traffic to Jubilee 2000's Web site, and some of that volume has remained. However, the difference between the actual number of visitors (2.5 million) and the hyped figure of 1 billion was a major disappointment. For Jubilee 2000, it reflected in part a failure of Netaid to provide a clear visual message for the concerts similar to those of Live Aid. Nevertheless, Netaid set an important precedent, and with a stronger focus, future online music events could reach massive global audiences, becoming powerful agents for social change.

---

addressing the issue. In contrast, the Netaid concert in October 1999 had a global online audience of only 2.5 million, despite a larger lineup of stars performing in three international cities (see sidebar, "Bringing Pop and Politics Together").

Despite the wider reach of television, connecting the Internet with the global and popular appeal of celebrities had distinct advantages for the campaign. This mainly comes back to the Internet's capacity to provide a flexible and controllable medium for communication. When Thom Yorke of pop group Radiohead went online for a chat in June 1999, he was able to talk to his large online fan base in depth about the campaign. He even refused to answer questions about his new album because he wanted to talk about the "real" issues. His unedited comments online are unlikely to have appeared in any other medium, yet reached a global audience, some of whom have since become highly committed campaigners. Similarly, on 23 September 1999, the meeting of the Pope with Bono, Bob Geldof, Professor Jeffrey Sachs, and Quincy Jones (see fig. 10.2) received significant press coverage (however, much of the coverage focused more on the personalities than on the issues). Jubilee 2000 via the Internet was able to give full coverage, including a live Webcast of the press conference, to emphasize not who was there, but why such a diverse range of people were speaking out on debt.

OUT WITH THE OLD, IN WITH THE NEW? OR, DOES TRADITIONAL CAMPAIGNING STILL HAVE A PLACE?

With all the advantages of the Internet, it might be assumed that more traditional methods of campaigning would be dropped. Certainly the Internet's ease of use has ushered in new ways of campaigning. It is now possible to e-mail many of

Figure 10.2 Bob Geldof, Professor Jeffrey Sachs, Bono, and Ann Pettifor at webcast press conference following meeting with Pope John Paul II, September 1999
Source: Photo courtesy Jubilee 2000 Coalition

the G7 leaders directly and easily by cutting and pasting material off a Web site. In May 1999, U.K. coalition partner Comic Relief inadvertently discovered the potential reach of the Internet when its Freephone number, advertised in a tabloid newspaper, found its way onto an e-mail incorrectly stating that the U.K. Prime Minister Tony Blair would "cancel the debt" if enough people called. More than 150,000 calls were made before the line was cut off. Beth Tegg, education officer for Comic Relief, said, "At first when calls started to pour in, we were baffled, but when we understood what had happened we were thrilled that so many people responded positively. It shows a great potential for e-communications." Using the Internet for local campaigning was also an exciting experience for some local activists. Sue Errington, Jubilee 2000 organizer in Devon, organized an "e-mail mountaineering" trip in January 2000. Campaigners climbed a nearby hill and e-mailed activists worldwide using a laptop and mobile phone. "For me the thrill was receiving messages from Malawi, Nigeria, Japan, and Uganda in response to our e-mails. I think people enjoyed the day because it felt exciting and at the cutting edge," she said.

For a movement allied with a communications revolution, Jubilee 2000 nevertheless depended in large part on historical and long-used techniques such as public meetings, rallies, leaflets, posters, and petitions—all of which were fundamental to the nineteenth-century campaign for the abolition of slavery. There is little evidence from Jubilee 2000's example that traditional methods have seen their day. This was most starkly evident with the Jubilee 2000 Petition, a core action of all the campaigns. Despite the ease of signing online, only 250,000 of the initial total 17 million signatures handed to G7 leaders in Cologne were online signatures. The Peruvian campaign, which collected almost 2 million signatures, did so in six months through a systematic mobilization of local networks—without the Internet. By contrast, a September 1999 attempt by Jubilee 2000 UK to boost online signatures using the latest in animated and interactive technology, although it won plaudits for its design, failed to circulate widely because the attachment was rejected by most e-mail systems.

The lack of direct e-campaigning is due in part to the insufficient number of people online. (For example, the German campaign Erlassjahr 2000 sent e-mail to only a few hundred supporters, yet has 6,500 subscribers to its print newsletter, and distributed more than 1 million leaflets in the year before the Cologne G7 summit.) Furthermore, sending e-mails directly to politicians remains less effective than drowning them with letters and postcards. Mary Bradford, campaigns officer at Christian Aid, an organization in the U.K. coalition, uses e-mail only as a backup to conventionally mailed actions. She says, "Decision makers can deal with electronic communications in a more sophisticated way than they can with piles of letters or postcards sitting in their offices!"

Perhaps the most significant limitation of the Internet in relation to direct campaigning at the local level is its impersonal nature. Barbara Crowther, former campaigns director of U.K. coalition partner Catholic Agency for Development (CAFOD), comments: "Campaigning is ultimately about people. Internet and e-mail can help bring people together but cannot replace [campaigning] in my mind." All regional organizers recount that the most important and engaging local events involved bringing people together. The most powerful of these events proved to be the sharing of experiences between campaigners from both hemispheres and the major demonstrations that were held at international creditor meetings, particularly the G7 summits. When 70,000 people formed a human chain around the G7 summit in Birmingham, England, in May, it not only awakened the world media to the debt problem, it also inspired local campaigners in a dramatic way that the Internet cannot achieve. James Stewart, a U.K. local campaigner and Web site designer, says, "I think that the fact that the Net doesn't provide anything tangible for users, as a physical protest does, means that it can never entirely replace traditional ways of protesting. It's very inspiring to physically join up with people who share your convictions on the issue."

The Internet played a role in all of these major events. For the Birmingham human chain, Roger Chisnall, a London Trade Union activist who organized buses in London, recounts that once his phone number was advertised on the Web in connection with the event, he received twenty to thirty calls a day for about ten days and rapidly filled his buses. In Spain, the organization of a referendum on debt conducted by a citizens' network in October 1999 (and in which 1 million citizens voted) relied a great deal on the Internet. However, the Internet played its role mainly in enhancing offline campaign actions, rather than replacing them. The strength of Jubilee 2000's most successful activities was derived from engaging with people and tying them into active networks. This involved a great deal of personal contact. The campaign may have had backup from the computer terminal, but its main arena remained the street.

LINKING WITH THE SOUTH

Jubilee 2000 was based on the education of individuals, especially in indebted countries, about the debt crisis. This education is essential for empowering ordinary people to take back control over resources, diverted through the collusion of elites in both the developed and the developing world. Involving people in the Southern Hemisphere was vital; the movement against debt first started in the South, and the only long-term solution to the debt crisis will come from the South. Consequently, the campaign had to confront the fact that poverty in indebted countries is worsened by information poverty—particularly on the issue of debt, for which all the data and decisions that impact people are collected from outside each country, in Washington, D.C.–based institutions like the International Monetary Fund (IMF).

This information divide is likely to be exacerbated, as the rapid polarizing of the world's economy and society is paralleled by a growing "technological apartheid."[5] As Roger Chisnall summarizes, "The Internet is so fast and easy to use, inevitably those with access are better briefed. Those we exclude tend to be the less affluent, the people we are working with in the first place. . . . This is a real challenge to us all."

At first glance, this does not seem to have been the case with Jubilee 2000—nearly all campaigners in the indebted countries stated that the Internet greatly assisted their campaigns and involved them further in international decision making. The Internet's inherent advantages that made it so central to Jubilee 2000 UK's work applied equally, and sometimes even more so, to campaigns in indebted countries. Many Southern campaign organizations were among the first online users due to early investment by academic, research, and nongovernmental organization (NGO) networks (Pruett & Dean 1998). Sharing information and perspectives cheaply and efficiently with an international movement, as well as being able to access previously hidden information, made a dramatic difference for southern campaigns. Camille Chalmers, coordinator of the Haiti Debt Campaign, says that e-mail transformed his work, enabling him to send information to thousands of people—an act that would otherwise have exceeded his entire budget and caused the messages to take weeks to arrive. Christine Nantongo of the Uganda campaign says that using the Internet to talk to international campaigners "like they are my next-door neighbors has been an inspiration and enables us to share information that we would otherwise not." The Zambian campaign has a Web site [http://www.jctr.org.zm] that it uses to inform journalists and northern campaigns while it focuses on mobilizing within Zambia.

Northern campaigning organizations report that e-mail has greatly assisted the sharing of information and has enhanced relationships with southern partners. Russell Price, of the church organization Church Mission Society (CMS), says that e-mail was "crucial for bringing raw data or stories from partners in Africa and Asia." This information laid the basis for CMS's education work on debt.

However, the Internet experience was much more difficult for campaigns in the South than the North. During the writing of this chapter, both the Haiti and the Ugandan campaigns suffered serious problems with their Internet service providers (ISPs), which blocked e-mails for several days. For such countries, downloading Web articles can be a very costly and sometimes fruitless experience due to poor and relatively expensive communication systems. Several campaigns, including those in Burkina Faso and Côte d'Ivoire, did not have e-mail access. Others, such as those in West African Francophone countries and countries throughout Latin America, were often excluded by the fact that more than 70 percent of the information shared via the Internet is in English—and this was largely the case within the Jubilee 2000 movement.

Realization that Internet could exclude as well as include quickly became apparent at an international Jubilee 2000 conference in Cologne in June 1999, at which even campaigns with access to the Internet had not received key information and campaign updates. This was backed up by analysis of international audiences visiting the U.K. Web site—of the users from the forty-four countries that regularly visited the site, only twelve were from southern countries, and these southern visitors ranked near the bottom in terms of the number of page requests. This prompted a rethinking in the Jubilee 2000 UK office, leading organizers to establish quarterly bilingual newsletters and a regular postal mailing to southern campaigns of key articles that were hitherto being shared via the Internet alone.

The repercussions of increasing reliance on Internet for communication in the context of a divided world are still being thought through. Barbara Crowther, formerly of CAFOD, says, "There is a legitimate worry that Northern agencies will increasingly prioritize communications with those southern NGOs with resources to keep up with online partnership models, and [that] others might get further excluded." Kofi Mawuli Klu, a Ghanaian debt activist, warns that reliance on the Internet could give a dominant voice to largely urban NGOs able and keen to respond to the North, rather than to more representative organizations that concentrate their efforts on working with local communities in which the Internet is irrelevant. Even if popular organizations are online, there is the danger that the varying e-mail experiences of North and South can distort perceptions of different campaign environments. For example, when a Northern campaign e-mails a consultation document, the deadline to respond tends to be only a few days. For Northern campaigns, a short deadline is easy to organize because it can be e-mailed to coalition organizations for consultation. However, for Southern campaigns, seeking a response is inevitably a longer process, and therefore valuable feedback may not be received.

The Ugandan campaign reported that any information received via the Internet, as valuable as it was, had to be simplified, translated into at least five languages, and delivered in segments before it was used publicly.

LESSONS FOR THE FUTURE

When Jubilee 2000 climbed onto the vehicle of the Internet in 1996, it had no idea where it was going to be taken. The Internet certainly carried the campaign a long way and was essential in driving Jubilee 2000 toward its goals. Five years later, it is also possible to look back at the journey traveled to get an idea of where we might be going next.

The first clear lesson is that future campaigns will be unable to ignore the vehicle of the Internet and still be successful. The Internet transformed the nature of the Jubilee 2000 campaign and of campaigning in general. For one thing, it quickly internationalized the campaign—now not only are many of the national organizations in constant contact, but local groups such as the Leeds Jubilee 2000 network still keep regularly in touch with communities in Zimbabwe and Germany. This internationalization ensures that future campaigns on global issues will not be contained within national boundaries. Popular and imaginative "big ideas" are likely to become as global as Jubilee 2000.

This process of internationalization also has a highly democratizing dynamic. The sharing of information, ideas, and perspectives via the Internet has created extremely well-informed local campaigners. Furthermore, as local campaigners develop Internet links with activists worldwide and as the diversity of information increases, the ownership of campaigns is likely to be increasingly decentralized. For example, at the time of this writing, most British campaigners receive campaign information from a few national organizations. As the Internet develops, however, campaigners will be able to bypass these communication channels. Jubilee 2000 UK, before its dissolution, started to pilot online community Web pages in which supporters could link up to share information, skills, and ideas without involving national offices. There are other campaigning organizations taking the ideas of online communities forward. This could substantially reduce pressure on tightly stretched national organizations that, too often, act as ineffective networking hubs for local campaigners, when supporters could network directly and more efficiently instead. This bypassing of national offices could have a profound effect on democratizing ownership of campaigns.

Set against the empowering nature of increased knowledge dispersed via the Internet is the danger of information overload. Many Jubilee 2000 campaigners reported an unsustainable growth in volume of e-mail and Internet material. Marlene Barrett, head of campaigns at Jubilee 2000 UK who received about fifty e-mails daily, says: "Because it's so easy and cheap to send an e-mail, people often are not thinking who needs this information and how much detail they need. The more e-mails you receive the less likely you are to answer or act upon them." As more campaigns take to the Internet, activists may become disempowered, daunted by the sheer weight of campaign requests arriving in their e-mail inboxes. Most likely, however, people will begin to develop new Internet strategies to deal with this volume of information, and campaigns will need to become more sophisticated in presenting its information online.

Although future campaigns will be unable to ignore the vehicle of the Internet, it will be essential that they do not rely on it. Despite all the hype, the vast majority of the world's population are excluded from the Internet, particularly in Southern nations. A digital divide to match the vast wealth divide is already widening—in reading the sidebar "Elinata Meets Gordon," one can appreciate just how wide this gap is. The situation is even more difficult to remedy given that one-third of the world's population must survive on the equivalent of one dollar per day.

Jubilee 2000 publicly questioned the priority of closing the digital divide at a time when many people lack basic necessities. In fact, protesters at the G7 summit in Okinawa (July 2000) burned a laptop computer to protest attempts by the G7 leaders to obscure their own failure to tackle the debt crisis by launching a new "digital divide" initiative. Indeed, the only way to tackle both the digital and the wealth divides will be through the success of campaigns—such as Jubilee 2000—that tackle the root causes of poverty, and through long-term empowerment of citizens of impoverished countries. Consequently, a campaign that relies on a methodology that excludes any group of people is shooting itself in the foot. While campaigns

---

Elinata Meets Gordon

On 14 June 1999, a few days before the Cologne G7 summit, U.K. Chancellor Gordon Brown picked up the phone in the U.K. Treasury to talk about international debt. This was not an unusual topic of conversation in advance of a major summit; what was unusual was that his call was to Elinata Kasanga, a poverty-stricken mother of seven in the remote village of Balakasau in Zambia, and his call was eavesdropped upon, live, by thousands of people on the Internet. The medium had succeeded in bringing one of the most powerful people in contact with one of the most powerless: A woman who suffered directly from the effects of her nation's debt was talking to a man with the power to stop collecting the debts of the poorest countries. Elinata Kasanga, completely unawed by the experience, challenged Gordon Brown to cancel Zambia's debts to enable her children to go to school. This innovative project, orchestrated by Tearfund (a Christian aid agency in the Jubilee 2000 U.K. Coalition), demonstrated the enormous potential of the Internet both to link people across the globe and to give a voice to people who have traditionally been excluded.

However, the project also highlighted the practical difficulties in using new media technology in impoverished countries. First of all, to realize the project, Tearfund had to rely on heavy financial backing from Microsoft Network (MSN), Mediawave, and other computer companies. Satellite phones were necessary for the linkup, and Tearfund was forced to use its backup plan of still images with audio instead of the planned live video when the power supply in the village blew up!

against poverty are still needed, traditional campaigning and communication methods will need to run alongside Internet communication.

Most of all, campaigns in the future must remember that changing society involves people and ideas. Campaigners should never mistake the vehicle for the message. Effective campaigning will continue to be based on persuading people of the need for change—whether that persuading is done from street stalls, at public meetings, in dialogue with campaigners from different parts of the world, or through the collective energy of a massive demonstration for social change. However, if campaigns have the right message and relish the challenge of taking campaigns out to people on the streets, they will find the computer terminal a revolutionary backup.

Notes

1. In 1989, UNICEF, in its *State of the World's Children Report,* said that the "debt crisis should not be discussed too politely, for polite discussion can imply a tacit acceptance of the unacceptable."

2. Jubilee 2000 UK officially dissolved on 31 December 2000, although the work of Jubilee 2000 is continuing in many countries or carried on by new organizations and coalitions such as in the case of the United Kingdom, the Jubilee Debt Campaign, and Jubilee Plus.

3. Jubilee 2000, as an international movement, is a vast field to submit to a case study. This evidence in this chapter is based on conversations with, as well as questionnaires and surveys sent to, campaigners at regional, national, and international levels. However, the study does focus on efforts in the United Kingdom because that country has led the way in using the Internet, as well as for practical reasons (this study was written in the midst of an ongoing campaign).

4. A full list of Jubilee 2000 Web sites can be found at [http://www.jubilee2000uk.org/]. [http://www.dropthedebt.org] was initially a popular education site on debt and was temporarily used after the end of Jubilee 2000 UK as the site for the short-term "Drop the Debt" campaign that worked up to the Genoa G8 Summit. It is now archived at the same address.

5. U.K. Chancellor Gordon Brown, in a November 1999 speech, made the salutary warning that the communications revolution could lead to "a society divided between information-haves and information have-nots[:] A society with a wired up superclass and an information underclass" (Brown 1999).

Suggested Readings

Brown, G. 1999. Speech made to U.K. Internet Summit, 28 October. Summary of speech available at [http://www.hm-treasury.gov.uk/press/1999/p175_99]. Retrieved on November 8, 2001.

Computer Industry Almanac. 1999. Press release, 18 August. Available at [http://222.c-i-a.com/199908iu.htm]. Retrieved on February 6, 2001.

Pruett, D., & J. Deane. 1998. The Internet and poverty: Real help or real hype? *Panos Media Briefing* 28 (April): 6–8.

Short, C. 1999. Speech made to the International Development Committee, 20 May. Available at [http://www.parliament.the-stationery-office.co.uk/pa/cm199899/cmselect/cmintdev/470/9052007.htm]. Retrieved on November 2, 1999.

Stone, J. 2000. *Losing perspective: Global affairs on British terrestrial television 1989–1999.* London: Third World Environment and Environment Broadcasting Project.

Chapter 11

Online Collaboration, Information, and the Resourceful Community

Joe Clarke

AS MANY GROUPS RACE TO BRIDGE THE DIGITAL DIVIDE, THE QUESTION OF how best to deploy technology in low- and moderate-income communities arises. The outcome of these decisions may very well be the determining factor that separates communities that prosper from those that do not. The use of information and communications technology (ICT) in community practice can include much more than the Internet. New technology can have significant positive impacts as an information management tool. This chapter presents an example of a working-class Philadelphia community that used ICT to identify local resources and to communicate their findings to one another, then went on to map the resources using information-management technology. Both a valuable community resource and newly developed ICT skills were the results.

The rapid pace of technological innovation during the past decade has surprised even the most forward-looking thinkers (Dertouzos 1997). A recent article in *Consumer Reports Online* (2000) stated that a personal computer, purchased in 1999, would "have 32 times the RAM (memory) and 65 times the hard-disk storage space," with roughly twelve times the processing power of an equivalent system purchased in 1994. Along with this meteoric rise in processing capacity has come a falling price tag for the additional power. The 1999 system costs about one-third as much as the 1994 model. These advances have put the computer within reach of social service agencies, community organizations, and moderate- and low-income families. They have also raised the bar for communities in their attempts to remain economically competitive.

A second, equally significant advance driving the rush to have access to technological innovations is the advent of the Internet and the World Wide Web, which offer a cornucopia of information for every age and education level imaginable. Thus it is understandable that the computer, when linked to the Internet with its seemingly infinite potential for delivering valuable information, is viewed by many policy makers as *the* instrument for correcting long-standing social ills. However, an elated rush to bring communities online without thoughtful preparation or purpose can reduce this communication phenomenon to merely another form of consumerism, and information to a trivialized commodity (Doheny-Farina 1996; Schuler 1996). With the cost of failure so high for stressed urban communities, both in dollars and in diminished hopes, it is important that we proceed carefully and develop a practical strategy for using these powerful tools within the community.

This chapter presents a model of community organizing that uses a strong information-management component as a means of realizing modern technology's potential to the urban community. The model is illustrated with a case example of a project undertaken by a faith-based organization in Philadelphia, Pennsylvania. Those of us working on this project hoped both to accomplish its ends and to demonstrate the utility of the computer. More important, the project intended to build community through the use of technology.

PROJECT DESCRIPTION

Our project was a year-long organizing effort with several urban churches in west and southwest Philadelphia. This is a working-class area with pockets of severe poverty. Our first objective was to assess the social service needs of each parish, and to recommend strategies for program development and implementation.

From the outset we used a model that was both community based and asset based (Kretzmann & McKnight 1993), focusing on resources, talents, and skills already available in the community. We followed Kretzmann and McKnight's proviso that "outside resources will be much more effectively used if the local community is itself mobilized and invested, and if it can define the agendas for which additional resources must be obtained" (8). In addition to the traditional community development goal, we pursued a second objective: to increase the capacity of and appreciation for information technology in the community by introducing computers, databases, and mapping software to assist the residents in resource collection, organization, reporting, and analysis. Our goal was to cultivate the necessary expertise to support and maintain these systems after we had gone. It should be noted at the outset that the digital divide is not entirely a technology issue. It also consists of training and education issues and the understated but important issue of motivation. If people lack the skills or desire to participate in technology, they will not participate even when the benefits are obvious.

Setting the Stage and Asset Mapping

We began by conducting an informal assessment of the community with a focus group. As an icebreaker, we asked each participant the number of years that he or she had been a member of the parish and thus a resident of the community.[1] As parishioners responded, we recorded their answers in a column on a large sheet of poster board; after the last person had checked in, we added the numbers in the column to show the total number of years spent within the parish community. Our total was always well in excess of 100 years, which was a surprise to the participants. We contrasted the collective duration of their presence in the community with our own brief tenure there, thus underlining the absolute necessity and value of their contribution to any successful community initiative.

Our first exercise accomplished two things: First, it introduced a process of recording in which personal information was displayed externally, giving group members a new perspective; and second, it empowered the church members to use their own experiences as the basis for knowledge generation. We emphasized that one's *expertise* in an area is one's raw experience subjected to the refining process of critical reflection. Through this they established that the center of expertise in the community is local and within the lived experience of the community members.

Next, we proceeded with an informal assessment of the needs and problems of the community. In some cases the participants needed our prompting, but usually they identified on their own each member of a list of problems endemic to many urban areas across the country: crime, blight, poor health care, joblessness, and lack of activities for youth. We then led the group in identifying the resources, or the assets, within the community. The group was able to name some resources, and the facilitators, employing some of the ideas suggested by Kretzmann and McKnight (1993), added others, including many public institutions (such as the library). This technique is called *asset mapping*.

What's Going On?

Even in this initial exchange, valuable information began to emerge regarding resources and programs in the community that had not been communicated, until now, by the participants through their usual avenues of communication. Our forum for sharing information began to yield raw data that would be useful later. We had not yet identified a means to store the information or to organize it for future planning or programming purposes. In our report after that first session, we attempted to begin this process by formalizing our findings in a structured way so that the group could view them critically. We produced two tables that could be used by the group for further reflection and analysis (see tables 11.1 and 11.2).

Information and Communication

As we continued our own research into the assets of the community, we discovered an overall lack of awareness of the programs and resources available in the vicinity. In one case the group members, some of whom were parents, did not know that the public libraries had been renovated, with computers installed and public access to them provided. In another instance, two parish leaders with whom we worked were unaware that their parishes were located in a federal Empowerment Zone, and that they could have participated in or benefited by these initiatives. After conducting several such focus groups and contacting other organizations in the area, we found that the most common problem within and among these groups was poor communication. This metaproblem—that accurate and timely information

Table 11.1: Resource Inventory Worksheet

Resource	Group Served	Types of Services
Immanuel Youth Center	Youth	Recreation, tutoring
PAL Center	Youth	Recreation
Bernice Arms Senior Housing	Elderly	Housing
Star Harbor Senior Center	Elderly	Recreation, case management
Salvation Army	All	Emergency food and clothing
St. Vincent de Paul Society	All	Emergency food and clothing
Health Annex at Myers Recreation Center	All	Health care
Southwest Community Development Center	All	Emergency fuel, housing
Paschalville Library	All	Tutoring, after-school program, computer classes
Point Breeze Art Center	Youth	Recreation, arts

Table 11.2: Problem Inventory Worksheets

Problem/Need	Priority	Groups Affected	Resource Match?
Lack of safe playgrounds		Youth, families	
Drugs sold on corner		All	
Lack of jobs		All, especially youth	
Illiteracy		All	
Trash and litter		All	
Crime		All	

about community events is *not* seen as an essential resource—was typified by the oft-repeated phrase, "I didn't know that you/ they/ we had that." This was usually the response to the news that a program, resource, or activity already existed within the community. We found that the problem existed within tight, homogeneous communities (*intracommunity*); across community groups (*intercommunity*); and between given groups and their agencies or central offices outside the community boundary (*extracommunity*). It also existed between service providers—private and public—and within their larger parent organizations. The geographic or cultural distance between the neighborhoods further compounded the problem.

Cultural Elements

From an institutional point of view, many urban churches were historically self-sufficient, relying on their own members for financial support. Individual parishes or congregations who needed additional support could rely on subsidies drawn from the healthy coffers of their congregations' central funds. In many cases, social services were also delivered to the congregation from these offices. This relationship is depicted in figure 11.1.

Other historical and theological elements impeded the free flow of community information. For instance, there was little if any sharing of information across differing denominational, racial, and partisan political lines. In order for individual faiths to coexist as good neighbors within our pluralistic democracy, they had erected very good "fences" (see fig. 11.2). These fences, which were intended to maintain civility between sects, were also effective in impeding information flow between institutions within the same geographic vicinity. Information about funding, events, and social services became proprietary to the specified group. Further, we found that even within denominational, political, or communal groups, there were still problems with communication and the dissemination of important information.

Fortifying these communication barriers was the culture of paternalism that existed between the local institution and its centralized political, religious, and

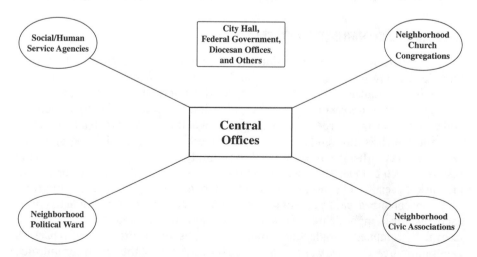

Figure 11.1   Traditional resource and information flow between community institutions and central offices

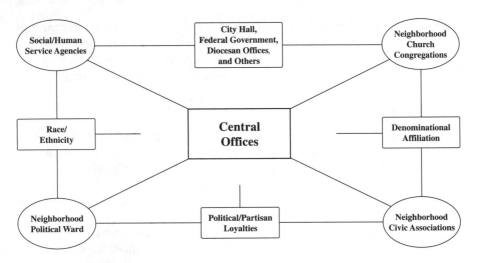

Figure 11.2 *Horizontal communication interrupted by traditional walls of denomination, race, income level, and orientation toward the central hub*

(most recently) social service authority. This relationship had citizens turning to regional leaders for answers to their local problems. This was true for the congregants, the pastors, the committee persons, and the citizens.

The concentration of power and thus the locus of control for these communities was seen as being outside the community. The power relationship was vertical in nature: Questions and requests went up the chain of authority and answers came down. This chain also represented the line of communication within the institution.

REFRAMING COMMUNITY INFORMATION

After concluding our first session with the group, we promised to return with any additional resources that we could find for the area. We checked numerous resource guides available to the community for this information. These guides were produced by local universities, churches, libraries, city, and social service agencies and varied in format, purpose, and design. Some of them were targeted to a certain age group, such as children or the elderly, or to residents of a certain geographically restricted area. Others, of interest to all community members, concerned a specific resource, such as food. These well-meaning guides presented a similar obstacle to our task. Specialized by discipline, target group, or geographic area, the information they contained was fragmentary, and their formats varied from guide to guide, each resource emphasizing different information. We scoured these guides and eventually compiled a single, but comprehensive, list of resources for each parish's geographic area. Our idea was to emphasize the centrality of the parish community, shifting the focus to its internal resource and information needs (Kretzmann & McKnight 1993).

We recorded this information in a database for ease of organization, reproduction, and reporting. My colleague, who had worked in direct services for more than twenty years and had used many different guides in her efforts, suggested a composite profile of information about each agency, church, or community organization. This effort was partly in response to some of the inquiries that we received from the group. In one instance, a working mother told us that day care was needed in her community. We did some research and discovered that there were numerous day care centers in her vicinity. When presented with this information, however, she amended her request, saying, "I meant *affordable* day care." Cost of services, then, was an important item for our group. Other important details, such as ages served or criteria for service, were also included in this agency profile.

During this time we had also acquired mapping software that interfaced well with our database software and allowed us to plot resource locations on a map of a geographic area. This allowed us to construct pictures of the parish community that offered the members a bird's-eye view that they had not realized before.

ENGAGING THE GROUP IN THE PROCESS

We returned to the second meeting with the first draft of the resource guide in hand and several color maps depicting the resource topology of the community (see fig. 11.3 for an example of the food-resource map). We circulated the guides and maps that we had put together thus far and asked for comments and questions. The group derived several insights from these representations of the resource topology for their community:

1. Many resources were available locally, but were sponsored by other churches or community organizations with which the group traditionally had little contact.

2. Systematizing this information at the parish level could help the parish become more effective and resourceful in responding to its own needs and to those of the surrounding community.

3. The group's own resources could be shared or exchanged with other groups in the neighborhood, thus reducing redundancy and expense.

4. Group members could identify service gaps graphically on the map, which supported their requests for additional services.

A STRATEGY FOR INVOLVEMENT AND OWNERSHIP OF THE DATA

We next drew the group's attention to the missing information for many of the resources that were listed in their guides (see table 11.3). We explained that our own sources were not always complete in listing the aspects or criteria of each service agency. However, as another function of the database software, we were able to produce a Resource Information Profile worksheet to help fill in the blanks. One needed only to fill in the worksheet using the agency's guide, and if any areas on the sheet remained blank, to contact the agency in question and requesting the missing information from its representative.

Table 11.3: Sample of Resource-Guide Layout with Partial or Missing Information

Resource Type	Agency, Address, Zip	Contact, Phone, Fax	Hours, Criteria
Food-cupboard	Mt. Carmel Baptist Church 5734 Race St. 19139	Rev. Albert F. Campbell 215-476-5320	
	Parents and Children against Drugs 4601 Market St. 19139	Frances Walker-Ponnie 215-476-5690 215-476-5505 (fax)	
	The Salvation Army 5501 Market St. 19139	215-747-1012	
	Walnut Hill CDC 252 S. 52nd St. 19139	215-472-3363	

We concluded our presentation with the question: "Would this group be interested in taking some of these worksheets and making the telephone calls or visits to the agencies to get this information?" A long pause often followed, broken in some cases when the pastor was present by the question, "Well, what do you think, Father?" The pastors at this point were very helpful in turning the decision back to the lay members, with a comment such as "I may be here another year or so, but you live in this community; you will be here for the long run." In many cases this was a turning point, where responsibility and authority for information management began to pass from the traditional source to the group and its experience in the community. This also represented an important shift in the direction and nature of information flow. Instead of the vertical flow up to or through the pastor, the flow was deflected down and sought a more horizontal or lateral direction. Through our engagement with the group we discovered that three key elements distinguished our participatory approach from traditional approaches to social science research: *people, power,* and *praxis.* Sohng (1996) and Finn (1994) found that the same three elements distinguished participatory research. Through the experience the community found that the "seed" of shared responsibility and power had been sown within the group. Each group embraced the task and began to come up with their own ideas about how the information might be obtained and who might obtain it. One group of people who were physically incapable of going outside but were able to serve from home made the phone calls to the agencies. Another had its youth group walk the streets to the listed organizations to obtain the information. Others developed a script that stated the purpose of the telephone call, which their members used when contacting other agencies or community groups. These contacts, we hope, will develop more personal relationships between parishes and other constituencies and will ultimately support each group's own continuing community initiatives.

TECHNOLOGICAL CONSIDERATIONS

Our approach accomplished several important objectives. It introduced the groups to the value of information—that is, to knowledge as a strategic asset. The community members, with their unique experiential vantage points, played an essential role in assessing, collecting, and interpreting the data. That is, it became their responsibility to partner with us and other agencies to help place the available facts into a meaningful framework that reflects their interests and priorities.

From a technological viewpoint, we used the resource guide as the "application," or the entrée into the concepts and capabilities of current technology. As we showed group members the maps and the guide, we explained in brief the software and hardware that made our tasks possible in such a short time. We also used the guide to encourage group members to build on their existing familiarity with the Internet, explaining how the guide could be made into a Web page and how it could be accessed and maintained thereafter. Thus, having established the value of the information, we were able to demonstrate how easily it could be organized, accessed, and maintained with the help of technology. This technology, we emphasized, was a useful tool for managing information in the service of the group's community plan.

We also mentioned local initiatives by the University of Pennsylvania, and regional ones by the Department of Housing and Urban Development (such as Call to Justice), to provide computers to communities for information access. We helped bring an important need, information, together with the medium of its delivery, information technology. In this way, by combining a theology of responsibility with the realities of the Information Age, we introduced a new and vital role to the local parish community: that of the parishioner as Steward of Information.

CONCLUSION

Communities can use technology to empower themselves and their members. This case study has demonstrated how technology can be used in conjunction with traditional community development processes to prepare communities to cope with the demands of the Information Age.

The following are some of the lessons that can be learned from this experience:

◆ It is of vital importance to use traditional techniques along with new technology. In this case, the traditional techniques led the way and were later supported by newer, technology-based techniques.
◆ Technology has the ability to break down authority and hierarchy. This case

demonstrates how this characteristic can be useful in a community-work situation.

◆ Although corporations frequently talk about their knowledge assets and the process of knowledge management, communities also have a knowledge base that is a valuable asset. Some of the same techniques that have been successful in the commercial world can be used to maintain and protect a community's store of knowledge. These new technologies can help citizens to learn about community issues, disseminate that information, and use it to create a better world for residents.

This is an interesting extension of the asset-based strategy of Kretzmann and McKnight (1993), who argued that the key to community empowerment is to mobilize the community's assets. Our project capitalizes on the knowledge assets of the community through the use of technology.

Knowledge has always been critical to community practice. Until recently, this vital stock of information was managed through a combination of the human memory and such simple devices as legal pads and card files. The new technology can help communities leverage their knowledge assets in ways they never knew were possible. They will need these assets as the Information Age unfolds.

Note

1. Catholic parishes are by tradition defined geographically. Until recently a person had to live in the area of the parish in order to be a member there.

Suggested Readings

Consumer Reports Online. 2000. Computers, then and now: Computer prices, shrinking 5/00. Available at [http://www.consumerreports.org]. Retrieved on 15 January 2001.

Dertouzos, M. 1997. *What will be: How the new world of information will change our lives.* New York: Harper-Collins.

Doheny-Farina, D. 1996. *The wired neighborhood.* New Haven, Conn.: Yale University Press.

Finn, Janet L. 1994. The promise of participatory research. *Journal of Progressive Human Services* 5 (2): 25.

Kretzmann, J. P., & J. L. McKnight. 1993. *Building communities from the inside out: A path toward finding and mobilizing a community's assets.* Evanston, Ill.: Asset-Based Community Development Institute, Institute for Policy Research, Northwestern University.

Schuler, D. 1996. *New community networks: Wired for change.* Reading, Mass.: Addison-Wesley.

Sohng, S. L. 1996. Particpatory research and community organizing. *Journal of Sociology and Social Welfare* 33 (4): 77–95.

Chapter 12

Technology-based Groups and Flash Campaigns

Goutham M. Menon

INTRODUCTION

Advances in information and communications technology (ICT) have allowed for the prolific development of technology-based communities in today's society. We are witnessing the emergence of virtual communities in almost all spheres of life. Rheingold (1993) states that "virtual communities are social aggregations that emerge from the Net when enough people carry on . . . public discussions long enough, with sufficient human feeling, to form webs of personal relationships in cyberspace" (5). Ranging from multiuser domains (MUDs) set up to revitalize the individual's virtual identity to newsgroups and online mailing lists developed to exchange ideas, share thoughts, and discuss issues, these virtual communities are shaping the way people collaborate, coexist, and advocate in the wide expanse of the Internet (Smith & Kollock 1999). Virtual communities bring people together regardless of their respective geographic locations that promote a sense of oneness among the people associated with them.

People use virtual communities for a variety of reasons (Rheingold 1993; Smith & Kollock 1999; see also chapter 3). Primarily, they act as a source of being in touch with others who share common ideas or support similar causes. We have seen the development of illness-specific support groups, announcement boards for advertising social causes, and a plethora of other tools that have made cause-related communication easier. One use of such tools is to organize and promote advocacy on behalf of people who are disenfranchised. This use is growing in stature due to the proliferation of user-friendly, Web-based protocols that are freely available to all. The implications for social work are extensive.

Advocacy is one use of a virtual community. This can be true even if the community is created for other purposes. This chapter highlights the use of online mailing lists as a forum for electronic advocacy. It also provides a set of procedures to follow when developing an electronic campaign.

TECHNOLOGY-BASED GROUPS

Online groups, using traditional e-mail, have helped in the development of virtual communities in a large way, transforming the use of the Internet from a one-to-one mode of communication to a more vibrant arena of multiple conversations. These groups can be broadly classified as either *synchronous* or *asynchronous.* Chat rooms offering real-time (RT) conversations in which users can chat with each other simultaneously fall under the first type. These rooms are the more refined versions of earlier multiuser domain (MUD) models (Menon 1998). In asynchronous groups, one uses the system to post or send messages but gets a response only when other users have logged on to read the messages. Usenet News and online mailing lists are examples of asynchronous networks. Usenet News can be viewed as a giant, worldwide bulletin board (McLellan 1997). Anyone can freely post or read something on it.

On the other hand, online mailing lists, often called *discussion lists* or *listserv[1]s,* are simply databases of e-mail addresses (Berge 1994). These lists are unique in that an individual or group who feels the need for sustained discussion and sharing of ideas within a discipline creates such a list for just that purpose. Operating out of complex software programs that more or less eliminate the need for a human administrator to manage the flow of e-mail through the system, these groups thrive on an asynchronous discussion framework. This means that not everyone must be online at the same time for a conversation to occur. Individuals interested in the specific topic under discussion must subscribe to the list (a process done by sending an e-mail to the list address) before they can contribute to or receive communications from other list members. Most of these groups carry node addresses starting with "Listserv," "Lstproc," or "Majordomo," representing three major software programs used for running mailing lists. The technical details on how to set up and maintain a discussion group are beyond the scope of this chapter; one can find more information on them in other publications (Berge 1994; Grobman & Grant 1998; L-Soft International 1998; Schwartz 1996). This is straightforward, tried-and-true technology that meets a number of needs. Among those needs are advocacy and empowerment.

ELECTRONIC ADVOCACY AND TECHNOLOGY-BASED GROUPS

Advocacy has been a part of the profession of social work for many decades (Specht & Courtney 1994). We have traditionally used direct mail, town hall meetings, rallies, and other methods to get our messages across and thus inform and change policies or public opinions. However, in recent years, we have made use of certain technology-based tools in the form of telephones, fax machines, and other communications equipment. Traditional electronic advocacy (FitzGerald & McNutt, 1999; Schwartz 1996) has been a powerful tool for many organizations and continues to be so. More recent, the growth of the Internet has provided more efficient modes—such as electronic mail, discussion groups, chat rooms, and Web sites—to spread information in a cost-effective and timely manner. FitzGerald and McNutt (1999) call this *emergent electronic advocacy.*

Electronic advocacy can be defined as the use of ICTs to disseminate information to and mobilize support from a large constituency to influence decision-making processes. It may include the use of telephone, fax, television, radio, e-mail,

Web sites, online discussion groups, network newsgroups, and other modes. Usually, an advocacy campaign is maintained by a combination of traditional and electronic modes of communication.

To illustrate how one can plan and create a campaign that catches the public's attention, this chapter highlights two examples from an online mailing list. The first example details a *flash campaign*—quick, planned activism that occurs spontaneously out of a single incident (Raney 1999). The second is a case of public-opinion mobilization that is slower paced and involves more discussions and suggestions. Both these cases come out of SCHIZOPH [http://www.schizoph@maelstrom. stjohns.edu], an unmoderated online discussion group dedicated to schizophrenia-related issues. It has been in existence for more than four years and has a membership of about 260 individuals at any given time. The membership is composed of individuals with a diagnosis of schizophrenia, their families and friends, and a handful of mental health professionals. Discussions usually pertain to issues of medication, treatment modalities, diet, and often, simply words of encouragement and mutual support. The membership is international.

Flash Campaign

A flash campaign is one in which online advocacy is conducted in a fast but systematic way (Raney 1999). The campaign is begun, and action is initiated while the issue at hand is hot and all involved are keyed up to do their parts. In March 1997, members of the SCHIZOPH group did just that. When they opened their electronic mailbox that day, they found a note about a mentally ill woman who had been arrested for not paying seventy-nine cents for a cup of coffee (Menon 2000). The posting ended with a casual statement, "Pretty big deal over a cup of coffee, I'd say." It turned out to be a big deal for the members in the group.

The next message that came through the network contained a question about the name of the diner where the incident had taken place and made another casual remark that maybe the members of the group should send seventy-nine cents to the diner to make a point. That idea created an unusual flurry of messages from the members of the list group. In place of the usual postings of questions about medication and treatment and the occasional "how are you feeling?" types of questions, suddenly the group woke up to take action.

What ensued shows how effectively the mode of online mailing lists can be used for advocacy purposes. The members soon began to post both their own experiences with the law and incidents of mistreatment of the mentally ill about which they had read. Words of comfort and support went back and forth. Beneath this were also numerous messages on what could be done to make the plight of the mentally ill known to the lay public. Anyone who has done traditional community organizing will readily recognize this situation. An injustice, made aware to the group, galvanizes the overall feeling of oppression.

The member from the area where this incident occurred made frequent postings about the case as she learned new details from the press. It was then suggested that instead of sending the seventy-nine cents to the diner, they should send the money and a letter condemning the incident to the local television station. This idea was embraced very quickly, and the nature of the campaign began to change. The members now needed to create professional-looking letters to make an impression with the news organizations. Some members posted that due to their illnesses they just could not sit down and write letters. To involve everybody, another member came up with the idea of drafting a form letter that could be mailed to everyone on the list, and even published on a Web site so that others would have access to it.

Soon a letter was floating around the list, its form changing as members made suggestions. This letter was finally posted on a Web site. Meanwhile, the members were constantly reminded to send their copies of the letter with seventy-nine cents in it via regular mail to the television station that had first carried the story, and to follow up with an e-mail. Within the span of thirty-six hours the members had an advocacy plan underway, and the television station was soon inundated with postal letters, each containing seventy-nine cents in the envelope. The television station carried this development in prime time news. Hearing of this, the group members felt elated and had a sense of achievement in that they had the power to do something constructive. This case demonstrates that a group can be mobilized to act quickly and effectively with relatively simple technology. It also demonstrates how organizing via technology is, in many ways, similar to traditional organizing.

Opinion Mobilization

The case discussed here is about a twenty-three-year-old male, Aaron Lee (names are not changed because the material reported here in is in the public domain). He is reportedly suffering from schizoaffective, bipolar, panic, and attention deficit disorders. He has been struggling with the problems associated with his condition but has been on regular treatment. He is married and has a son who is six years old. In 1992, Aaron had another son who died when he was about seven weeks old. He had suddenly stopped breathing, and Aaron not knowing what to do, shook the baby to try to make him breathe. The child died. Aaron was arrested in 1996 and was accused of murder and injury to a child.

The case gained momentum after Aaron's mother posted the plight of her son to the SCHIZOPH discussion group. While he was in the prison, his mental illness was not recognized, and he was given no medication to treat the problems from which he was suffering. Eventually, with some pressure from elected officials, his medication was reinstated. Aaron's family dealt with a number of issues while he was in the prison; a detailed description of the case can be found at [http://www.geocities.com/Heartland/Ridge/8616/aaronleegeorge.html].

Immediately after the scenario was posted in the discussion group, the members responded with empathy. They provided emotional support to Aaron's mother and gave her some idea of her options in providing for his care, and in getting the justice department to take into consideration his mental health when deciding the case. Some of the postings are listed next.

If you would send that list of contacts that you sent me privately on to the list, I am sure people here would be glad to write a letter if your lawyer feels that would help Aaron's case and not hurt it. If you will check and let us know, then those who wish to and can will write a letter or two. We would not want to do anything to make matters worse in the situation, so please let us know. Hugs.

Thanks for your offer. The attorney said the more people [that] get upset about this kind of thing, no matter their location, the better our chances of helping Aaron and so many others like him. I will send out the list again. God Bless You Dear for your help!

I feel The Urgency And Importance of this matter . . . For Some Reason This Issue with Aaron Calls to me for my attention, please keep fighting, I will muster whatever I am able, to generate pressure and support for Aaron's cause I "will" Be In Closer Touch.

Aaron asked me to convey his appreciation to each of you who have sent him Christmas cards and other correspondence. . . . He cannot think of words to write and when he thinks of the words he cannot remember the spelling. . . . So . . . from Aaron (and always from me) thank you for being who you are and fighting for what is right. I am honored to be among you!

The members of the list group composed letters to elected officials, suggested lawyers who would be able to take the case pro bono, and in general were very supportive of Aaron's plight. The Web site that Aaron's mother created gave constant updates of the case, and people could follow its development as time went on. This is another example of effective organizing through the Internet. Stakeholders were engaged and empowered through online interaction.

A MODEL FOR AN ADVOCACY CAMPAIGN

As noted in the previous section, electronic advocacy can be a simple and cost-effective method to disseminate and share information about a cause. It can be used both by large organizations to inform and mobilize their members, or by a handful of individuals passionate about a cause to enlist and encourage others to act. As more people become familiar with the Internet and its tools, organizations will be in a position to run cost-effective campaigns quickly while the issues are still hot (Bennett and Fielding 1999; Schwartz 1996; see also chapter 7). I suggest the following set of procedures for organizations to use when planning a campaign over the Internet.

Campaigns must follow a structured process when using a highly unstructured entity such as the Internet, else the message and the enthusiasm of the campaign will be lost in the cyclic repetition of the same information. To help organize and run a campaign, four broad steps can be followed, namely, 1) collection of tools, 2) conceptualization of the issue, 3) contribution of members, and 4) coordination of the campaign.

Collection of Tools

The first step in organizing an electronic campaign is to ensure that the organization and its members have the necessary tools to undertake the task. Organizations must keep in mind that accessibility to computers and connectivity to the Internet by its members cannot be taken for granted. There are issues of differential access, in which certain groups of people are disadvantaged due to socioeconomic status, ethnicity, or other reasons. In these circumstances, members must be informed of public-access sites (e.g., libraries) in their neighborhoods, and of how and where to get Web-based e-mail accounts through sites such as Yahoo! [http://www.yahoo.com], Hotmail [http://www.hotmail.com], or others that provide these free services. Thus costs to individual members can be kept to a bare minimum.

There are two things that organizations themselves must have in setting up a campaign. First, they must have a presence—a home page—on the World Wide Web (WWW). Once again, spending on expensive Web server software and hardware is unnecessary. Sites that provide free home pages abound on the Internet. Second, organizations must have an e-mail address. The free Web hosting sites just mentioned also provide free e-mail addresses for the organizations.

Once the Web page and e-mail addresses are in place, the next step is creating a distribution list for the members. These lists allow members to send and receive multiple messages using only the list's e-mail address, so that individual members need not develop address books containing all of the other members' addresses. Once again, these lists are available at no cost; Yahoo! Groups and Listbot, for example, provide free distribution-list services.

Now that the tools have been collected, the next step is to conceptualize the issue.

Conceptualization of the Issue

The issue for which to advocate can arise from a discussion-list member's casual observation about something that might affect the organization, or it can be a planned process coming from the board of directors or the agency team. Either way, it is important to discuss and come to an understanding of what is to be done by the organization.

Casual Observations
Once in a while, a member on the discussion list might throw out an observation that catches the interest of the rest of the membership. In an earlier example, when a member of the SCHIZOPH list group posted news that a mentally ill woman in Wisconsin had been arrested for nonpayment of seventy-nine cents for a cup of coffee, the other members were so angered that they launched an e-mail–facilitated letter-writing campaign directed at the TV station that had originally reported the story, in the hope of raising awareness of the difficulties the mentally ill face in society. This campaign effectively used both a Web site and e-mail to achieve its goal.

Planned Campaign
Although spontaneous campaigns based on casual observations can be effective due to the emotional involvement of the people, a planned campaign is generally

more effective. For one thing, a campaign springing from a casual observation can be an emotional roller coaster for the members, who become highly attuned to the situation. Planned campaigns, although not unemotional, do not require highly charged emotion in order to take place. They also allow for better use of time and resources, and for the sending out of a consistent message that reflects the mission of the organization.

A planned campaign begins when an organization or its board posts an issue for the list members' discussion. Once the discussions have derived a plan of action, decisions are made on the nature and process of the campaign.

Contribution of Members

Electronic advocacy can be effective only as long as the members have a sense of involvement in the campaign. Care must be taken to encourage members to participate in whatever capacity they can—and there are many capacities. First, someone must be in charge of making a list of e-mail addresses of people to target for the campaign (senators, local leaders, etc.). Others who have good writing skills can draft letters to post to the distribution list for members to read and modify. Still others who have skills in HTML scripting can help put the information on the Web site. This does not mean that individual members need be wizards at Web-based programming or own sophisticated Web-design software. Almost all off-the-shelf software, such as Microsoft Word or WordPerfect, comes with features that enable the user to write a document in "plain English" and then save it as an HTML document.

In all cases, the lack of face-to-face contacts and the sense of alienation in virtual settings should be kept in mind, and efforts must be undertaken to get everyone involved. Initially, a checklist of skills of all members can be put up on the Web site, allowing subgroups to form to finalize the campaign.

Coordination of the Campaign

This is the most important stage of a campaign. Without coordination, there will be chaos. Campaigners should keep in mind that the needs of a local campaign will be much different from those of a national one, and that they need to be planned carefully based on their campaign's needs.

Local Campaigns

A local campaign can be coordinated by one person who will take the lead in posting information to the distribution list and uploading information to the Web site. Using the distribution list, members can converse about and debate the issue and reach consensus on the tactics they want to adopt to tackle the issue. It could be that the campaign requires letters to be sent to various leaders; if this is the case, form letters should be drafted and sent to all the members. (Some of us either find it difficult to write an effective letter or lack the time to do so. Receiving a form letter that needs only a signature before being passed on helps.) The letter can also be placed on the Web site so that visitors can see it and possibly take part, a typical strategy in campaigns dealing with groups who are mentally or physically disabled.

National Campaigns

These campaigns are best handled by dividing the area into regions. The organization as a whole will have one distribution list, while chapters of the organization will have their own local lists. For example, if the National Association of Social Workers (NASW) needs to mobilize support for a particular national campaign, the Washington Office of NASW will have a distribution list set up for all members who have expressed an interest in participating in public policy. Each state chapter will also have its own list. The discussions are best handled at the state level; then the chapter presidents can contact each other and share the views of their respective chapters, come to a consensus decision, and report their decision to the entire list via the national office. Delegating the work is necessary to keep the campaign organized. Without delegation, a horrendous amount of electronic messages will pass through one person's mailbox, and much time will be wasted in sifting through it.

CONCLUSION

Advocacy is an integral role social workers play in the lives of the people we touch. It has a rich history of empowering disenfranchised groups and a tremendous influence in the processes of today's society. The advent of new ICT tools makes it imperative that social workers learn to use them in the service of the people with whom we work. The explosion of information on the Internet makes it is easy to find virtual communities that support one's own areas of interest, and to become integral parts of these communities will be beneficial. Many of these communities are loosely bound groups of people who have a great interest in the topic they support but who may lack the skills necessary to conduct a fruitful campaign, should they need to organize one. Social workers, with their career training and with the interest and skills they may acquire in ICT, have an important role to play in the development of these communities and in shaping the debate in various social causes. One hopes that programs of social work across the country will heed these developments and include relevant course material. Social-work students need such training, and to be open to the idea that, yes, virtual communities do exist, and we must study them constructively to help "Netizens" be productive members of the communities in which they take part.

Electronic advocacy is a viable option for small and large organizations or groups. It is an effective tool, not only for lobbying policy-making institutions, but also for raising public awareness on issues that are close to the heart of social work. As with any campaign, care must be taken to plan and conduct the process in an effective and efficient manner.

Notes

1. Listserv is the name of a brand of software but is often used to describe e-mail discussion lists.

Suggested Readings

Bennett, D., & Fielding, P. 1999. *The Net effect: How cyber-advocacy is changing the political landscape.* Merrifield, Va.: E-Advocates Press.

Berge, Z. L. 1999. Electronic discussion groups. *Communication Education* 43 (2): 102–111.

FitzGerald, E., & J. G. McNutt. 1999. Electronic advocacy in policy practice: A framework for teaching technologically based practice. *Journal of Social Work Education* 35 (3): 331–341.

Grobman, G. M., & G. B. Grant. 1998. *The non-profit Internet handbook.* Harrisburg, Pa.: White Hat Communications.

L-Soft International. 1998. LISTSERV(r)—The mailing list management classic as of February 6th, 1998. Available at [http://www.lsoft.com/listserv.stm].

McLellan, T. 1997. Free advice on Usenet News. *Dispatch.* University of Alberta, Computing and Network Services. Available at [http://www.islandnet.com/~tmc/html/articles/usentnws.htm]. Retrieved on 23 October 1999.

Menon, G. M. 1998. Gender encounters in a virtual community: Identity formation and acceptance in cyberspace. *Computers in Human Services* 15 (1): 55–69.

———. 2000. The 79-cent campaign: The use of online mailing lists for electronic advocacy. *Journal of Community Practice* 8 (3): 73–81.

Raney, R. F. 1999. Flash campaigns: Online activism at warp speeds. *New York Times Online.* Available at [http://www.e-elections.com/html/political_pages_B4_nyt3.html]. Retrieved on 3 June 1999.

Rheingold, H. 1993. *The virtual community: Homesteading on the electronic frontier.* Reading, Mass.: Addison-Wesley.

Schwartz, E. 1996. *NetActivism: How citizens use the Internet.* Sebastopol, Calif.: O'Reilly.

Smith, M. A., & P. Kollock (eds.). 1999. *Communities in cyberspace.* New York: Routledge.

Specht, H., & M. Courtney. 1994. *Unfaithful angels.* New York: Free Press.

Part **III**

Social Policy
and
Community in
an Information
Society:
Implications
for Advocacy
and Organizing

Chapter 13

Social Policy and Advocacy in Cyberspace

Steven Hick
John McNutt

SOCIAL POLICY IS AN AREA IN WHICH SOCIAL WORK ADVOCACY AND AC-
tivism have been effective—promoting, and at times securing, policies that advance
social and economic justice. As the industrial era unfolded, social workers were active in the passage of workers' and children's rights legislation, early welfare benefits, and a host of other programs and policies that led to an increase in human well-
being (Specht & Courtney 1994; Trattner 1994). After the Depression of the 1930s
and World War II, the role of governments in society changed. Governments were
seen as playing an important role in society and the economy to protect its citizens'
security. During this era, social workers in the developed capitalist countries advo-
cated for new and improved social programs. Later, however, economic globalization and large government deficits made the 1980s and 1990s an era in which social
programs were eroded.

As we enter the new millennium, the political economy has changed. Both policy makers and policy advocates face a new globalizing economy, with information
as its base and knowledge as its store of value. This has implications for the nature
of work, the type of organization within which people will be employed, and the future of wealth and poverty (McNutt 1996). These forces have made a significant impact on social policy as we conceive of it.

As we discussed in previous chapters, the globalizing and opening up of the
economies of the world have curtailed the ability of nations to manage their
economies and develop social spending and systems of protection (Mishra 1999). It
has resulted in devolution and decentralization, changes in the nature of government organizations, the rise of the "hollow state" (Peters 1994), and the decline of
the Keynesian welfare state. Money and capital are now free to move across national
boundaries as never before. This has curtailed the autonomy of national governments and their capacity for Keynesian macroeconomic management (Meenaghan
& Washington 1980). Social spending and full employment policies are severely
limited in this environment. Another growing phenomenon is *social dumping,*

whereby corporations threaten to move operations to locations with lower wages, less social protection, fewer regulations, and lower taxes.

This globalizing of the economy and the relative decline of the nation state has immense implications for the strategies and tactics that advocates and activists undertake to influence and change social policy. These changes will have massive effects on the nature of the social policy enterprise and on policy advocacy and social change efforts. Some of those changes may include

- ◆ The development of new forms of poverty and social exclusion as a consequence of the changing nature of the workforce. The digital divide will exclude many from future participation in the economy by denying access to needed technological and skills resources (Ebo 1998; McConnaughey Everette, Reynolds, and Lader 1999). This will become even more serious as technological resources become prerequisite for political, as well as economic, inclusion.
- ◆ The weakening of the nation state as devolution, combined with the globalization of the economy, remove control of critical decisions from national government. This will lead to more diffuse decision-making environments, which may be more difficult to influence.
- ◆ Changes in the delivery system of social services, reflecting a change in the nature of organizations. It is likely that public and private nonprofit organizations will follow the trend toward virtual or network models characterized by outsourcing and very small permanent staffs. This might cause major drifts in the delivery of services and the enforcement of client rights.
- ◆ Scarcity brought about by environmental destruction and resource consumption. The declining resource base will eventually result in fewer available resources for services and benefits. In addition, environmental destruction will have major impacts on the life chances of the poor and powerless.
- ◆ Changes in the nature of work and worklife that may render traditional systems of social welfare inappropriate. The prospect for long-term employment with a single employer has deteriorated, replaced by more uncertain work situations. This long-term employment is an underlying assumption behind many western welfare states. This will require reorientation toward a less secure economic future.
- ◆ Changes in the decision-making process as technology makes direct participation in government possible.

None of these changes is likely to emerge immediately. It is much more likely that each will evolve over time, and that some elements will be evident sooner than others. This will create new challenges for social workers to devise new strategies and tactics to advance social and economic justice.

These changes in the global political economy have affected social work advocacy and have made the use of new technologies even more critical. In particular, the increasingly globalized economy necessitates the use of Internet communication, for two reasons. First, the forces of economic globalization are increasing their hold on the social protection and social justice policies of state governments through the use of international trade agreements such as the World Trade Organization (WTO), North American Free Trade Agreement (NAFTA), and Free Trade Agreement of the Americas (FTAA). To fight these agreements and the restrictions on social policy contained in them, citizens must organize global coalitions. To do so requires a low-cost means of sharing information and communicating globally. The Internet provides an important component of this. Within the new political economy it may not be enough to organize locally or even nationally. The reach of corporate power is enforced using international trade agreements, which necessitates that activists organize globally.

Second, corporate power is using Internet technology to pursue global operations and communications. It is imperative that social work advocates use the latest Internet technology to monitor the developments in international trade agreements and the activities of large corporations around the world. The information discovery must be instantaneous as the events unfold. As corporations act quickly, using new technology, so to must the advocates who resist them. It is imperative that social work advocates use the same tools as corporate powers.

POLICY PRACTICE AS MACRO-PRACTICE

Social workers have always engaged in advocacy and activism on behalf of the poor, the disadvantaged, and the oppressed. The creation of policy-advocate roles for social workers, however, is more recent (Jansson 1998). A knowledge base specific to policy advocacy is developing and is distinct from community organization and community practice. In the United States and Canada, this practice is called *policy practice* (Jansson 1998), but it goes under other names as well. Policy practice includes such activities as policy analysis, planning and evaluation, lobbying, supporting candidates, political and social action, grassroots organizing, and so forth (Haynes & Mickelson 2000).

The development of information and communications technology (ICT) has vastly transformed the capacity of human service organizations to build coalitions and networks and to advocate for their clients, causes, and principles. These organizations frequently advocate and initiate action dealing with health care, child welfare, poverty, human rights, environmentalism, physical and sexual abuse, suicide prevention, substance abuse, homelessness, and all the other human problems in modern society. Activism in cyberspace really does not much differ from activism anywhere else. E-mail, newsgroups, discussion lists, Web sites, chat, virtual communities, computer conferencing, and online publishing are a few of new methods that the Internet enables. They all, in many ways, either replace or augment activities that were previously done by other means. For example, e-mail action alerts are the electronic version of the flyers that grassroots organizers hand out on street corners or at rallies. The difference is that e-mail alerts reach more people instantly, and cost nothing.

Policy practice is performed by various kinds of organizations, from direct-service agencies to advocacy groups (Boris & Mosher-Williams 1998; Hoefer 1998, 1999a,b, 2000a,b). Advocacy groups may be small and in some cases may exist only on the Internet. Other groups may be large and advocate for a variety of issues, social policy issues among them. In the United States, larger advocacy groups, such as the Children's Defense Fund and the Sierra Club, have significant impacts on their respective policy areas.

In recent years, the capability of these organizations has been limited by the concentration of corporate power and its effect on political decision making. Campaign finance reform is an attempt to deal with this, but the concentrated power of corporate actors and their immense wealth are still problematic. In addition, the devolution of social policy decision making in the United States and several other Western countries has created more decision-making units, resulting in a demand for smaller advocacy groups to create more expansive advocacy efforts than previously were needed.

Small and local activist groups use the Internet in a variety of ways. The Ottawa Coalition to Stop the FTAA, a small local activist group, effectively used the Internet to communicate the activities of the group to its members and nonmembers. Their Web site [http://www.flora.org/ftaa/] reported all upcoming events, meetings, and actions, as well as the results of past events. It contained a calendar of the events with details available via hot links. It also contained an online petition that captured thousands of local signatures. The petition asked that the Ottawa City Council pass a resolution against the Free Trade Area of the Americas (FTAA), the General Agreement on Trade in Services (GATS), and any other agreements that would allow multinationals to overrule local governments. In the space of twenty-nine days, 450 local Ottawa citizens signed the petition digitally. Additionally, the Ottawa Coalition Web site linked people with local working groups and with other national and international groups, and even sold scarves online. (The scarf was a response to draconian bylaws passed by the Canadian city governments of St. Foy and Quebec City, banning the wearing of scarves during the FTAA summit.)

Large national and international groups use the Internet in ways similar to those of small groups but often have additional resources to use advanced features. The Council of Canadians [http://www.canadians.org/], a national advocacy and activist organization in Canada, uses the Internet as the foundation of its national and international advocacy work. The Web site takes advantage of more advanced Internet technologies, such as video streaming and online publishing. It contains a complete guide to online organizing, and an index of issues around which an individual or a group can organize. Finally, the Council has instituted an automated Fax Your Member of Parliament (MP) program that guides the user through the process of choosing a campaign issue, getting the facts, drafting a letter, and automatically faxing the letter to the MP. Similar systems are available in the United States and internationally (Turner 1998). Most of the larger advocacy groups have extensive online facilities for legislative advocacy (McNutt 2000), and consulting firms produce a number of related commercial products. These usually include resources for finding representatives' names and addresses, downloadable letters, facilities for fax and e-mail communications, and, in some cases, tracking of bills and regulations. These developments have led many policy practitioners to see the Internet as a potential savior or equalizer. As social policy advocacy and change efforts become increasingly global in nature, social workers are turning to new ICT to link internationally. This is not the case for social activists only; groups from all areas of the political spectrum have embraced the Internet as a valuable tool and a way to network globally. In fact, there are concerns in Europe over the growth of extreme right-wing groups facilitated, in part, by Internet technology. In the United States, militia groups and hate groups have been a major force on the Internet. This has concerned both law enforcement and advocates of liberal causes.

The use of electronic techniques in advocacy is a growing. Beginning a decade ago with e-mail–based systems, the practice has grown to include sophisticated Web-based systems that incorporate geographic information systems (GIS), and videoconferencing. Earlier systems continue to be useful as the leading edge advances to newer and more sophisticated technologies, such as online fund raising and recruitment. Despite evidence that the use of these techniques is growing in social work advocacy and activism, little research has been done on the impacts and benefits.

POLICY PRACTICE ONLINE

The development of online policy practice, like that of online organizing, is a new phenomenon. Advocacy groups have only recently come online, although some organizations have made considerable effort to develop high-end systems (see Hick & Halprin 2001; McNutt & Boland 1999; McNutt, Keaney, Crawford, Schubert, & Sullivan 2001). The extent of Internet use by advocacy groups is growing rapidly enough, however, that a thorough analysis of the methods, potentials, and dangers of the medium is necessary.

Methods and Strategies

The methods used in policy practice are similar to those used by community-based organizations. The differences are in the strategies used and the ways they are employed. This is often a function of both setting and arena. Early campaigns used e-mail and very limited Web-based approaches. Current strategies vary by organizational size and scope. Based on the distinction between technology-assisted and technology-dependent practice, current strategies include the following.

Technology-assisted practice:
- E-mail to coordinate efforts at policy change
- Web-based public education and awareness campaigns
- Databases
- Mapping and targeting programs
- Online fund raising
- Blast faxing

Technology-dependent practice:
- Intranets and extranets for policy communication
- E-mail to decision makers
- Online communities
- Internet-only advocacy groups
- Video streaming of speeches and educational resources

Commonalities and Differences

Within the technology-assisted group, similarities outweigh differences. Many of these new tools simply automate processes long used by activists. The more advanced tools require differential thinking and organizing and may require additional funding. Industry is also using some of these tools, which greatly expands both the possibilities and the costs. Several commercial policy-change packages, such as Capital Advantage, are within reach of well-funded organizations. Although there is evidence of their use, it is not altogether clear that these methods have gained the needed credibility in some circles.

Research has demonstrated that, at this point, decision makers are less convinced of the value of online support. This may change in the future, but at present, activists must make liberal use of traditional techniques to deliver their messages.

The chapters in this section provide a spirited discussion of these issues. In chapter 14, George Haskett gives an overview of the changing nature of social-policy making and advocacy. He discusses the traditional advocacy methods and how they are used in practice.

In chapter 15, On-Kwok Lai provides an interesting discussion of teledemocracy and its role in reinventing governance for social welfare. The chapter integrates a great deal of current material on the information society along with the implications of change in the political economy for public participation and democracy.

The next two chapters examine the critical digital divide issue. Jan Steyaert (chapter 16) discusses the issue for local communities. For Steyaert, the digital divide is an inequality between those connected to the Internet and those not connected. He concludes that a central component of Internet-based advocacy and activism is that of people coming together online and acting to change structures and policies that negatively affect them. The people who most need to come together, however, are often those who are left out by the digital divide. As Steyaert's chapter demonstrates, even if the excluded and oppressed in society gain physical access to the Internet, the digital divide will not disappear. Only when opportunities for the excluded to increase their information and technology skills are made available will the digital divide be closed.

In chapter 17, Jamal Shahin explores the digital divide from an international viewpoint. He gives an overview of how the information society is fast becoming a core policy concern for most governments. The chapter looks at the driving forces behind the Information Society, focusing upon electronic commerce and the issue of access. It puts forward the notion that commercial concerns are providing the main impulse for the global information society's growth and thus highlights the relationship between consumers and citizens. The chapter describes a few projects that promote the Information Society in the developing world and concludes that much must be done to enhance the citizen's role in the information society and to enable citizens and civil groups to organize and advocate for their rights and the rights of others.

CONCLUSION

The natures of social policy, social welfare, and social-work policy advocacy and activism are changing. The tools are growing in sophistication and ability, but the forces arrayed against us are also growing more sophisticated. Corporate power and the potential for control of cyberspace are important threats. This underscores the need for activists to use these new technologies to their best advantage. Not only must activists use the latest technological techniques to achieve our goals, but we must also struggle to ensure that new technologies such as the Internet remain open, accessible, and public. Within both the global and national contexts it is imperative that the Internet remain open to all classes and sectors of society.

Suggested Readings

Boris, E. T., & R. Mosher-Williams. 1998. Nonprofit advocacy organizations: Assessing the definitions, classifications, and data. *Nonprofit and Voluntary Sector Quarterly* 27 (4): 488–506.

Ebo, B. (ed.). 1998. *The cyberghetto or cybertopia: Race, class, gender and marginalization in cyberspace.* New York: Praeger.

Haynes, K. S., & J. S. Mickelson. 2000. *Affecting change* (4th ed). Needham, Mass.: Allyn and Bacon.

Hick, S., R. Halpin, & E. Hoskins. 2001. *Human rights and the Internet.* London: Macmillan.

Hoefer, R. 1998. *Human services interest groups in four states: Lessons for effective advocacy.* Presentation at the twenty-seventh annual meeting of the Association of Voluntary Action Scholars, 5–7 November, Seattle, Wash.

———. 1999a. Protection, prizes or patrons? Explaining the origins and maintenance of human services interest groups. *Journal of Sociology and Social Welfare* 26 (4): 115–136.

———. 1999b. The social work and politics initiative: A model for increasing political content in social work education. *Journal of Community Practice* 6 (3): 71.

———. 2000a. Human services interest groups in four states: Lessons for effective advocacy. *Journal of Community Practice* 7 (4): 77–94.

———. 2000b. Making a difference: Human service interest group influence on social welfare program regulations. *Journal of Sociology and Social Welfare* 27 (3): 21–38.

Jansson, B. S. 1998. *Becoming an effective policy advocate: From policy practice to social justice* (3rd ed.). Belmont, Calif.: Brooks/Cole.

McConnaughey, J., D. W. Everette, T. Reynolds, & W. Lader (eds.). 1999. *Falling through the Net: Defining the digital divide.* Washington, D.C.: U.S. Department of Commerce, National Telecommunications and Information Administration.

McNutt, J. G. 1996. National information infrastructure policy and the future of the American welfare state: Implications for the social welfare policy curriculum. *Journal of Social Work Education* 6 (3): 375–388.

————. 2000. *The Internet and non-profit advocacy: Patterns of Web-based online advocacy in different organizational fields.* Paper presented at the International Society for Third-Sector Research biennial conference, "The third sector: For what and for whom?" 5–8 July, Dublin, Ireland.

McNutt, J. G., & K. M. Boland. 1999. Electronic advocacy by non-profit organizations in social welfare policy. *Non-Profit and Voluntary Sector Quarterly* 28 (4): 432–451.

McNutt, J. G, W. F. Keaney, P. Crawford, L. Schubert, & C. Sullivan. 2001. Going online for children: A national study of electronic advocacy by non-profit child advocacy agencies. In *The impact of information technology on civil society: Working papers from the independent sector's 2001 spring research forum,* 213–228. Washington, D.C.: Independent Sector.

Meenaghan, T. M., & R. O. Washington. 1980. *Social policy and social welfare: Structure and applications.* New York: Free Press.

Mishra, R. 1999. *Globalization and the welfare state.* Cheltenham, U.K.: Edward Elgar Publishing Limited.

Peters, B. G. 1994. Managing the hollow state. *International Journal of Public Administration* 17 (3-4): 739–756.

Specht, H., & M. Courtney. 1994. *Unfaithful angels.* New York: Free Press.

Trattner, W. 1994. *From poor law to welfare state* (5th ed.). New York: Free Press.

Turner, R. 1998. *Democracy at work: Non-profit use of Internet technology for public policy purposes.* Washington, D.C.: OMBWatch.

Chapter 14

Social Policy and Social Change in the Postindustrial Society

George Haskett

FROM ITS EARLIEST DAYS, THE SOCIAL WORK PROFESSION HAS PROMOTED social reform (Trattner 1995). Our advocacy and reform tradition distinguishes social work from many other helping professions that focus only on the individual, giving little or no thought to larger social and economic forces that constrain human development and "life, liberty, and the pursuit of happiness." As social work enters a new century, the profession continues to fight oppression, to focus on the vulnerable in any society, and to promote the general welfare of all.

The purpose of this chapter is to discuss how trends in the policy environment since 1990 will influence policy making in what has been called our "postindustrial information society," and to consider what approaches might be necessary if social workers and other human service workers are to become effective advocates in this new setting. In this chapter I examine some of the major trends that are changing society and the work of social work advocates. In addition, the chapter looks at the current major advocacy methods and explores how changes in political economy might affect these methods in the future.

In this chapter I argue—to paraphrase McLuhan—that the medium (new technology, e-mail, and electronic advocacy) is *not* the primary message—yet. As society develops and the decision-making system changes radically, new forms of advocacy will gain prominence. In the current situation, the new technology-based advocacy serves mostly to complement to existing advocacy tactics and techniques.

CHANGES IN POSTINDUSTRIAL SOCIETY AND SOCIAL WELFARE

The growing prominence of the information sector in the global economy has made significant changes throughout the world (Dillman 1991; McNutt 1996). The most significant changes have probably come in the economic sector, but changes in government, culture, family, and other aspects of society are not far behind. Although a complete treatment of these issues is beyond the scope of this chapter, a number of these transformations are salient to the discussion here. The major areas for consideration are changes in the economy, in governance, and in social welfare.

Economic Systems

The economic system has undergone the most profound changes, many of which have direct implications for the social welfare system. These include globalization, decentralization, and the rise of the knowledge worker and of knowledge as a store of wealth (Huey 1994; McNutt 1996).

The growing importance of knowledge work is an unmistakable trend in the new economy (Beniger 1988; Dillman 1991; Huey 1994). This is a central issue in the transition from an industrial to an information economy. Although goods and services will still be produced, much of what is most valuable in the economy will be information. Already, organizations are developing the capacity to conserve this resource through a technique called *knowledge management*.

The world of the individual knowledge worker is also different (Huey 1994; Wallace 1989). Since knowledge work can be done at diffuse locations (as opposed to industrial work, which must be done in a factory), the trend toward urbanization may eventually reverse itself. As Garvin and Cox (2001) note, the growth of industrialization and the factory system made urbanization inevitable.

Knowledge work will require higher levels of education (McNutt 1996). Those without sufficient education will have to find work in the shrinking agricultural and industrial sectors. Even those jobs will require more education as technology automates many of the positions.

This need for education, combined with access to technology, creates a situation known as *information poverty,* or the *digital divide.* This means that, because access to these resources is essential to full participation in the information economy, those deprived will become the new poor. Research done in the United States and abroad documents the seriousness of this problem (Ebo 1998; McConnaughey, Everette, Reynolds, and Lader 1999; McNutt 1996, 1998).

The information economy is also a global economy. The ease by which information and communications technology (ICT) transcends distance makes reaching out to other areas, even over national boundaries, much easier. It also means that competition is more direct and immediate.

Technology and the nature of knowledge work will also change how organizations are structured and how they operate. Technology flattens and decentralizes organizational structures and allows for the creation of new organizational forms, such as *virtual organizations* (Cleveland 1985). The nature of knowledge workers creates change in the way that organizations manage their workers and creates the opportunity for new work-life options, such as telecommuting (Wallace 1989).

Governmental Systems

Changes in the nature of government are also inevitable as technology and the related social transformations occur. Perhaps the most important trends are devolution and decentralization.

Devolution is an international trend that refers to the moving of control not only to lower levels of government but also to the private sector. In the United

States, much of domestic policy over the past twenty years has sought to reverse the concentration of power at the national level and return it to the states. At the same time there has been a move toward privatization of formally government responsibilities (Peters 1994).

How successful this has been is open to question. Although there certainly has been the appearance of movement toward a devolved, decentralized service-delivery system, it is unclear whether the federal government has actually lost any significant power. A number of political scientists (Davis 1999; Hill & Hughes 1998) question the ultimate impact of the Internet itself on the governmental system, at least in the near term.

Social Welfare

How will social welfare change as a consequence of all of these transformations in the economic and political systems? Although these forces are likely to dominate, we must also assume that sociocultural changes and changes in human services technology will also be critical.

The forces of decentralization and devolution will have clear consequences for both social welfare policy and the organizations that deliver its benefits. This will probably mean that the current devolution trend will extend into the future, and that agencies will probably adopt the "virtual organization" form—a highly decentralized organization that outsources most functions to other organizations and individuals. This means that social agencies will be smaller and will handle most of their work by contracting and other mechanisms. This development, often called the *hollow state phenomenon* in political science, clearly will change the nature of agency-based practice.

Technology will add some new interventions to the practice regimen, as in the case of the development of telehealth interventions that will change the nature of clinical practice (Slack 1996). Innovations in the administration of safety-net programs, such as electronic benefits transfer (EBT), will make possible both economic benefits for agencies and, for recipients, stigma reduction and ease of use.

Although it is difficult to predict the exact course of future developments, it seems fair to say that changes will occur in areas critical to social policy and advocacy. As society and its governmental systems become more decentralized, policy making will change—followed by changes in advocacy methods to address this new reality. At present, traditional techniques are working in cooperation with emergent ones. The next section will examine current ideas about advocacy and the political environment.

ADVOCACY AND SOCIAL CHANGE

Advocacy is a long-honored tradition in social work. Although it is often taken to mean client-centered work, it is more commonly used to describe policy change or class advocacy. In recent years, this type of advocacy has been combined with other aspects of policy work to create *policy practice.*

The idea of policy practice dates back to 1984 (Jansson 1984, 1994). The concept is that social workers and other human-service professionals must go beyond the theoretical and analytical study of social policy to embrace the more pragmatic, proactive aspects of advocacy.

In order to become effective advocates, social workers and other human-service professionals must be familiar with basic practices and principles of advocacy. Most social work education programs include at least one course to prepare students for advocacy work, and numerous texts focus on policy practice.

Advocacy techniques range from lobbying, to grassroots organizing, to (eventually) running for public office (Haynes & Mickleson 2000; Jansson 1999). These techniques vary in effectiveness and resource requirements. Much of this depends on the arena and the political environment.

Lobbying

One of the most frequently used policy-change techniques in the United States is lobbying (Birnbaum 1992; Birnbaum & Murray 1987; Drew 1995, 1996, 1997; Haynes & Mickelson 2000; Smucker 1999; Wolpe 1996;). Wolpe (1996) provides excellent coverage of the fundamentals in an easy-to-use guide. Some of these fundamentals are

- ◆ Define the issues in any lobbying visit;
- ◆ Know the players;
- ◆ Know the committees;
- ◆ Go to the outside when required;
- ◆ Anticipate the opposition;
- ◆ Understand the process;
- ◆ Become cross-partisan eyes and ears; and
- ◆ Observe basic courtesies.

Wolpe (1996) also offers five commandments: "Tell the truth; never promise more than you can deliver; know how to listen so that you accurately understand what you are hearing; staff are there to be worked with and not circumvented; and, spring no surprises" (20–47). His six lobbying corollaries are equally useful: "It is much easier to stop something than to start something; precedent controls process; defer to your leaders; don't burn votes—you may need them tomorrow; the best ideas are worthless without the votes; if you don't ask, you don't get" (55–68).

Grassroots Action

Another useful technique, *grassroots action,* involves building support for social and economic justice at the local level. It aims at empowering oppressed, disenfranchised, and forgotten people. Activity often revolves around mobilizing a local population to take action.

Grassroots action can also consist of public education about issues (Rees 1998; Smucker 1999). An aware public is one that can influence voting on a community or policy issue. This can include research and dissemination activities. To achieve change, particularly where there is opposition, one must make the case that a social problem is of such magnitude that something must be done, or offer a potential solution so enticing (effective, efficient, economical) that it must be employed—or both. Politics is omnipresent. The political winds are either at your back or in your face. Henrick Smith, former *New York Times* Washington bureau chief as well as chief Washington correspondent for twenty-five years, contends that in any political fight there are two parties: those engaged in the fight, and *the audience.* The audience can determine the outcome, which, obviously, can work both ways. Sometimes public opinion supports an important idea such as a minimum wage increase or other strategy to make work pay. At other times, clever interest groups convince the American people that ideas such as universal health care do more harm than good.

Political Action Committees

Political action committees (PACs) also affect the political process (Colby & Buffum 1998; Haynes & Mickelson 2000). These organizations provide financing for political campaigns and initiatives. They also issue report cards on candidate voting records and organize constituent groups around various issues. PACs require considerable amounts of funding, so there are few of them in social work. The National Association of Social Worker's (NASW's) political action committee is PACE (Political Action for Candidate Election) and has a modest capacity to fund candidates. Its most successful application is to mobilize social workers to support certain candidates.

Referenda

Referenda are citizen-created legislation. The procedures vary, but basically these proposals are put before the voters in an election. If they pass the voters, they can become law. Alternatively, they may be put before a legislature or other decision-making body. One particularly interesting type of referendum is a *recall petition,* which is aimed at removing an elected official.

Working for Political Candidates

Voting the right kind of people into public office is important (Haynes & Mickelson 2000). Social workers can use their organizing skills to build support for a candidate who will support social causes. This involves many tasks, from door-to-door, get-out-the-vote campaigns to working with the local media. Finally, running for public office is open to social workers themselves and involves creating a political campaign to insure victory on Election Day. Throughout the world, a number of social workers have won races for public office.

Judicial Intervention

The use of the court systems for intervention policy change has also proved an effective technique. Attorneys are responsible for much of this kind of activity, but social workers can be invaluable in identifying clients, collecting evidence, doing background research, and so forth. After the judgment is handed down, social workers can help monitor the judgment to ensure that changes are actually made.

All of the techniques mentioned in this section are widely used by social workers and constitute the current toolbox for advocacy. They require skills that are generally similar to Internet-based advocacy—and they are also, in general, labor intensive and expensive skills to use. In a diffuse decision-making environment, the cost may be prohibitive. In any case, the traditional methods are still of great help to the social work activist.

Advocacy, like any other type of social work practice, is predicated on the development of an appropriate strategy that addresses the situation in such a way as to ensure goal attainment. It works best when the most effective methods are skillfully employed by a knowledgeable practitioner who has carefully evaluated the issues and barriers.

Judgment and experience provide some of this knowledge. There is no substitute for working with these issues every day, knowing which actors are important and which processes cannot be shortchanged. In addition, skill in using the various tools is essential. How this works can be seen in the following case example.

CASE EXAMPLE: FAMILY VIOLENCE PREVENTION AND SERVICES ACT

This is a personal story about the origins and development of the Family Violence Prevention and Services Act (Public Law 98-457). It serves well as a policy practice illustration. The U.S. Congress considered domestic violence programs from 1979 to 1983 but appropriated no money until 1984. I can tell this story in fifteen minutes or fifteen hours. Students usually like the shorter version, but the longer version contains lifetime lessons I am still using in advocacy efforts.

My employer, the Association of Junior Leagues (or AJL, an international women's organization with 243 member leagues in the United States, representing approximately 148,000 individual members in 1979, when this story begins) worked on this issue as a top priority in the early 1980s. AJL's advantage was one I used repeatedly in legislative updates, appeals to members of Congress and their staffs, and in testimony:

> We have nothing personally to gain from this; we are making a financial and voluntary commitment because we know this is a nationwide problem requiring federal attention. We are doing as much as we can. We . . . urge you to work to ensure that legislation is enacted to begin to deal with this serious problem.

In February 1984, after much advocacy, lobbying, investigation, and formal hearings, the House of Representatives passed the Family Violence Prevention and Services Act (FVPSA) as an amendment to the Child Abuse Amendments of 1984 (itself a reauthorization of existing child abuse legislation that had passed in 1978). By 1983, public policy support for child abuse programs had created a window of opportunity to recognize spousal abuse, sexual assault, and other violence within the home. Advocates collected data on action in local domestic violence programs and began to use this information to lobby Congress, both in Washington and from the home districts.

Connecting these pieces of legislation was the ingenious idea of Congressman George Miller (D-Calif.). Although it had been difficult to make the case for a "new" domestic violence initiative, it could be argued that spousal abuse is another piece of the child abuse problem. The House bill passed 367 to 31. In March, family violence legislation virtually identical to the House bill was introduced in the Senate. In July, the Senate passed a compromise version, necessitating a conference committee. In September 1984, the House and Senate passed the conference version, and in October, President Reagan signed the bill into law.

However, because this legislation was passed late in the session, no money had been appropriated. AJL staff continued to work on a supplemental appropriation. The Democrats on the House Appropriations Committee were initially supportive, but the Republicans were not. Of course, we thanked the Democrats (regularly) and continued to seek Republican support. The ranking Republican was Representative Silvio Conte (R-Mass.). His staff conveyed Rep. Conte's indifference, if not his opposition.

Proving the truth of House Speaker Tip O'Neill's phrase, "All politics is local," this changed for us when AJL staff encountered a local Junior League president from western Massachusetts. In casual conversation about our plight, the League member said something to the effect that, "Oh, our League has been supporting a domestic violence program, and it needs help. I'll bet Uncle Silvio doesn't know about that." The following Monday morning we were on the phone with the congressman's office. Mr. Conte was indeed interested in supporting an appropriation for this important legislation. The rest, as they say, is history. Congressional Research Service Report 1997-675 EPW notes that the FVPSA received an appropriation of $6 million in fiscal year 1985 and $62 million by fiscal year 1997. The Violence against Women Act was added later, with a 1997 fiscal-year funding level of $251 million.

Davis and Hagen (1988) summarize the political development of FVPSA. My own account extends their discussion by reporting on inside advocacy activities and strategy to pass House Resolution 1397 (97th Congress), introduced by a social worker, Representative Barbara Mikulski (D-Md.). A brief chronology, noted earlier, describes the work of AJL, which was working in a coalition of more than forty organizations from 1981 to 1985. The more detailed story would emphasize the importance of coalitions, bipartisanship, defining problems, finding solutions, staying in touch with one's grassroots, courting elected officials and their staff, and persistence. In summary, the "problem" was defined in such a way that action became necessary; a solution was proposed (with constant compromise); political work paid off; a bill was passed; and local advocates across America had a new source of support in the struggle against domestic violence.

The story of FVPSA is an example that could be replicated. Advocates who worked on the act from 1979 to 1983 encountered much resistance. What could they do about the growing problem of battered women? How could they overcome the resistance of elected officials and staff who argued that intervention into the lives of troubled families would violate the sanctity of the family and possibly do direct harm? At a time of economic recession and government cutbacks (1981–1983, the first years of President Reagan), how could advocates expect even to get this issue on the agenda?

Most new advocates are surprised by the trials and tribulations of coalition building. A coalition can broaden support for legislation, but each member group of the coalition has its own priorities. Negotiating among the diverse interests becomes a separate task, calling for political, interactional, and values-clarification skills.

To paraphrase Edmund Burke, all that it takes for evil to prevail in any society is for good people to do nothing. To that should be added that sentiment expressed by civil rights activist Frederick Douglass: There is no progress without a struggle—which should be the first and last word for any advocate. In the future, technological advances will no doubt enhance advocacy. Communication will be instantaneous. Speed, however, is not necessarily the way of political change. Advocates will need long-term vision and the energy and commitment to keep working on issues.

We see in this case the triumphs and travails of traditional methods. The newer methods, in the short run, can add to these tried-and-true approaches.

INTEGRATING TRADITIONAL AND ELECTRONIC METHODS

The dominance of the traditional techniques of advocacy will probably continue for the foreseeable future. The expectations of many stakeholders in the policy process almost ensure this situation. Even within the traditional techniques, however, ICT can facilitate simple tasks and make human efforts go further—word processing, for example, is much more efficient than using a typewriter.

The current use of technology in advocacy is both extensive and growing. Although it is clear that the traditional methods are still both useful and necessary, it is less clear when to use technology and when to use traditional methods.

It is somewhat clearer, however, that all decision makers are not equally comfortable with technology. Studies of the impact of e-mail on the U.S. Congress and in one state legislature raise the issue of whether e-mail campaigns are ignored by the very decision makers they are intended to reach (Lemmon & Carter 1998). This technology gap might also extend to coalition partners and other stakeholders. As long as these issues remain, the traditional techniques will still be important.

Advocacy is usually developed within a host organization that may be dedicated to social change or may include a number of additional functions (Boris and Mosher-Williams 1998; Gibbelman & Kraft 1996). This organization's issues may modify the actions that its advocates can take. The organization's resources may be another serious issue. All of these affect the advocate's decisions about using technology.

CONCLUSION

The changes that we discussed in the first part of this chapter will eventually revolutionize advocacy and activism in the social work profession. We can expect that some of the economic and political forces that have a minor impact today will be major issues in the future.

Advocacy will change as society changes. The economies of scale gained by going to the nation's capital may not be enough. Globalization will limit the power of the national government to make effective policy, and the shrinking power of the nation state may mean international policy change is needed. At the same time, devolution will shift power to lower levels of government and to private organizations. What this means for advocates is becoming clearer every day—there must be a shift in advocacy methods to meet these new threats.

This change will not come overnight, and the traditional methods will retain their potency far into the future. The principle of comparative advantage is important: Use the technique that works most effectively in the situation at hand. It is critical that social work activists and advocates master the range of available techniques. It is also vital that they retain the traditions and the commitment of the profession to creating a world that is just and fair for all.

Suggested Readings

Beniger, J. 1988. Information society and global science. *Annuals* 495: 14–29.

Birnbaum, J. 1992. *The lobbyists: How influence peddlers get their way in Washington.* New York: Random House.

Birnbaum, J., & A. Murray. 1987. *Showdown at Gucci gulch: Lawmakers, lobbyists and the unlikely triumph of tax reform.* New York: Random House.

Boris, E. T., & R. Mosher-Williams. 1998. Nonprofit advocacy organizations: Assessing the definitions, classifications, and data. *Nonprofit and Voluntary Sector Quarterly* 27 (4): 488–506.

Cleveland, H. 1985. The twilight of hierarchy: Speculations on the global information society. *Public Administration Review* 45: 185–195.

Colby, I. C., & W. E. Buffum. 1998. Social workers and PACs: An examination of National Association of Social Workers P.A.C.E. Committees. *Journal of Community Practice* 5 (4): 87.

Davis, R. 1999. *The Web of politics: The Internet's impact on the American political system.* New York: Oxford University Press.

Davis, L. V., & J. L. Hagen. 1988. Services for battered women: The public policy response. *Social Service Review* 62: 649–667.

Dillman, D. 1991. Information society. In *The encyclopedia of sociology,* ed. E. Borgetta & R. Borgetta, 925–927. New York: Macmillan.

Drew, E. 1995. *On the edge: The Clinton presidency.* New York: Simon & Schuster.

———. 1996. *Showdown: The struggle between the Gingrich Congress and the Clinton White House.* New York: Simon & Schuster.

———. 1997. *Whatever it takes: The real struggle for political power in America.* New York: Viking.

Ebo, B. (ed.). 1998. *The cyberghetto or cybertopia? Race, class, gender and marginalization in cyberspace.* New York: Praeger.

Garvin, C., & F. Cox. 2001. A history of community organization since the Civil War with special reference to oppressed communities. In *Strategies of community intervention* (6th ed.), ed. J. Rothman, J. L. Erlich, & J. E. Tropman, 65–100. Itasca, Ill.: F. E. Peacock.

Gibbelman, M., & S. Kraft. 1996. Advocacy as a core agency program: Planning considerations for voluntary human services agencies. *Administration in Social Work* 20 (4): 43–59.

Haynes, K. S., & J. S. Mickelson. 2000. *Affecting change* (4th ed.). Needham, Mass.: Allyn and Bacon.

Hill, K. A., & J. E. Hughes. 1998. *Cyberpolitics: Citizen activism in the age of the Internet.* Lanham, Md.: Rowman and Littlefield.

Huey, J. 1994. Waking up to the new economy. *Fortune* 129 (13): 36–46.

Jansson, B. S. 1984. *Theory and practice of social welfare policy: Analysis, processes, and current issues.* Belmont, Calif.: Brooks/Cole

———. 1994. Social welfare policy. In *The foundations of social work knowledge,* ed. F. Reamer, 51–87. New York: Columbia University Press.

———. 1999. *Becoming an effective policy advocate: From policy practice to social justice* (3rd ed.). Belmont, Calif.: Brooks/Cole.

Lemmon, P., & M. Carter. 1998. *Speaking up in the Internet age.* Washington, D.C.: OMBWatch.

McConnaughey, J., D. W. Everette, T. Reynolds, & W. Lader (eds.). 1999. *Falling through the Net: Defining the digital divide.* Washington, D.C.: U.S. Department of Commerce, National Telecommunications and Information Administration.

McNutt, J. G. 1996. National information infrastructure policy and the future of the American welfare state: Implications for the social welfare policy curriculum. *Journal of Social Work Education* 6 (3): 375–388.

———. 1998. Ensuring social justice for the new underclass: Community interventions to meet the needs of the new poor. In *The cyberghetto or cybertopia? Race, class, gender and marginalization in cyberspace,* ed. B. Ebo, 33–47. New York: Praeger.

Peters, B. G. 1994. Managing the hollow state. *International Journal of Public Administration* 17 (3–4): 739–756.

Rees, S. 1998. *Effective non-profit advocacy.* Washington, D.C.: Aspen Institute/Nonprofit Sector Research Fund. Available at [http://www.aspeninst.org/dir/polpro/NSRF/enpatoc.html]. Retrieved on 20 October 1998.

Slack, W. 1996. *Cybermedicine.* San Francisco: Jossey-Bass.

Smucker, R. 1999. *The nonprofit lobbying guide: Advocating your cause—and getting results.* Washington, D.C.: Independent Sector.

Trattner, W. I. 1995. *From poor law to welfare state* (5th ed.). New York: Free Press.

Wallace, M. 1989. Brave new workplace: Technology and work in the new economy. *Work and Occupations* 16 (4): 363–392.

Wolpe, B. 1996. *Lobbying Congress: How the system works* (2nd ed.). Washington, D.C.: Congressional Quarterly.

Chapter 15

Teledemocracy

Reinventing Governance for Social Welfare

On-Kwok Lai

INTRODUCTION

This chapter examines the role of information and communications technologies (ICTs) in welfare advocacy and empowerment in the emerging teledemocracy (TD) regime of governance. Given the erosion of the welfare state through post-welfare capitalism and promarket reforms, the important question for activists is: How should we reinvent the structure of public governance using ICT enhancements for better health and welfare? Highlighting both the differential impacts of TD on social agencies and its redistributive policy outcomes, this chapter critically analyzes the growing production/supply-side bias in the use of ICT. It further argues that for the betterment of welfare projects, political and administrative institutions and individuals should become willing to learn about and adapt to the integrated, multimodal ICT-networking environment of teledemocracy, both online and in real time.

The first section of this chapter discusses the crisis of welfare capitalism and the shift toward "digital capitalism," paying special attention to the resulting problems of social inequality and governmental inadequacy. The next section examines the emerging supply-side bias in the use of ICT in service of health care reform. In the subsequent section, the chapter discusses the alternative reform agenda and governance structure that are compatible with TD praxis and that can facilitate both advocacy and social learning processes. The final section remarks on the issues and prospects of this project of reinvention.

FROM THE WELFARE CAPITALISM CRISIS TO DIGITAL CAPITALISM

Welfare capitalism is a predominant form of government in the twentieth century. Its history has shown how the state promotes collective welfare in the interest

Research support by the Visiting Fellowship of the Social Science Division at Hong Kong University of Science and Technology, and students' stimulation from the School of Policy Studies at Kwansei Gakuin University enabled the author to complete this paper.

of having economic growth with minimal labor conflicts. Welfare-state benefits are mostly bound to the worker's value in the labor market: unemployment allowances, social insurance, or at minimum, the enhancement of the individual's performance in production sector (Castles & Mitchell 1990; Esping-Andersen 1990).[1] Yet all these welfare provisions and (more important) their related decision-making processes are mostly beyond the influence of citizens in general and of the service recipients in particular. More specifically, even under the so-called representative democracy system, the nonparticipatory welfare-governance structure (under professional domination and party politics) is more than obvious.

Bismarck's prototype of insurance-*cum*-welfare policy (and the United Kingdom's Beveridge Report) tend to support an approach of economic pragmatism in ensuring wealth generation and social stability. The welfare state has the function of keeping the citizens loyal but lacking in any sense of self-actualization, as a direct consequence of having no decision-making power (Mommsen 1981). Critics with totally different worldviews have challenged this set of collective value orientation and its indirectly related (but more directly created) welfare state polity (Taylor-Gooby 1991). Two major aspects that have been structurally and historically associated with the welfare state are problematic:

1. The welfare state has failed to achieve its repeatedly stated Utopian goals and its formerly agreed-upon objectives (such as full employment) of social equality, equity, justice, and human rights.

2. The welfare state has, in different ways, created socially undesirable and unjust conditions for society and citizens at large: Minority groups, the underclass, the unemployed, and women have been discriminated against not only because of their given social status but also—ironically—through their relationship to the welfare state, and through the hegemonic professionalism (Bryson 1992).

The failure of welfare capitalism has been criticized from both the political (New) Left and (New) Right: from the Right for its inefficiency in generating wealth and its creation of redundant and ineffective (with regard to market principles) bureaucracy; and from the Left for the state's control of individual livelihoods in the interest of furthering capital accumulation. These criticisms have, paradoxically, put the state through waves of collective protest movements on the one hand, and emerging fiscal crisis on the other. Hence, the structural crisis of the welfare state mirrors its regressive policy outcomes and is a direct reflection both of nonparticipatory governance and of contradictions in the sociopolitical constitution of welfare capitalism. The success of welfare-state governance has, paradoxically, undermined its own legitimacy. New forms of self-realization and spontaneity are generated, supported by welfare provision, which then finally *exceeds* the capacities of state politics. It follows that both the "crisis of crisis management" and "ungovernability" are embedded in welfare state governance.[2]

Retrospectively, the welfare-state project is an unsustainable one, both economically and politically. In response to global competitiveness, most welfare states have begun to adopt policy measures that favor supply-side economics, including lowering taxes on personal and corporate income; imposing labor discipline, lowering labor costs, removing labor rigidities, and removing regulatory rigidities— for example, reducing budgetary commitments to social welfare vis-à-vis considerations of entrepreneurial-*cum*-consumption freedom (Falkner 1998; Hine & Kassim 1998). In other words, the new global economic conditions have "diminished the effectiveness of the old welfare state arrangements even without any budget cuts or other restrictive measures" (Pfaller, Gough, Therborn, & Therborn 1991, 280f). The consequence is a common trend in *social dualism:* widespread poverty within affluent societies, in line with a set of deregulatory policy initiatives that favor privatization.

Welfare Neglect in Technopolis

Times change, technology changes, and we move inexorably into the twenty-first century. We live in a new economy of global capitalism that is both informational and networked. Juxtaposed against the decline of welfare capitalism the new, ICT-based governance structure of the information society is emerging (Castells 2000; McChesney, Wood, & Foster 1998). The role of ICT in global capitalism (what Dan Schiller (1999) refers to as *digital capitalism*—the condition in which ICT networks directly generalize the social and cultural range of the capitalist economy) is greater than ever before. For instance, a U.S. Department of Commerce report reveals, among other things, that information technology (IT) accounts for half or more of the improvement in productivity growth since 1995; that IT is lowering inflation; and that, between 1994 and 1998, employment in IT industries expanded by 30 percent, from 4.0 million to 5.2 million jobs. In addition, these jobs average $58,000 a year, 85 percent higher than the average for the private sector (U.S. Department of Commerce [DOC] 2000). Although the idea of digital capitalism is predominantly for the developed world, the assertion that the corporate-led market system has been somewhat globally transcended is very important:

> What is historically new is a change in the sweep of corporate rule. For the first time since its emergence in the early twentieth century, the corporate-led market system no longer confronts a significant socialist adversary anywhere on the planet. Digital capitalism also is free to physically transcend territorial boundaries and, more important, to take economic advantage of the sudden absence of geopolitical constraints on its development. Not coincidentally, the corporate political economy is also diffusing more generally across the social field. (Schiller 1999, 205)

Responding to trends in globalization, the state's project on the "Technopolis" becomes the iconography for futuristic high-tech society, particularly the ICT-intensive mode of production (Castells & Hall 1994). These projects are for national economy competitiveness, mostly being initiated by the strong states in the East (China, Japan, and Singapore) and the West (the European Union and the United States). The creation of "technopoles" is no longer divided across political (Left and Right) ideologies. Some questionably "Asiatic democratic systems" have invested heavily for decades in upgrading their technologies and their selective utilization in society—the Singaporean and socialist Chinese states represent such an endeavour (Olds 1997; Singapore Government 2000).

Social life in the emerging ICT-based Technopolis will be different judging from the present high-tech system. First, productivity enhancement of both firms and individuals is one of the major achievements of integrating ICT into the production domain—although its contributions to quality of life may be dubious because the individuals must cope with, among other things, incoming messages from other time zones during night-time sleeping hours. Second, the division between working and leisure times, and between the domestic and the official, will become more blurred. More specifically, information networking will likely become the only mechanism of defining one's own identity, and entitlements, because most of the gate-keeping functions of information-processing systems (Katz 1997).

Third, sophisticated network systems originating in the Technopolis will compose the essential infrastructure for engorged transnational corporations that pursue export-oriented and regionally (or even globally) integrated production and marketing strategies. Corresponding to the ongoing buildup of transnational production, therefore, are powerful, pan-corporate, international financial institutions (such as the International Monetary Fund [IMF] and the World Bank) whose aim is to subject global social development to neo-liberal regulatory norms (Schiller 1999).

Fourth (and most important of all), welfare neglect will become more than obvious, with the juxtaposition of poverty and social exclusion against bourgeoning e-commerce in the global cities such as New York and London. The capitalist state's investments are (or will be) more on ICT and future technologies than on social investments for the protection of the socioeconomically vulnerable, disadvantaged, and underprivileged—particularly when economic crisis (such as the recent Asian financial crisis) occurs. More specifically, "The Internet is contributing to an everwidening gap between rich and poor which has now reached 'grotesque' proportions" (United Nations Development Program [UNDP] 1999b, 1; see also UNDP 1999a). Here, the critical issue is not only that of further development of ICTs, but also of equity and equality, and of redistributive justice in the transformation of global systems in general, particularly involving a shift from welfare capitalism to digital capitalism.

Last, but not least, the behavioral repertoire of individuals is being shaped in accordance with the information available on-time, real-time, just-in-time, and across former geographically bound time-zone differences. In actuality, the foremost development of the information age in every aspect of society and economy can be represented by the global, round-the-clock regime of production, communication, and exchange (Castells 1989, 1997). This trend is being reinforced by a global regime of capital financing, supported by ICT and its integration with the emergence of the so-called informatic or telematic city (Fathy 1991; Graham & Marvin 1996; Leyshon & Thrift 1997). More challenging is the new demand for individuals and communities to react, with good interpretive power and judgment, to real-time global events as mediated by ICT with massive loads of information and representation.

HEALTH CARE REFORM: THE SUPPLY-SIDE ICT APPLICATION

The dynamics and logic of welfare-state reform, as well as the specific role of ICT, can be epitomized in health care reform. The global and dominant health care themes are containment of health care costs; the shift from hospital care to primary health care and health promotion; and the shift from acute-illness treatment to chronic-illness prevention. Furthermore, the commodification of health care services by bringing in market forces (following, say, the purchaser-provider split model), becomes a globally accepted formula for health care reform.[3]

Under the new managerial regime and the full-scale "invasion" of ICT into the medical and health care sectors, global health care reform has three key targets:

1. The principle of cost cutting, value for the dollar, bringing in the business, and creating a market for health care services, backed by ICT-based information science.

2. The shift from valuing clinical judgment to valuing clinical efficiency, usually backed by a new health informatics regime using different Diagnosis-Related Groups or Unit Cost categories to monitor health treatment (Wiley 1994).

3. The movement toward some form of collective insurance and copayment—again, supported by information (insurance, financial, actuarial) science and ICT.

Yet, not many of the cost containment strategies (such as a cost-effectiveness or recovery approach) in health care reform actually have an optimal policy outcome, either because they wrongly target pricing on health products and services or they exacerbate the already inequitable distribution of resources in the public sector—or because market failures exist in the health-insurance system (Chernichovsky 1995; Hammer & Berman 1995). More problematic, the outcome of health care reform can be neither prescribed nor accounted for by information science or by a microeconomic managerial approach to better health care.[4] To recapitulate, the global strategies for health care reform, as well as the reinvention of the welfare state, are backed mostly by a new regime of informational governance: The main instrument is clearly defined by *supply-side biased ICT application.*

Conversely, the underutilization of ICT on the demand (human) side of welfare and the health care sector is due to a combination of the following reasons:

- ◆ The information services do not meet the needs of indigenous people;
- ◆ Governmental support is lacking;
- ◆ Funds for high-cost ICT infrastructures are insufficient;
- ◆ Information technology is inadequate and inappropriate; and, more fundamentally,

◆ Governments do not recognize the role of ICT in political goodwill-building as an important part of socioeconomic development (Boon 1990).

Furthermore, as in the United States (where 65 percent of households have at least one computer and 43 percent of all households are connected to the Internet), the Internet today is a giant public library with a decidedly commercial tilt (Nie and Erbring 2000). More specifically, the penetration of ICT into different socioeconomic arenas generally follows a trickle-down approach: first (and most heavily) into the entertainment and economic (profit-making) arenas, then into educational and health-related ICT applications, and finally into the "unproductive sector" of social welfare (Khosrowpour & Loch 1993; Kraemer, Gurbaxani, & King 1992).

More often than not, ICT is considered to be the growth engine only for productivity and the generation of wealth, rather than for social development; for economic growth rather than for the progressive welfare of the people (especially the less privileged). To recapitulate, the impact of ICT is substantial and global, differential, unequal, and inequitable—yet there is potential for social development via the synergy of ICT and the welfare regime of governance.

PUTTING TELEDEMOCRACY TO THE TEST: REINVENTING WELFARE GOVERNANCE

Despite regional differences in the degree of ICT interconnectivity (Moss & Townsend 2000), the creation of cyberspace through the heavy integration of ICT both locally and globally has been extending the ways, modes, and forms of communicating, doing business, and setting policy, and hence the development of new and distinct (cyber) culture, (virtual) communities, and (virtual) reality (Arnonowitz, Martinsons, & Menser 1996; Featherstone & Burrows 1995). These developments, in turn, are shaping both social processes and political culture (Rash 1997).

There is no doubt that the ICT-based flexible production regime generates more wealth and global economic activity. Yet, far from developing an equitable and better society, our ICT-driven postmaterial society has produced more social calamity than existed before: the digital divide and the formation of an almost permanent underclass, for whom high unemployment and redundancy (even in the forties) are common. Critiques of the information society highlight the contradictions of our "new world"—a world generally mediated by ICT under global corporate governance (Luke 2000; Menzies 1996; U.S. National Telecommunications and Information Administration [NTIA] 1999; see also [http://www.digitaldivide.org]). The dominance of ICT in our work and social (i.e., virtual) encounters has reinforced a division of society in which the ICT-rich minority stands above those being controlled by the ICT. This is the so-called *dual city* phenomenon: The information-based formal economy, when juxtaposed against a downgraded, labor-based informal economy, results in a spatial structure—a city that combines segregation, diversity, and hierarchy (Castells 1989). Obviously, a call for a normative development agenda for the humanization of ICT is urgently needed—and this is the project of teledemocracy: equity, participation, and social justice in the system of global/local governance.

Empowering the Underprivileged

Equitable ICT distribution cannot be achieved exclusively through the market. In the future, it should be the goal of governments, nongovernmental organizations, and private firms to ensure universal access to ICT (Patterson & Wilson 2000). If and when the government can promote ICT at the demand side for the empowerment of end users of health and welfare services, the social lives of the underprivileged may finally change; homebound pursuits may be linked to the global network, with a higher and better quality of life as a result.

Many discussion lists and hyperlinks, for example, have been serving multifunctional and multidimensional activities: policy advocacy, informational exchanges, and consultation. These have been changing the ways in which the underprivileged participate in sociopolitical life—locally, regionally, and globally (Simpson 2000; Wax 2000).

Second, the underprivileged and disadvantaged are, in most cases, less mobile than their counterparts and thus must anchor upon the communities in which they live. The physical constraints on these groups also limit their access to information and contacts with outside world. To remove the environmental barriers, ICT and the information to which it gives access can enable them to live and work in their limited places (domestic settings) yet with similar, if not equal, and equitable life chance.

Last, *Net activism* has revolutionized the mode of interaction for advocacy and empowerment, power relationships between providers and users, and the structure of governance in the health and welfare sector (Walch 1999). The key issues here are interactivity, active participation, and the progressive agenda setting of activists upon their respective policy systems. Virtual political communities could be the opportunity for individuals to become instrumental in policy making.

Thanks to the digitization of information and its multiple representations (text, audiovisual, and others), we are in a new era of digital economy, polity, and society (Tapscott 1996; U.S. DOC 2000). Participatory politics and teledemocracy with emphasis on the social could be enhanced if the new and alternative modes of communication are designed to incorporate one-to-one, one-to-many, many-to-one, and many-to-many true communications in Habermasian sense. Perhaps this is the real offering, and challenge, of the Internet, which is evolving around different (cable, wireless, and satellite) modes of communication that represent both micro- and mass-media functions (Morris & Ogan 1996). Strategically, the new, alternative, and teledemocratic modes of communication can, at least in theory, enable online, real-time, and full participation of citizens in governing their societies.

Enhancing the Formation of Political Will

Lately, many U.S. citizens have begun to be able pay their local property taxes and parking tickets on commercial sites such as [http://www.govworks.com] or [http://www.ezgov.com]. This indicates that e-commerce is more flexible and advanced than e-politics or e-policy. Undoubtedly, ICT has a differential impact, be it positive or negative, on governance and politics. Most of the empirical studies at present are mixed, but they tend in general to reflect positively on the impact of ICT on public administration and politics (Andersen 1995; Andersen & Danziger 1995; Margetts 1999). The influence of ICT on actual administrative and political settings (i.e., "soft" systems, involving political will and dynamics) is complex and multifaceted, although the impact of improved system capabilities (i.e., "hard" systems, especially as they affect administrative efficiency) is more than obvious. More specifically, information quality for government and political activities are enhanced, although it is perhaps not surprising that negative consequences are underreported. From this observation, it is clear that the quality of information can be improved with an appropriate ICT-based regime in place to substantiate the policy-making process.

Yet, ICT is used more to enhance *data quality* for the politico-administrative processes of government than *policy-making quality,* and the benefits of using ICT accrue mostly to the elite, powerful, selected few among the governing bodies. Again, this reflects the predominantly production- and supply-side bias of ICT use in public policy governance (Margetts 1999).

In other words, the overall performance of ICT on soft, fluid data—the most critical and controversial aspects of government—is far from satisfactory. In many instances the consequences of ICT use on individual privacy, empowerment, and legal rights are obvious and unfavorable (Bennett & Grant 1999). Although the impacts on personal or societal values have not been overwhelmingly negative, this trend does raise a serious question about the role of ICT in the most important dimensions of society and politics, namely, the ethnical, sociocultural, and moral dimensions. Hence, ICT cannot replace real-life politicking—making politically binding choices in various circumstances, either at the individual level or in society at large (Alexander & Pal 1998).

Because the current use of ICT applies more to the processing of hard data information than to enhancing decision-making process, analysts identify the positive impacts of ICT far more frequently than the negative. Up until now, ICT has not provided enough leverage to those who stand outside the formal, elitist systems of politicking and who would use different critical standards (and whose criticisms would thus be more negative). This is parallel to the state of ICT use in the areas of health care and welfare development: again, a production- and supply-side bias.

THE SYNERGY OF TELEDEMOCRACY AND WELFARE ADVOCACY

The Internet and ICT in general have much to offer in the way of facilitating the reinvention of participatory politics, safeguarding health, and furthering welfare rights. For obvious reasons, in order that the Internet be fully realized as a new form of democracy, we must overcome a number of problems—not least of which is the need for public ownership of and access to airwaves and the information superhighway (Barnett 1997; McChesney et al. 1998; and Wright 1995). For this to happen, we must be aware of two major areas of conflict: differing individual "information personalities," and differing world cultures.

Engaging Information Personality and Alternative Networks in Teledemocracy

Information personality is the individual's personal style of communication and information exchange when engaging in political articulation for democracy, whether in the real or the virtual community. For instance, one person may have better public-speaking skills, whereas another may have a better knack for critical, information-based reasoning. Such diversity of skills and creativity should flourish in teledemocracy. These information personalities, enhanced by the diversity and power of alternative networks, create progressive, sociocivic forces to oppose the dominant, one-brand mode of media engagement promoted by state and corporate influences (Castells 2000; Luke 2000; Walch 1999). It is important to continue to enhance the powerful force of the information personality (both within and outside cyberspace) to further the social democracy project—indeed, to enhance that force as far as the diversity of social systems and the emancipating forces of social development can be extended and developed.

There is a future for social change toward a better world via the praxis of teledemocracy, provided we can continuously develop alternative, action-oriented media and networks beyond the dominant, mainstream one, and strengthen the alternative participatory networks. These are built around alternative projects, such as environmentalism, feminism, and the human rights movement, that compete, from network to network, to build links to other local and global networks using communications media.

In sharp contrast to the present mainstream development toward commercializing and depoliticizing ICT under state and corporate governance, we need an overhaul of the "doing" of politics in both real and virtual settings. Power relationships and networking should be renegotiated—or, alternatively, citizens should take back their power from the representative democracy system and their autonomy from the market mechanism, which no longer work procedurally, substantially, or sustainably. At this historical juncture, the issues of e-equity and justice, and of social inclusion and integration (as well as biodiversity) should be articulated in TD praxis.

Cultural, Ethnic, and Moral Mismatches

We must overcome the indeterminacy of ICT's role in the democracy project (Tehranian 1990). Individuals should be empowered and mobilized, in and beyond the mass media and virtual reality, to critically challenge the given order and the hierarchies of power relationships—between the haves and have-nots, between the informed and the uninformed. In short, the present agenda for change is to bring the Net back into the public domain and hence the control of the people, rather than allow it to be captured by global capitalism (Barnett 1997; McChesney et al. 1998; Rheingold 1995).

A key issue is the compatibility of ICT with human society. In praxis terms, the incompatible element is the denial of the network logic through the affirmation of values and norms that cannot be processed in any network, but that may only be obeyed and followed—in Manual Castells' terminology, *cultural communes* (such as those with religious, national, territorial, and ethnic specificity), which are not necessarily linked to fundamentalism but which always center around their own self-contained meanings (Castells 2000). Such groups make it necessary in, say, the sociocultural arena, to safeguard the development of ICT against possible cultural domination or imperialism. Information provided via channels of communication represents *ideas*—neither passive data nor a commodity to be bought or sold in the marketplace, but rather, images or information conveying the powerful meanings that influence and persuade the minds and orientations of the receivers (Horton 1992; Stover 1984). The development of ICT depends on the global organization and division of technology; hence, developing economies are bound to devise their own instruments for research and development to foster the growth of locally compatible modes of application—in other words, to "indigenize" technology (Stover 1984).

To conclude, ICT by itself, without the human element, can do little for the project of democracy and the empowerment. Unfortunately, the situation may worsen if ICT is captured by corporate interests. The trend to date indicates just such a trend (Stallabrass 1995). On the other hand, it is possible to change the dominant logic and structure of governance by challenging the existing networks, affirming cultural-communal power and autonomy, and strengthening and continuously developing progressive civic forces and alternative networks.

Advocacy for Inclusive Society and E-Equity

If we are to achieve synergy between our social development and the development of teledemocracy, we must take note of three interrelated issues: First and foremost, just as we promote welfare rights, we should *promote the basic rights of ICT users.* The legal and political infrastructures must be such that users can participate in and be empowered by the political process, and that all users may enjoy similar (if not the exact same) levels of ICT rights—that is, the rights to own, use, and have access to ICT should be incorporated into the social rights of citizens. Supportive aids following principles of justice and equity should be provided when and where appropriate. Around the world, some forms of social rights and security for the needy are already in place; ICT rights should be considered an extension of the existing provisions of social rights.

This basic, necessary provision within the legal and political infrastructures will further empower the underprivileged, beyond the welfare and health care arenas. ICT-based empowerment is, in short, for all citizens in general and for the needy in particular. Only by enacting legislation that both promotes the health and welfare of individuals and guarantees their access to ICT can we develop a sustainable society.

Citizen participation is crucial for the success of these efforts. In particular, a basic step toward improved health and welfare for the underprivileged is the support of facilitators—namely, significant others, parents, spouses, or friends in their daily milieu—to help them gain access to technology (particularly ICT). The state could enable this process, using a system involving cash payment to help provide facilitators and ICT hardware and software.

A second—and related—issue is *the building of a supportive community among alternative networks and cultural communes.* Extensions of social and network groups provide the informational support needed from both the virtual and real worlds to help individuals make the right decisions when faced with sociopolitical dilemmas. This is *networking,* a term that should describe the activities of the locally underprivileged as much as those of users in the corporate world. Networking via ICT can build direct, personal contacts in the community, thus enhancing the user's sense of belonging and neighborhood, enlarging the individual's personal knowledge base, and diversifying his or her outlook, attitude, and lifestyle within the global culture. It is obvious that ICT can thus make the world a smaller place— and that it can also actually prevent normal, face-to-face encounters in the traditional community setting in some cases. The most important aspect of human community is its lively participatory dynamic. Activists must be aware of the dual power of ICT, both to enable communication between individuals and to form a barrier to it.

Keeping this in mind, we can ensure that ICT and its networking capabilities *increase* the level and intensity of communal participation and, in time, the development of a better informed and caring community, in which the underprivileged can benefit from ever-evolving mutual and self-help behaviors. Thus, the extent to which nation state and civil society should guide or even assume control of the development of ICT and media networks (e.g., by encouraging private or public ownership, or by legislating for centralized or decentralized control) is and will remain a major sociopolitical issue (Takahashi 1990; Truman & Lopez 1993).

The last—but not least—issue is that *the development of people-centered welfare governance* should be part of our future (Davenport 1994). The role of ICT in the promotion of health and welfare is its promise of individually adapted and tailored systems to help professional advocates and activists better serve the underprivileged. This should be an achievable goal even in the short term.

A LAST REMINDER: THE RISKS OF THE INFORMATION SOCIETY

The known benefits of ICT may be fewer and may have less impact than its unrecognized or unknown consequences—it is doubtful, for instance, that the ability to process an ever-increasing volume of information via sophisticated electronic media can sufficiently reduce the extent and risks of bad decision making. How will individuals react to the round-the-clock information society, with direct, online, real-time ICT set up to access and be accessed by anyone, anywhere in the world? More troublesome than the answer to that question are the emerging concerns about system failures and malfunctions, resulting both from mistakes by end users and from intentional misuse by experts. Computer hacking, fraud, sabotage via computer viruses such as the recent "Love Bug," and inadvertent system failures emphasize our new social vulnerability, particularly where personal identity, privacy, and intellectual property rights are concerned (Brooks 1990; Forester 1992; Wersig 1993; Whittle 1997).

To cope with the one-dimensional development that is taking place, we need to develop both our own *sensitivity* regarding ICT applications in sociocultural arenas, and the built-in system's *self-reflectivity* on teledemocracy. Hence, participation of the users (broadly defined) in ICT development is the Golden Rule. The further strengthening of users' and producers' groups, alternative movements, networks, and cultural communes for the sustainable development of global society and local communities should be encouraged. Without these, there is little chance of success for a better world with equitable welfare governance.

Notes

1. See the discussions on the division of welfare in Titmuss (1987) and on the role of social welfare as collective consumption in capitalist state governance in Castells (1977).

2. See the discussions of the regressive nature of the welfare state in Baldwin (1990) and of the welfare state crisis in Habermas (1989) and Offe (1984).

3. The context of health reform is that there are high technology, labor, and capital costs for health services as the advancement of medical knowledge allows the global population to live longer than before (see Organization for Economic Cooperation and Development [OECD] 1990, 1992, 1994).

4. Backed up by ICT, information science, and medical informatics in particular, the reform agency has been successful in uncoupling or blocking some professional influences from policy making. Yet, the information science and ICT applications are in the hands of the privileged group (powerful elites and the state) and mostly benefit the supply side rather than the underprivileged and end users.

Suggested Readings

Alexander, C. J., & L. A. Pal (eds.). 1998. *Digital democracy.* Oxford: Oxford University Press.

Andersen, K. V. (ed.). 1995. *Information systems in the political world.* Amsterdam: IOS Press.

Andersen, K. V., & J. N. Danziger. 1995. Information technology and the political world: The impacts of IT on capabilities, interactions, orientations, and values. *International Journal of Public Administration* 18 (11): 1693–1725.

Arnonowitz, S., B. Martinsons, & M. Menser (eds.). 1996. *Technoscience and cyberculture.* London: Routledge.

Baldwin, P. 1990. *The politics of social solidarity.* Cambridge: Cambridge University Press.

Barnett, S. 1997. New media, old problems: New technology and the political process. *European Journal of Communication* 12 (2): 193–218.

Bennett, C. J., & R. Grant. 1999. *Visions of privacy.* Toronto: University of Toronto Press.

Boon, H. 1990. Information and development: Some reasons for failures. *The Information Society* 8 (4): 227–242.

Brooks, H. 1990. Unrecognized consequences of telecommunications technologies. In *Telecommunications, values, and the public interest,* ed. S. B. Lundstedt, 17–35. Norwood, N.J.: Ablex.

Bryson, L. 1992. *Welfare and the state: Who benefits?* New York: St. Martin's.

Castells, M. 1977. *The urban question.* London: Edward Arnold.

———. 1989. *The informational society.* Oxford, U.K.: Blackwell.

———. 1997. *The rise of the network society.* Oxford, U.K.: Blackwell.

———. 2000. Materials for an exploratory theory of the network society. *British Journal of Sociology* 51 (1): 5–24.

Castells, M., & P. Hall. 1994. *Technopoles of the world.* Oxford, U.K.: Blackwell.

Castles, F. G., & D. Mitchell. 1990. *Three worlds of welfare capitalism or four?* Discussion Paper no. 21, Graduate Program in Public Policy, Australian National University, Canberra.

Chernichovsky, D. 1995. What can developing economies learn from health system reforms of developed economies? *Health Policy* 32: 79–91.

Davenport, T. H. 1994. Saving IT's soul: Human-centred information management. *Harvard Business Review* (March/April): 119–131.

Esping-Andersen, G. 1990. *Three worlds of welfare capitalism.* Cambridge, U.K.: Polity Press.

Falkner, G. 1998. *EU social policy in the 1990s.* London: Routledge.

Fathy, T. A. 1991. *Telecity.* London: Praeger.

Featherstone, M., & R. Burrows (eds.). 1995. *Cyberspace, cyberbodies, cyberpunk.* London: Sage.

Forester, T. 1992. Megatrends or megamistakes? What ever happened to the information society. *The Information Society* 8: 133–146.

Graham, S., & S. Marvin. 1996. *Telecommunications and the city.* London: Routledge.

Habermas, J. 1989. The new obscurity. In *The new conservatism,* ed. J. Habermas & S. Weber Nicholsen, and trans. S. Weber Nicholsen, 48–70. Cambridge: Polity Press.

Hammer, J. S., & P. Berman. 1995. Ends and means in public health policy in developing countries. *Health Policy* 32 (1–3): 29–45.

Hine, D., & H. Kassim (eds.). 1998. *Beyond market: The EU and national social policy.* London: Routledge.

Horton, F. H. 1992. Why information management is an international issue. *The Information Society* 8 (2): 123–124.

Katz, J. E. 1997. The social side of information networking. *Society* (March/April): 9–12.

Khosrowpour, M., & K. D. Loch (eds.). 1993. *Global information technology education.* Harrisburg, Pa.: IDEA Group.

Kraemer, K. K., V. Gurbaxani, & J. L. King. 1992. Economic development, government policy, and the diffusion of computing in Asia-Pacific Countries. *Public Administration Review* 52 (2): 146–156.

Leyshon, A., & N. Thrift. 1997. *Money space.* London: Routledge.

Luke, T. W. 2000. *The "Net" effects of e-publicanism.* Paper presented at the annual meeting of the International Studies Association, 14–18 March, Los Angeles.

Margetts, H. 1999. *Information technology in government.* London: Routledge.

McChesney, R. W., E. M. Wood, & J. B. Foster (eds.). 1998. *Capitalism and the Informational Age.* New York: Monthly Review Press.

Menzies, H. 1996. *Whose brave new world? The information highway and the new economy.* Toronto: Between the Lines.

Mommsen, W. J. (ed.). 1981. *The emergence of the welfare state in Britain and Germany.* London: Croom Helm.

Morris, M., & C. Ogan. 1996. The Internet as mass medium. *Journal of Communication* 46 (1): 39–50.

Moss, M. L., & A. M. Townsend. 2000. The Internet backbone and the American metropolis. *The Information Society* 16: 35–47.

Nie, N. H., & L. Erbring. 2000. *Internet and society: A preliminary report.* Stanford, Calif.: Stanford Institute for the Quantitative Study of Society.

Offe, C. 1984. *Contradictions of the welfare state.* Cambridge, Mass.: MIT Press.

Olds, K. 1997. Globalizing Shanghai: The global intelligence corps and the building of Pudong. *Cities* 14 (2): 109–124.

Organization for Economic Cooperation and Development (OECD). 1990. *Health care systems in transition.* Paris: Author.

———. 1992. *The reform of health care.* Paris: Author.

———. 1994. *Health: Quality and choice.* Paris: Author.

Patterson, R., & E. J. Wilson. 2000. New IT and social inequality: Resetting the research and policy agenda. *The Information Society* 16: 77–86.

Pfaller, A., I. Gough, I. Therborn, & G. Therborn. 1991. *Can the welfare state compete?* London: Macmillan.

Rash, W., Jr. 1997. *Politics on the Nets.* New York: W. H. Freeman.

Rheingold, H. 1997. *The virtual community: Surfing the Internet.* London: Minerva.

Schiller, D. 1999. *Digital capitalism: Networking the global market system.* Cambridge, Mass.: MIT Press.

Simpson, G. R. 2000, May 17. The Web's final frontier: City hall. *The Wall Street Journal,* n.p.

Singapore Government. 1996. *Information technology development towards 2000.* Singapore: Government Printer.

Stallabrass, J. 1995. Empowering technology: The exploration of cyberspace. *New Left Review* 211: 3–32.

Stover, W. J. 1984. *Information technology in the third world.* Boulder, Colo.: Westview.

Takahashi, J. 1990. Main issues involved in IT-led development. In *Information technology-led development,* 45–60. Tokyo: Asian Productivity Organization (APO).

Tapscott, D. 1996. *The digital economy.* New York: McGraw-Hill.

Taylor-Gooby, P. 1991. *Social change, social welfare and social science.* New York: Harvester-Wheatsheaf.

Tehranian, M. 1990. *Technologies of power.* Norwood, N.J.: Ablex.

Titmuss, R. 1987. The social division of welfare: Some reflections on the search for equity. In *The philosophy of welfare,* ed. B. Abel-Smith & K. Titmuss, 39–59. London: Allen and Unwin.

Truman, K., & F. C. Lopez. 1993. The community: Perspectives for its sustainability. *Technological Forecasting and Social Change* 44: 291–314.

U.S. Department of Commerce (DOC). 2000. *Third annual report (2000) on the information technology revolution and its impact on the economy.* Washington D.C.: U.S. Department of Commerce. Available at [http://www.doc.gov].

U.S. National Telecommunications and Information Administration (NTIA). 1999. *Falling through the Net: Third Report.* Washington D.C.: NTIA. Available at [http://www.ntia.doc.gov/ntiahome/digitaldivide/index.html]. Retrieved on 20 November 1999.

United Nations Development Program (UNDP). 1999a. *The human development report: Globalization with a human face.* New York: UNDP.

————. 1999b. Press release, 12 July.

Walch, J. 1999. *In the Net: An Internet guide for activists.* London: Zed Books.

Wax, E. 2000, February 3. Immigrants use Internet as a link with past. *Washington Post,* n.p.

Wersig, G. 1993. Information science: The study of postmodern knowledge usage. *Information Processing & Management* 29 (2): 229–239.

Whittle, D. B. 1997. *Cyberspace: The human dimension.* New York: W. H. Freeman and Company.

Wiley, M. M. 1994. Quality of care and the reform agenda in the acute hospital sector. In *Health: quality and choice,* 25–44. Paris: OECD.

Wright, R. 1995, January 23. Hyper democracy. *Time,* n.p.

Chapter 16

Inequality and the Digital Divide

Myths and Realities

Jan Steyaert

INTRODUCTION

In the context of the emerging information society, one of the most talked-about concerns in the area of social equality is the *digital divide:* the potential gap between those connected to the Internet and those not connected, sometimes called the divide between the information haves and have-nots. For some, the digital divide is about more than access to information. It includes the repercussions that the restriction of access can have on existing or new patterns of social exclusion and inequality. The Internet, although used by community organizations and advocates to fight exclusion and inequality, may also be part of the problem. As well, in order for the Internet to be an effective advocacy and social activists' tool, it must be available to all sectors of society throughout the world.

This chapter describes and analyzes the digital divide, drawing on data from both Europe and North America. It outlines how technology replicates the existing social stratification, rather than creating a new social divide. Subsequently, the chapter analyzes three elements of the digital divide: the importance of time in the diffusion of innovations, the multidimensional nature of the concept of *access,* and the imbalance in information availability. Based on this analysis, the chapter proposes an alternative conception of the digital divide—one that goes beyond problems with physical access to the technology. Physical access to technology is not enough to enable the Internet to have a significant and lasting impact on social change.

THE INTERNET AND INEQUALITY

In 1995, *Newsweek* described the average Internet user as being politically conservative, male, white, single, English speaking, living in North America, and a professional, manager, or student. Beyond doubt, that description is no longer valid—but is the availability of the information superhighway more democratic now than it was in 1995? Many are concerned that the digital divide creates new social exclusion, on both a global and a national level. Although much of the debate on access to the Internet focuses on differences at a national level, the differences on a global scale are phenomenal, as Jamal Shahin indicates in chapter 17. The telephone directory of the whole African continent is slimmer than that of Manhattan. The situation is even worse for access to the Internet. Consequently, whole parts of the world are on the brink of total exclusion. Castells (1998, chap. 2) introduces the concept of "technological apartheid" to refer to this process of disconnecting poor neighborhoods and entire countries from the world's economic and social systems.

Internet Citizens: Not a World of Equals

With great frequency, the Western media report on new statistics regarding the spread of the Internet into society. Governments, corporations, and scientists have joined forces in a unique eagerness to "keep a finger on the pulse," so to speak. The overwhelming majority of these reports conclude that the number of people with access to the information superhighway is rapidly increasing.

In addition to this observation, all available survey results indicate that the diffusion is not equally spread across all layers of the population. Between the different surveys there is, however, a great diversity in the quality of available information and the level of analysis carried out. Certainly, for commercial surveys little background information on the respondents is gathered and made available. Consequently, for a more in-depth analysis of Internet-use diffusion patterns, we must rely on only a handful of studies. These include the almost annual survey by the U.S. Department of Commerce; the National Telecommunications and Information Administration, or NTIA, (see [http://www.ntia.doc.gov/]; (McConnaughey, Everette, Reynolds, & Lader 1999, 2000); and the more recent study of the Dutch Social and Cultural Planning Office, or SCP (see [http://www.scp.nl/]; van Dijk & de Haan 1998; van Dijk, de Haan, & Rijken 2000).

Both studies indicate that Internet diffusion patterns follow the general patterns of social stratification in many societies: among men more than women, the young more than the old, the well educated more than the less educated, and the high income more than the low income. The NTIA also indicates differences in ethnic origin (Whites and Asians more than Blacks or Hispanics) and location (urban more than rural). The not-connected groups of the population can be described relatively easily: "It is the by now well known groups of our population which are not connected: (single) women, 65-plus, low-educated citizens and people with low-income" (van Dijk et al. 2000, 137).

Both the NTIA and the SCP surveys indicate that the inequalities in Internet access are increasing. This increase in inequality holds across many criteria (e.g., gender, ethnicity, age, etc.); inequality by ethnic background illustrates the trend. The 1997 NTIA survey (see fig. 16.1) found that the rates of Internet access in the United States were, for White, non-Hispanic citizens, 21.2 percent, and for Hispanic citizens, 8.7 percent—a difference of 12.5 percent. In 1998 this had increased to a 17.2 percent difference (McConnaughey et al. 2000). Only in the high-income groups did inequalities seem to be decreasing.

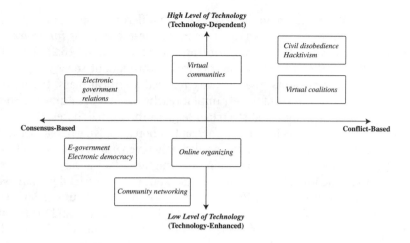

Figure 16.1   Rates of Internet access across the United States, by largest racial groups
Source: *National Telecommunications and Information Administration survey (1997; see text for Web address)*

The picture that emerges is that the digital divide does not create new exclusions or inequalities in society, but that it by and large replicates the existing social stratification (at least in terms of physical access). This observation seems to contradict some of the social projects in which technology is used to give disadvantaged people or deprived neighborhoods a head start (e.g., telework for functionally impaired citizens; technology courses for low-skilled, long-term unemployed citizens; community access centers in deprived areas; etc.). Although these projects make a substantial difference for those concerned, they are not yet able to generate a multiplication effect beyond their direct participants.

Governments and corporations around the world communicate their statistics, points of view, concerns, and good intentions to address the issue quickly and profoundly. At least three key elements seem to be missing from the mainstream debate: the dynamic perspective on the diffusion of innovations, the multidimensional nature of access, and the imbalance in available information on the information superhighway.

TIME AND THE DIFFUSION OF INNOVATION

Some innovations appear to conquer the world in no time (e.g., television). Most, however, go through a relatively slow process of development and diffusion into society. At any given time, a certain percentage of the population has access to the innovation in question, uses it, and has acquired the necessary skills. *Time* is a critical element in the diffusion of innovations.

The diffusion processes for previous innovations (e.g., telephone, radio, television) can be described on an **S**-curve in which different groups of the population adopt the innovation. Rogers (1996) refers to these groups as *innovators, early adopters, early majority, late majority,* and *laggards* (see fig. 16.2). According to Rogers's theory, the diffusion of an innovation throughout society begins with a small group of innovators; then, having reached a critical mass, the innovation seeps through to all layers of society until it reaches a point of saturation. Some diffusion curves can be long and stretched (e.g., in the United States, the telephone needed sixty-seven years to reach 75 percent of households), whereas some can be very short and dense (the television needed only seven years) (Putnam 2000).

The diffusion of the information superhighway had a very slow start. For decades the basic infrastructure was available but not user friendly, there were no Internet service providers (ISPs), and the technology was unreliable. This all changed on short notice: A whole industry of ISPs has emerged, and the technology has now become reasonably reliable (although most people would never dare to drive a car with an equivalent level of reliability). Diffusion of access seems to be coming up to speed. After the introduction of graphical browsers, the availability of free Internet accounts has, in many European countries, been a significant stimulus for increased diffusion. (Free Internet accounts, however, do not guarantee equal access.)

Not only do the diffusion of access to and the usage of an innovation change with time, but the innovation itself transforms. As time progresses, the innovation matures; it becomes more reliable, functional, and user friendly. Such developments will heavily affect the speed of diffusion in the second half of the **S**-curve. The early innovators who can cope with the lack of user friendliness and unreliability have already adopted the technology. The speed with which the late majority join in will depend on the maturity of technology and its perceived value.

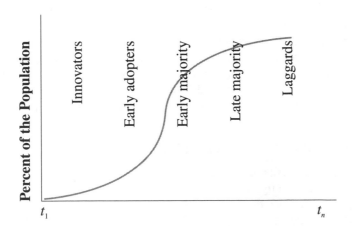

Figure 16.2   Rogers' theory of diffusion of innovation
Source: *Rogers (1996)*

Near the end of the curve, the diffusion pattern is characterized by differentiation in quality. On the information superhighway, we see this in emerging differences in price, type, and quality of access. Access can be had via regular telephone lines, ISDNs (integrated services digital networks), ADSLs (asymmetric digital subscriber lines), or television cable, and each service provider offers a range of options and prices. As a result, some people no longer define the digital divide in terms of access to a computer and the Internet, but in terms of available bandwidth (Wilhelm 2000).

As time progresses and as we move farther up the typical **S**-curve of dissemination, the percentage of households with Internet access will grow. The question will then be whether *more access* will also imply *more egalitarian* access. At what point can we be satisfied with the diffusion and social distribution of access, and when should we be concerned about a digital divide? Several scenarios are possible. In one, the diffusion of Internet access progresses but several regions in the world are excluded. At this moment North America is in the lead position, with the Scandinavian countries taking the lead in Europe. The diffusion of Internet access could increase to 85, 90, or even 95 percent, but, as with the telephone system, a specific group of citizens will remain unconnected. Once the normal diffusion processes have done their work, will such a group still exist? Will any category of citizens remain structurally unable to have access? Any such group that would exist in another form of digital divide should be addressed by appropriate policy measures. In another scenario, there could be a group of citizens who are not connected and do not wish to be connected, as with the television system. Even now there are indications that some persons acquire access, make use of the Internet, and subsequently disconnect (Wyatt 1999).

Will society enable citizens to choose not to be connected (as when one chooses not to watch or own a television), or will such choice be burdened with heavy consequences (as when one chooses, say, not to have a bank account)? For research and policy on the digital divide, we must differentiate among those groups that are not connected as a result of informed choice, as a result of a lack of awareness, or as a result of some structural threshold (financial, skill-related, etc.).

The dynamic perspective on the diffusion of these technologies is sometimes used to argue against policies that address the digital divide. The conservative Heritage Foundation writes that "clearly, the vibrant PC market is doing more than an adequate job of providing computing technologies to all Americans. Free computers and inexpensive technologies are filling any digital divide that remains. Washington should be patient and not interfere with this well-functioning process" (Thierer 2000). Such discourse, however, neglects the multidimensional character of the concept of Internet access. Access to the physical infrastructure is only the first building block of the information society.

THE MULTIDIMENSIONAL NATURE OF INTERNET ACCESS

To be truly able to access the Internet, users require three elements beyond physical access: 1) informacy, 2) usage skills, and 3) information skills. These additional elements have also been defined as technology literacy (elements 1 and 2) and information literacy (element 3). *Technology literacy* refers to one's ability to operate the technology; *information literacy* involves the ability to translate this into relevant information and implement it in one's life. It involves the ability and attitude to search for relevant information, translate it to one's own situation, and implement the necessary actions.

Informacy: Skills to Handle the Technology

The ICT revolution plays an important role in the functioning of the labour market, through the reshaping of work, skill structures and the organisation of work. As the new technology is an information technology, it requires not only stronger basic skills in numeracy and literacy, but also a new form of basic skill, the skill of interaction with the new technology, let us call it "informacy." (European Commission 1996)

Despite myriad studies on access to the Internet, the data on informacy—on how well people can handle the technology—are scarce. One Dutch study from 1997 gives an overview of digital skills of the Dutch population (Doets & Huisman 1997). The following is a sample of their findings:

◆ One-third of the population never plays or puts on a compact disc.
◆ Slightly more than half of the population never uses teletext and never programs the video recorder.
◆ One-fourth of the population never takes money from a cash dispenser or automatic teller machine.
◆ Almost half of the population never uses plastic money.

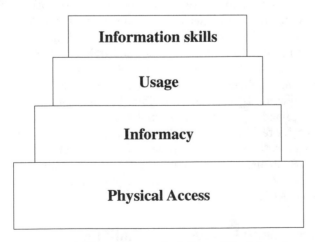

Figure 16.3   Elements needed by users to make full use of the Internet

Each of these figures refers to the population members with access to the technology—not to the overall population! Although 60 percent of the Dutch population (in 1997) had access to a personal computer at home or at work, only one-third used a computer regularly. It is not surprising to observe that in all these data, the elder population made limited use of the technology and had fewer digital skills.

The already mentioned SCP study also contains data on digital skills. Concerning the level of general literacy, 1 percent of the respondents indicated they cannot search for a telephone number in the phone book, 10 percent cannot read contracts, and 39 percent cannot fill out their tax forms. Regarding numeracy, 18 percent indicate they cannot read graphs or tables, and 4 percent cannot estimate the final cost when they go shopping. Concerning informacy, 53 percent admitted having trouble with searching for information on Internet, and 15 percent indicate that Internet use is a sheer impossibility for them.

Usage Skills

The currently available data on Internet access (see fig. 16.4) do not give a clear picture of what is done with that access. There are some indications that, on the level of physical access, the digital divide along lines of gender is closing (women get access on equal terms with men), but that there is a substantial difference in usage patterns. This applies as much to the quantity of usage (men spend more time online) as to the kind of usage. Men use the Internet more to download software and search databases than do women (van Dijk et al. 2000), and there are some indications that men use the Internet more for work-related issues, whereas women use it more for educational purposes (McConnaughey et al. 1999). As with other media such as telephone and television, equal access still generates different patterns of usage along the traditional fault lines of gender, education, income, and the like.

As physical access becomes more democratic, we will observe a shift in survey data away from physical access into the area of usage. Important issues that will emerge are whether differences in usage patterns result from personal choices or from context (e.g., access at work versus at home, the socioeconomic context of the user, etc.), and to what extent differences in usage have socioeconomic implications for the citizen and society.

Information Skills

Even with equal physical access, equal informacy, and equal usage patterns, we would lack some of the elements needed to build an egalitarian information society. A recent study from the Dutch Technology Assessment Institute (Steyaert & Mosselman 2000) distinguishes among three layers of information skills that are relevant for the emerging information society:

◆ *Instrumental skills*—the ability to use technology, to handle the basic functionality of the hardware or software involved. These instrumental skills are

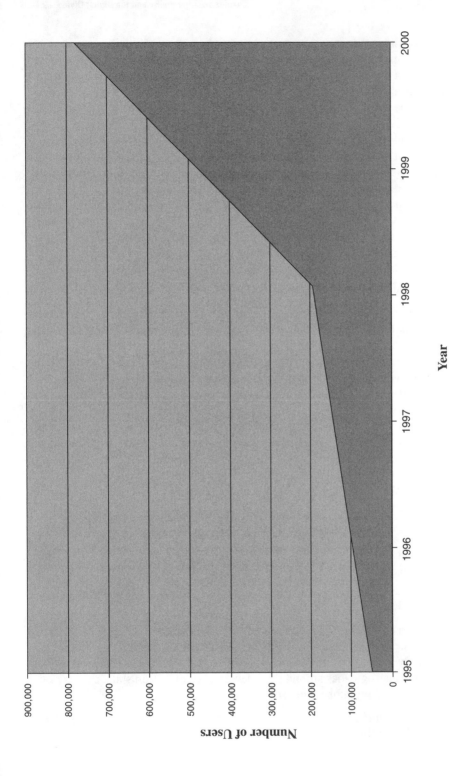

Figure 16.4 Changes in the number of Internet users worldwide

similar to the notion of informacy and are targeted by such initiatives as the European Computer Driving Licence [http://www.ecdl.com/].

◆ *Structural skills*—the ability to handle the new formats in which information is communicated. These involve, for example, the skill to look for information interactively (e.g., through listservs) or to make good use of the hyperlink structure of electronic information. These skills are relatively new and are induced by the technology.

◆ *Strategic skills*—the personal disposition to use information as a basis for decision making, involving an attitude to look for information before taking action, to scan continuously the information environment for relevant items, to translate information into consequences, and to implement necessary or possible actions. This level of strategic skills is as relevant in relation to traditional media (television, newspaper) as for new media. However, the technological innovations not only have provided us with tangible products and services but have also provided one building block for a society that is very information intensive. Consequently, these strategic information skills will become of paramount importance.

THE IMBALANCE IN INFORMATION PROVISION?

The digital divide cannot be reduced to having or not having access to the information superhighway. The differences in the supply of information must also be taken into account. In the early days of the Internet, information was basically available only if it concerned computers or some other tangible form of technology. That era is over. The Internet now offers not only a much bigger quantity of information, but also much more variety. Both can be described as progress, but such a description would be simplistic. Neither increasing the quantity nor increasing the variety of information makes it better information.

Internet growth statistics, such as the number of Internet users, number of Web servers, or number of Web pages, treat all data as equal. It is consequently not surprising that all data show upward trends. However, if one were able to differentiate among kinds of data and identify (for example) all pornographic or violent content, a different picture would probably emerge. A large part of the appealing, information-sharing character of the Internet loses its attraction. This is not unlike television studies. In the early days of television, the medium was welcomed as the platform for the education of the future—people could see a bright future for a "learning society." It is difficult to imagine such optimism when one reflects on the content of today's television broadcasts.

The expansion of information available through the electronic highway turns the latter into a more useful instrument, but the increased utility does not necessarily apply equally to all groups in society. A sample of the information needs of citizens in lower socioeconomic groups is provided in *The Information Poor in America* (Childres & Post 1975):

◆ Where is the most accessible and cheap child care in this neighborhood?
◆ How can I get rid of the rats in the vacant house next door?
◆ My husband left me—what can I do?
◆ How can I know whether there is lead in the plumbing or painting of my apartment?
◆ Where do I get the money to buy food until the next paycheck?

None of these information needs are addressed by the present content on the information superhighway. The Web sites of local authorities might provide information on the agenda and minutes of town council meetings or the address of the mayor, but contain nothing of relevance to these down-to-earth and real-life issues. Why is it, then, that lower socioeconomic groups have lower rates of Internet access?

A recent study by the North American Children's Partnership identifies four barriers in the current information supply that make the Internet less relevant for low-income Americans (Lazarus & Mora 2000):

◆ *Lack of local information:* Information about employment opportunities, the local housing market, local activities, and so on, is immediately relevant for the community in which one lives.
◆ *Literacy barriers:* Most information is made available in a format that requires a substantial level of reading skills.
◆ *Language barriers:* The overwhelming majority (estimated to be 87 percent) of all Internet information is in English, which is not the first language of many low-income Americans. On a global scale, this dominance of English is even more disproportionate.
◆ *Lack of cultural diversity:* Very little Internet content is generated by ethnic (non-White) communities.

Given these barriers, and taking into account the overlap among the different population groups facing them, the study estimates that about 20 percent of the U.S. population "face one or more content-related barriers that stand between them and the benefits offered by the Internet"(Lazarus & Mora 2000, 9). Again, this illustrates that physical access to the Internet is only one of the many building blocks of the digital divide.

REDEFINING THE DIGITAL DIVIDE

In the communications media and in government policy, we can witness profound concern over the emergence of a digital divide. National and supranational proposals are being developed to secure access to the Internet for everyone. The focus of these, however, is mostly on physical access, one of the less critical elements in achieving an egalitarian information society. Providing physical access lies within the interests of commerce and government (establishing a critical mass). Moreover, physical access will diffuse into society as the Internet becomes more readily accessed via television—a future development that is predicted by many and already happening with WebTV. More than physical access is needed for community organizing and activism with disadvantaged sectors of society and the world. Individuals must be able to operate the technology effectively, to find information that is relevant to their lives, and to use the information as leverage for change.

Although physical access to computers and networks appears to be problematic in the short run, there are two more critical and long-term issues for the digital divide. Unless individuals have the skills to operate the technology efficiently and effectively (technology literacy), as well as the ability and attitude to search for relevant information and translate that to their own situations and implement the necessary actions (information literacy), then the Internet stands to contribute little to the progress of social change. Even with physical access, the existence of technology illiteracy and information illiteracy will maintain a digital divide.

Not all citizens have the same level of information literacy, thereby creating a knowledge gap. This is the most critical element that makes the digital divide a social issue of extreme importance. However, it is not so much a digital issue as one that applies equally to traditional media. It was first identified in the late 1960s and became known as the *knowledge gap theory* (Gaziano 1997):

> As the infusion of mass media information into a social system increases, segments of the population with higher socio-economic status tend to acquire this information at a faster rate than the lower status segments, so that the gap in knowledge between these segments tends to increase rather than decrease. (Tichenor, Donohue, & Olien 1970, 159)

To use the previous analysis in developing policy to reduce the digital divide, such policy must include three ingredients:

- *Availability of access:* The inequality in access to new media can be targeted by offering all citizens a choice among alternative access scenarios, such as through the local library, with the use of free e-mail accounts, or with some other form of community access point. Policy and activities in this area are being initiated throughout the Western world, but there is a wide variety among the different activities: Some are focused on the individual (e.g., free e-mail), and some target groups (e.g., [http://www.seniornet.org] targets a certain age group, and community-access centers target people from the neighbourhood). Some activities stimulate the demand side (provide access), whereas others address the supply side (digital cities and content provision). Such variety is no weakness but reflects the variety of contexts from which these initiatives emerged.
- *Universal access:* When telephone technology emerged, a legal framework of universal access was developed. Although the background of this concept has been debated, the outcome was to make access to this new technology more democratic than market forces alone would have been able to accomplish. For the new media, no such legal framework currently exists, although some developments are taking place (McConnaughey 1999).
- *Skills:* Availability and universality of access are strategies on the level of physical access. As indicated before, this is only one of the conditions for

democratic availability of new media. Likewise, policy and initiatives must focus on technical and information skills, through either education (e.g., [http://www.big6.com/]; [http://www.microsoft.com/enable/]; [http://www.corel.com/accessibility/]; [http://access.adobe.com/]) or other alternatives.

CONCLUSION

There is significant hype around the notion of a digital divide at the moment. Mainstream analysis and solutions tend to focus exclusively on physical access, thereby neglecting issues of technology and information skills. Physical access is important, but without the required information and technology skills the digital divide remains.

A central component of Internet-based advocacy and activism is the coming together online of people who act to change structures and policies that negatively affect them. Within this scenario, the people coming together are often those who are left out by the digital divide. Furthermore, as this chapter demonstrates, even if physical access to the Internet is obtained by the excluded and oppressed in society, the digital divide will not disappear. To address the digital divide effectively, opportunities for individuals to increase their information and technology skills must be made available. As society increasingly becomes technology- and information based, these new skills not only enable community organizing and advocacy, but also underlie many of the employment opportunities.

Consequently, addressing the digital divide is a necessary, but not sufficient, condition to have true Internet-based social activism and advocacy. The alternative scenario in which the digital divide issue is not resolved can result only in the emergence of regions of "technological apartheid" across society.

Suggested Readings

Castells, M. 1998. *The information age: Economy, society and culture: Part 3. The end of the millennium.* Oxford, U.K.: Blackwell.

Childres, T., & J. Post. 1975. *The information-poor in America.* Metuchen, N.J.: Scarecrow Press.

Doets, C., & T. Huisman. 1997. *Digitale vaardigheden, de stand van zaken in Nederland. [Digital skills: State of affairs in the Netherlands.]*'s Hertogenbosch, Ned.: Cinop.

European Commission. 1996. *Green paper: Living and working in the information society— People first.* Brussels: Author.

Gaziano, C. 1997. Forecast 2000: Widening knowledge gaps. *J&MC Quarterly* 74 (2): 237–264.

Lazarus, W., & F. Mora. 2000. *Online content for low-income and underserved Americans: The digital divide's new frontier.* Santa Monica, Calif.: Children's Partnership.

McConnaughey, J. 1999. Universal service and the national information infrastructure (NII): Making the grade on the information superhighway. In *Making universal service policy: Enhancing the process through multidisciplinary evaluation,* ed. B. A. Cherry, S. S. Wildman, & A. S. Hammond, 189–212. Mahwah, N.J.: Lawrence Erlbaum Associates.

McConnaughey, J., D. W. Everette, T. Reynolds, & W. Lader (eds.). 1999. *Falling through the Net: Defining the digital divide.* Washington, D.C.: U.S. Department of Commerce, National Telecommunications and Information Administration. Available at [http://www.ntia.doc.gov/].

————. 2000. *Falling through the Net: Towards digital inclusion.* Washington, D.C.: U.S. Department of Commerce, National Telecommunications and Information Administration. Available at [http://www.ntia.doc.gov/].

Putnam, R. 2000. *Bowling alone: The collapse and revival of civic America.* New York: Simon & Schuster.

Rogers, E. 1996. *Diffusion of innovations.* New York: Free Press.

Steyaert, J., & I. Mosselman. 2000. *Digitale vaardigheden, geletterdheid in de informatiesamenleving.* The Hague: Rathenau Institute.

Thierer, A. 2000. *How free computers are filling the digital divide.* Washington, D.C.: Heritage Foundation.

Tichenor, P., G. Donohue, & C. Olien. 1970. Mass media flow and differential growth in knowledge. *Public Opinion Quarterly* 34 (2): 159–170.

van Dijk, L., & J. de Haan. 1998. *Moderne informatie-en communicatietechnologie en sociale ongelijkheid: Tussenrapportage.* Rijswijk, Ned.: Social and Cultural Planning Office.

van Dijk, L., J. de Haan, & S. Rijken. 2000. *Digitalisering van de leefwereld, een onderzoek naar informatie-en communicatietechnologie en sociale ongelijkheid.* den Haag: Social and Cultural Planning Office.

Wilhelm, T. 2000. *Democracy in the digital age.* New York: Routledge.

Wyatt, S. 1999. *They came, they surfed, they went back to the beach: Why some people stop using the Internet.* Paper presented at the Society for Social Studies of Science conference, October, San Diego, Calif.

Chapter 17

The Global Information Divide and Online Organizing for International Development

Jamal Shahin

INTRODUCTION

The impact of new information and communications technology (ICT) is being felt across all sectors of society, and within both domestic and international policy. This increasingly important global phenomenon affects many aspects of the way we live. If the politicians are to be believed, the information society will improve the lives of all who live within its reach. The Internet will bring citizens closer to their governments by providing more information that will be more easily obtained; it will also provide more opportunities for social activism the sharing of information, and a means for rejuvenating democracy.

This chapter presents the key issues that must be considered if we are to hope the information society will provide a just environment, where access is equitable and available to people as citizens—not just as consumers. We need to understand the driving factors behind the development of the information society, so that we can understand how to bridge the gap between the haves and the have-nots. We must determine whether individuals who are computer illiterate can survive in the informationalized world that surrounds us (even at this nascent stage). Is education the answer? Are the information-society initiatives of nations and international organizations enough to ensure that this digital divide does not grow, and that the Internet can be used to develop citizenship and public participation?

This chapter will examine the digital divide within the context of a global capitalist economy and its inherent push to commercialize the Internet. First, I describe several possible optimistic applications of the Internet that developing countries could use to aid sociopolitical organizing. Next, I examine the European Union (EU) while also taking a broader look at a few European Commission projects that aim to develop the global information society. This chapter then discusses the issue of public and private investment in the information society, the notion of global access, and the implications for social work advocacy and activism. One aspect in particular of the development of the information society must be considered: If Internet access is treated as a public service, we must bring the question of social exclusion to the fore and look at whether governments should provide access and accessibility to the information society. This is not solely a concern of the world's economically advanced nations. The universal nature of the information society, and the separation of governance from territorial sovereign control, make it more difficult to determine where responsibility lies for its development. In a world where "[forty-nine] countries have fewer than one phone line per hundred people and that 80 per cent of the world population lacks basic telecommunications, such as telephone service" (Shapiro 1999, 242), we must carefully consider the development of the global characteristics of the information society. In addition to infrastructure concerns, which dominate the debate in the international development literature, it is also important to discuss the concerns of application and usage of the Internet in these regions.

The EU has been providing support for international cooperation in creating global information networks ever since the G7 conference on the subject in Brussels in February 1995 (see [http://www.ispo.cec.be/g7/keydocs/g7en.html]). Within the European Commission, the unit dedicated to the regional aspects and international diffusion of the information society is called the Information Society Activities Center (ISAC2). This center, the Bangemann report (1994), the EU-U.S. dialogue on the information society, and the EU-MEDIS (European Union–Mediterranean Information Society project), to name a few, would all testify to the importance of the notion of "globalness" to the information society. Another reason for choosing the EU as a focal point is that it is in the midst of determining its own identity, much of which hinges on the concept of Trans-European Networks (TENs) and upon the EU's relations with its neighbors.

THE INFORMATION SOCIETY, ECONOMIC DEVELOPMENT, AND THE STATE

To begin, it is necessary to offer a definition of the concept of the *information society*. Such definitions are very important due to the novelty (and ambiguity) of the subject matter. Castells (1996) recognized the pervasive nature of the information society when he wrote:

> Technology and the management of technology involving organizational change could
> be diffusing from information technology manufacturing, telecommunications, and
> financial services (the original sites of technological revolution) into manufacturing
> at large, then business services, to reach gradually miscellaneous service activities
> where there are lower incentives for the diffusion of technology and greater resistance
> to organizational change. (79–80)

Castells (1996) implies that the ramifications of developing ICT are slowly filtering down from sectors where their importance was greatest and are now providing motivation for organizational change in areas that initially lacked any incentive to adopt the technology. The idea that the technology provides an impulse for organizational change has also been argued by Dordick and Wang (1993) through their concept of *informatization*. Underlying this body of literature is the implication that the information society is pertinent to individuals from all walks of life. In such books as *Being Digital* by Nicholas Negroponte, *Release 2.0* by Esther Dyson, and Howard Rheingold's *The Virtual Community,* there is an assumption that ICT will go one stage farther and change the way that we actually interact within our communities. For these authors, being connected becomes a way of life, although others may see it as a very particular style of living. As Tang (1998) noted, the information super-highway "has become a metaphor for wealth creation, sustained economic develop-ment, enhancement of the quality of life and social cohesion" (183).

The Internet provides the perfect analogy for defining the information society. The fundamental assumption that being connected to the Internet affects all ways of life (the socialization of ICT into the information society) reveals that the impli-cations of its development are greater than those for the development of (for ex-ample) broadcasting. The Internet has a deeper impact on society than did previous media and communications technologies due to its global and interactive nature. The Internet provides a vast, one-to-many communications network, and is essen-tially different from the television or the telephone. It is appropriate to call the phe-nomenon *interactivity*. Other attributes of the Internet include *hypertextuality* and *connectivity*, both of which are staple constituents of the information society. These are not new concepts, but they are combined in such a way through the Internet that they are once again novel.[1]

These attributes combine to create a whole new host of potential applications that take full advantage of the global communicative aspects of the Internet. These can be broadly placed in two different areas: education and online government. Within both areas the concept of advocacy or activism is central, although perhaps more so within the latter. If the Internet is to operate successfully and completely, then access must be globally feasible within these two areas.

Another fundamental characteristic of the information society is the level of commercial interest apparent in its development. Information and economic de-velopment are closely connected. The centrality of economic development to the in-formation society was raised by Ferenc Glatz, at the World Conference of Science held in Budapest in 1999. He said that we are living in "a society where knowledge is an enabling base for both fostering economic growth and creating intellectual wealth" (cited in e-mail distributed to the Netizens discussion list and written by J. Horvath, 27 June 1999).

Thus there is clearly a direct connection between information/knowledge on the one hand, and economic factors on the other. It is crucial to recognize that the information society reflects the economic ambitions that Glatz propounds. On the Internet, commerce and investment have blossomed to dramatic heights. The in-terest taken by corporations in technical and legal issues posed by the Internet re-veal that the economic benefits of the Internet are certainly connected to its un-precedented growth rates and profit potential. Nation states have recognized this and subsequently are attempting to cooperate both with one another and with commercial interests in the matter of technology policy decisions.

From this discussion, we can make a few assumptions:

- ◆ The information society affects the way we live—it is more than just "information."
- ◆ The information society must have a universal telos if it is to be functional in any public sense or if it is to enable social activism or advocacy;
- ◆ The information society *fundamentally affects the role of the state as a provider,* as cooperation both among states themselves and with commercial interests and actions are seen as increasingly important.

These assumptions lead us to recognize that the sociopolitical context of the development of the information society is not defined solely by state-based actors, and that its development affects all people in all walks of life. The Internet should be seen primarily as a public good, but at the same time it should be understood that commercial interests are what fuel its growth. Factors such as e-commerce are promoting the development of the information society, and this will undoubtedly affect both access to the Internet and its role in social activism.

INTERNET DEVELOPMENT AND ELECTRONIC COMMERCE

Electronic commerce (or *e-commerce*) refers to more than business-consumer operations on the Internet. A broader definition views e-commerce as "the ways that firms are engaging in the conduct of business by using advanced electronic information and communication networks" (Mansell & Silverstone 1996, 103). This goes beyond the recent dot.com phenomenon and can be traced back to networks such as SWIFT, the international bank clearance system developed in the late 1970s.

Of course, the consumer (as the end point of commerce, whether traditional or electronic) has an important role to play, and this is as important online as offline. The desire to be connected is in some way related to the utility of the Internet. In the industrialized world, this seems to be driven by corporate push.

A recent report by Forrester Research, *The Net-Powered Generation,* concluded that the Internet has become internalized for today's youth in North America. A quotation attributed to a senior member of the research team states: "This is a watershed for the Internet—when a generation of consumers internalizes a technology, its dissemination becomes self-sustaining and pervasive" (Forrester Research 1999). It is interesting to note the use of the word *consumer* in this context. We have discovered that the information society is a way of life—surely, then, to reduce studies of the Internet to consumer analysis makes our appreciation of being a citizen online difficult.

Because the development of the information society is inherently connected to investment in technology, and because the role of e-commerce is closely connected to this investment, we can see there is a close connection between the two. Many

ICT-related companies take special interest in social applications of their products. Microsoft's partnership with the government of the United Kingdom to provide computers and software to schools is merely one example of this.

Commercial concerns require access to the Internet to ensure maximum market penetration. Mansell states that "electronic commerce is feasible only to the extent that an appropriate network infrastructure or substructure is in place" (Mansell & Silverstone 1996, 103). For e-commerce to succeed, it must be based on widely accepted protocols that are openly accessible, to ensure that the maximum audience is reached. The Internet model combines perfectly with this understanding of e-commerce, as its standards are open.

This means that a broad system of protocols must be adopted. Secure purchasing mechanisms are one area in which commercial concerns are most noticeable. In this sense, we can see that commercial input into the development of the technical protocols of the information society is playing a large role. Governmental organizations are also playing their roles, however. International organizations such as United Nations Conference on Trade and Development (UNCTAD) are attempting to agree on procedures to free e-commerce of everything but the most minimal governmental restrictions; thus the freedom of markets (and equality of market access) ensues. The importance of market access as highlighted by reports from governmental and international organizations reveals that national governments accept the point made earlier, that economic growth and technological development follow hand in hand.

This incursion of private corporations into the domain of public policy is not limited strictly to the information society sector. Governments also support commercial interests; many public initiatives in promoting the information society are *match funded,* that is to say, public funding is given to match the private funding received as part of the project. Many programs that promote the information society have a commercial aspect, and this reveals the increasing importance of corporate investment (and thus e-commerce) to the development of the information society.

The danger in letting commercial interests take hold of the ICTs that underlie the information society is revealed in a strictly commercial sense by Whinston, Choi, and Stahl (1997):

> The public would need to guard against the possibility that the upper-level management of the network authority might attempt to distort prices or restrict capacity in ways that increase revenues. (124)

Although this mainly concerns monopolization for commercial ends, there are also implications for the benefits to citizens if commercial concerns take too much control of the Internet.

Commercial interests drive the development of the Internet in advanced capitalist nations. We have seen that governments are handing over control of this crucial communications network to commercial concerns, and that commercial concerns are taking the lead in Internet's development. Given this, what are the implications for other benefits and social goals that the Internet could provide? What are the implications of this for the Internet's possible use as a social activism tool or forum? Corporate control of the Internet raises numerous concerns and issues for online activism and electronic advocacy. For the Internet to continue to be a space for social activism, it must be openly accessible and not tightly controlled by corporations. As Noam Chomsky details in the foreword to this book, corporate control of the Internet will make it increasingly difficult to find alternative information or discussion. Corporations will attempt to control bandwidth, filter noncommercial users, slow pipelines, and guide users to commercial sites.

ACCESS AND ACCESSIBILITY

Given the utility of the Internet as a public service tool, it is the state's responsibility to ensure that access to the Internet and related technologies is not commercially defined, and that certain sectors of society are not excluded. For the purposes of this chapter, access issues comprise both *access* and *accessibility*. The former deals with physical connection; the latter, with usage issues as discussed in chapter 16.

Most individuals will gain access to the Internet through their homes, but, of course, this cannot be seen as the standard method of access in areas where homes lack telephones or other communications facilities. Although there have been astonishing changes in the means of access to the Internet, there are also some trends that can be defined. Internet access points are never free of charge. They require a computer, a communications device such as a modem, and bandwidth, all of which must be paid for. The connection is generally supplied by a cable or telecommunications company; additionally, an Internet service provider (ISP) must be used.[2] Thus, access to the Internet—and membership in the information society—is restricted in some sense to those who can afford it. It can only be assumed that cost of access to the Internet will decrease as time goes on, and that this will expand access—but whether this access will be to a commercialized information society will be something we must examine closely. As other chapters in this book have stated, individuals will have to organize and fight to keep the Internet a public entity under public control. As Noam Chomsky points out, the Pentagon will not simply hand over, as a gift, a tool that can be used for free communication and social action.

It is not only the cost of making the physical connection that provides a disincentive to becoming connected. The problem of accessibility—the complexity computer use—is also a substantial barrier for some people. In the recent Eurobarometer survey (European Commission 1999a), 10 percent of Europeans fifteen to twenty-four years of age believed the Internet was too complicated. The recent eEurope initiative proposed by the European Commission requires that "every home, every school, every business and every administration" is brought online in the coming years (Liikanen 2000). Indeed, UNESCO has been concerned about "new communications technologies" since 1989, when it instituted its medium-term plan's communication program to "strengthen communication capacities in the developing countries, so that they may participate more actively in the communication process" (Sparks 1991, 3). The problem goes well beyond physical access. People need both information access and usage know-how.

CITIZEN VERSUS CONSUMER

The story of the conflict between state and market is not a new one. The conflict has been redefined in the information age, however, because of the market's increasingly powerful role in providing the crucial ICT infrastructure. Although in certain cases the same could be said of previous technologies, the global nature and particular characteristics of the Internet make defining the boundaries for the purpose of regulation much more difficult. Indeed, the World Trade Organization (WTO) has gone as far as to say that national control of these infrastructures is limiting technological progress (WTO 1998). The EU's approach to the information society is clearly documented in various papers, all of which conclude that the role of government should be to regulate (minimally) the commercial control of ICT infrastructures. This approach is common throughout the world and raises some concerns. The individual's role as consumer should not act to the detriment of his or her role as a citizen. This principle should be at the center of the debate on the development of the information society.

It is difficult to imagine how the information society can develop without corporate involvement, given the rise of neoliberal capitalism in the world today; but to allow this involvement to the detriment of the ethos of the information society is undesirable. Thus, government investment and input are crucial to ensure that citizens and their concerns are not pushed offline in the quest for consumers who can increase profit margins. Indeed, our access to the Internet as citizens, and not only as consumers, is a necessary precursor to our ability to undertake social activism on the Internet.

To this extent, electronic government and nongovernment (nonprofit) initiatives are important. Application of these at local, national, and regional levels will encourage participation in the information society for more than merely commercial purposes. The examples throughout this book of local and international groups' use of the Internet for noncommercial purposes show that the role of the citizen is not currently being ignored in the information society.

THE GLOBAL CONSEQUENCES OF THE INFORMATION DIVIDE

If we believe the information society takes its sole impulse from commercial interests, then its final aim is restricted to one of an extended universal market. This does nothing for the benefit of citizens in the information society. The global technology of the Internet, however, does not help the state in maintaining legal and political control of the information society. This presents us with a paradox. Given the continuing tension between social interests and commercial forces, the road ahead will be a confusing one for policy makers. In order that this global society does not contain inherent structural inequalities, we must carefully examine the issues outlined earlier. This chapter has revealed the commercial interest in these technologies. The social divide that could occur in this arena is potentially devastating for the sociopolitical prospects of the global information society—but the experiments noted in this chapter reveal that the citizen is a crucial stakeholder in that society.

It has been noted that "a notion has developed that the electronic marketplace is the great equalizer, which accommodates big and small firms on equal terms" (Whinston et al. 1997, 464). The developing world might actually be able to take advantage of this and to "leapfrog" into the information society, but as Bessant (1987) noted, "the only alternative is to try to cope with [the implications of ICT for development] on relatively advantageous terms. With so much of the control over [ICT] in the developed North and in the hands of the multinational corporations, the prospects do not look good" (179).

The technologies behind the information society are of crucial importance to the structuring of society. There is an inherent commercial drive behind these technologies, but due to the public-service aspect to the Internet, many governments are attempting to ensure widespread and, if possible, universal access.. Governments are also attempting to take advantage of the potential of the Internet as an information utility. Whether the information society will be seen as a place where citizens can be accommodated on equal terms is something that will emerge as a result of these experiments and social struggles by citizens. The dual roles of citizen and consumer are incredibly blurred in the information society, and it is the task of public policy makers to ensure that the balance is maintained.

Notes

1. For a discussion of whether the Internet is radically new or merely a novel innovation, see Graham (1999), chapter 2, especially pages 24–27.

2. The International Telecommunications Union (ITU) divides Internet access into three components: hardware/software, access provision, and telephone service (ITU 1999).

Suggested Readings

Bessant, J. 1987. Information technology and the north-south divide. In *Information technology: Social Issues (a reader)*, ed. R. Finnegan, G. Salaman, & K. Thompson, 163–180. London: Hodder and Stoughton.

Castells, M. 1996. *The rise of the network society*. Oxford, U.K.: Blackwell.

Dordick, H. S., & G. Wang. 1993. *The information society: A retrospective view*. London: Sage.

Dyson, E. 1997. *Release 2.0: A design for living in the digital age*. Harmondsworth, U.K.: Viking.

European Commission. 1999a. *Eurobarometre 50.1: Les Européens et la Société de l'Information*. Brussels: International Research Associates.

Forrester Research. 1999, August 10. The Net-powered generation. *Online News*. Available at [http://www.computerworld.com/home/news.nsf/all/9908102youth]. Retrieved on December 5, 2000.

Graham, G. 1999. *The Internet: A philosophical inquiry*. London: Routledge.

International Telecommunications Union (ITU). 1999. *Internet for development: Challenges to the network*. Geneva: Author.

Liikanen, E. 2000. An information society for all. Speech delivered to the Infoworld Conference: "The liberalization of the telecommunications sector in Greece," 21 January, Athens.

Mansell, R., & R. Silverstone (eds.). 1996. *Communication by design: The politics of information and communication technologies.* Oxford: Oxford University Press.

Negroponte, N. 1995. *Being digital.* New York: Knopf.

Rheingold, H. 2000. *The virtual community: Homesteading on the electronic frontier* (rev. ed.). Cambridge: MIT Press.

Shapiro, A. 1999. *The control revolution.* New York: Century Foundation.

Sparks, C. (ed.). 1991. *New communication technologies: A challenge for press freedom.* Paris: UNESCO Press.

Tang, P. 1998. Managing the cyberspace divide: Government investment in electronic information services. In *Cyberspace divide: Equality, agency and policy in the information society,* ed. B. Loader, 183–202. London: Routledge.

Whinston, A., S. Y. Choi, & D. O. Stahl. 1997. *The economics of electronic commerce: The essential economics of doing business in the electronic marketplace.* Indianapolis: Macmillan Technical Publications.

World Trade Organization (WTO). 1998. *Electronic commerce and the role of the WTO.* Geneva: WTO Publications.

Chapter 18

Cyberadvocacy as Social Work Practice

The Continuing Challenge to Reinvent the Profession

John McNutt

Steven Hick

SOCIAL WORK PRACTICE IS EVOLVING IN THE MIDST OF A RESTRUCTURING of society quite unlike any other that has happened in the recent past. The primary force driving this change is the shift from an industrial society to one whose economic system is based on information and knowledge. The current restructuring of the economy represents a social transformation equivalent to the Industrial Revolution (Menzies 1996). This transformation will change social work practice in three ways:

◆ The context of practice will be altered. Many of the problems that we now face and our policies for handling them will be changed by the new economy.
◆ The agencies within which we work will be different. They will be smaller, more decentralized, less accountable, and more residual in nature. Some will have less connection to the community than they do today.
◆ Newer, technologically more sophisticated tools will be available to us. Electronic advocacy is one of those tools, but developments in telehealth (Slack 1996; VandenBos & Williams 2000) and related areas will be important for the clinical social work community.

These forces will make changes in the theory of social work practice inevitable. This book marks a place at the beginning of this process of change—a process that will transform the study of advocacy and activism in social work. The authors herein have described the foundations of this transformation, which we can sum up as follows.

◆ *Cyberadvocacy is a viable form of macro practice.* The chapters in this book have shown that electronic or online advocacy and activism is in use in numerous policy and practice settings, with both a beginning literature from its practitioners and an empirical base. We also have initial evidence of its effectiveness.

◆ *Integration with traditional practice, however, is essential*—for a number of reasons: the newness of the techniques, traditions in decision making, and so forth. There is little fear that traditional advocacy techniques will disappear.

◆ *Human infrastructure and the technology dimension must support each other.* There is also ample evidence that electronic advocacy depends on both a human element and a technological element. These two components must work together for the overall effort to be a success. In addition to satisfactory technology, adequate training and technical support are essential.

◆ *The digital divide is one of the more severe social-exclusion issues facing the world today.* It will limit the effectiveness of those interventions that involve excluded groups. Thus, as a barrier to practice, it must also become a practice target.

THE FUTURE OF CYBERADVOCACY

Because the practice of online or electronic advocacy is still in its infancy, is it fair to ask what the future holds? The technology is changing so quickly that the future may be a short matter of several years (Dertouzos 1997).

Advances in information and communications technology (ICT) will be important determinates of the future course of practice. Wireless applications are becoming cheaper, more dependable, and more capable—and because activism tends to be a mobile practice, the use of wireless systems with smaller computers seems to be a natural fit. Another technological breakthrough is the growth of artificial intelligence, particularly neural networks. Artificial intelligence will help the activist by pre-processing huge volumes of data to find the material most useful to the task at hand. One application of this new technology is data mining, a technology that combines statistical analysis with neural networks (a form of artificial intelligence) to discover patterns in very large data sets (Schoech, Quinn, & Rycraft 2000).

The growth of activist-specific software is also clearly in the offing (Turner 1998). One product available now is E-Base, a database system that runs on File-Maker Pro. E-Base includes categories that are useful for membership development, tracking, and so on (Turner 1998). Other types of software that are proprietary in nature are available for activists, but they can be costly. The possibilities for other developments are endless, and the growth of the movement toward open-source software (which developers offer for free public use; Wang & Wang 2001) makes it likely that more material will be available in the future.

Internet-only organizations and activist portals are two additional developments that will change the nature of practice (Brainard & Siplon 2000; Price 2000; Skocpol 1999). *Internet-only organizations* are activist groups that exist only on the Internet. These organizations have minimal local presence and do most of their work in cyberspace. Although the literature on these groups is sparse, they are the logical outcome of a movement toward professional advocacy groups without members and with virtual activism. *Activist portals* are sites that organize other sites. They may be based on conservative [http://www.townhall.org] or liberal [http://www.epn.org] ideology or may exist specifically for activists [http://www.protestnet.org].

One of the major developments in the area of nonprofit ICT has been the rise of application services providers, or ASPs. These organizations provide the services that a traditional information technology department would provide. Their services include the upgrading of hardware and software, technical assistance, installation, and so forth. ASPs have found a ready market among both larger nonprofits and small businesses, and an ASP that specializes in activism is not too far in the future. An activists' ASP not only would be familiar with general software and hardware issues but also would understand the nature of activism on the Internet and the range of technology choices that have been helpful.

In addition to ICT and the organizational issues that arise from it, we can anticipate changes in the profession itself. The use of technology in social work and social work education is now reaching critical mass. This means that social work students in the future will receive more instruction in ICT and that more attention will be paid to technology-related practice. Current textbooks (Haynes & Micklesen 2000; Hick, Halpin, & Hoskins 2000; Jansson 1999; Schneider & Lester 2000) already include Internet material, and papers that suggest ways to incorporate this material into courses and curriculum designs are available (FitzGerald & McNutt 1999; McNutt 1996; McNutt & Boland 1998). This material will be included in social policy, social work practice, and field education.

A more exciting development will be the emergence of the *cyberadvocacy specialists:* social workers trained to develop and manage cyberadvocacy programs. A concentration in this area would include coursework in traditional advocacy methods and strategies, as well as several courses in Internet-based advocacy and ICT. A field placement with a cyberadvocacy program would also be required.

Funding, Networking, and Research

A number of issues influence the likelihood that cyberadvocacy will be successfully developed as a major practice method. These issues generally fall into the categories of funding, development of support networks, and further research.

Funding
Although funding for most efforts will come from agency budgets, the funding for training programs, software development, and the development of new practice methods must come from other sources. Government funding has been problematic in some countries because of conditions placed on advocacy that is performed with governmental money. Charitable foundations are one possibility. Historically, such foundations have been reluctant to fund both advocacy and technology, but some are beginning to break that mold. One possible innovation would be a donor-

advised fund pertaining especially to technology. Donors put money into a fund and then agree to contribute to projects that seem to provide the philanthropic opportunities they desire. Another likely source would be the new technology foundations. These foundations, established by technology companies, understand technology and may be willing to fund new efforts. They are, however, unlikely to fund advocacy efforts that would weaken their own power or profitability.

Support Networks

As with any new practice, the success of an individual endeavor is dependent on the available support networks. Some such networks are informal, existing both within and outside the organization and providing ready sources of support and consultation (especially important to new and inexperienced practitioners). These networks are also important to the adoption of new technologies (Rogers 1995).

More formal networks include the ASPs and activist portals discussed earlier, as well as a series of additional organizations. Found at the high end of complexity are organizations that can develop and test new electronic advocacy techniques; at the lower end are informal technology providers, such as the TechFoundation's Geek for America program, which places computer-science-trained workers with local nonprofits, and Web Networks, a Canadian, Internet-based gathering place for individuals and nonprofit organizations working online.

Research

The third issue influencing the future success of cyberadvocacy is *research.* Social work is committed to developing, to the extent possible, an empirical base of knowledge about social work practice. In this section we will discuss research issues in evaluating electronic advocacy.

Outcomes measurement is a major trend in social services (Schorr 1997), and a great deal of time and effort is being invested in documenting the results of social intervention. Any discussion of outcomes in advocacy should proceed from the realization that there are a number of unique challenges to evaluating this type of effort. These include (McNutt & Burke 2001) the following:

- ◆ *Multiple factors and causality.* Disentangling causality in an advocacy situation is particularly difficult. It is unlikely that we would be able to say, with any degree of assurance, that one element of an advocacy effort was the most important or that another element was less critical. The participants in the process are not likely to be forthcoming in these matters. It is also not usually possible to use the kinds of designs that lead to easy isolation of causal relationships.
- ◆ *Shifting focus in advocacy efforts.* Advocacy is a very dynamic activity that can change at a moment's notice. To put it another way, in the morning one might be evaluating intervention *A,* and in the afternoon, intervention *B.* This adds new dimensions of difficulty to evaluation, which tends to prefer a stationary target to a moving one.

◆ *The political nature of evaluation.* If all evaluation is political (Weiss 1972), can we expect that the evaluation of political advocacy will be any different? Accountability is resisted by political actors, which makes credible data collection difficult.

Given these problems, it seems unlikely that any one approach to research will be successful. Multiple strategies will be needed, and a number of them have been advanced to deal with these issues. None is without problems, but used together they can help us understand what types of new tools are most useful.

◆ *User-perceived effectiveness approaches.* These strategies involve asking current users about the effectiveness of their tools. Although it is unlikely that they would provide completely objective information, given the right circumstances, the results could be useful.

◆ *Theory-based approaches.* These approaches test the links between concepts in a theory of intervention (Connell, Kubisch, Schorr, & Weiss 1995). For example, one assumption intrinsic to a given theory might be that e-mailing a message to a decision maker may sway his or her vote. Asking legislative staffs how they regard e-mail messages could test this assumption. If it does not seem to be reliable, we can disregard other parts of the theory that rely on this assumption.

◆ *Effective-organization approaches.* These approaches look at organizations that are thought to be effective and examine the techniques they use. Rees (1998) used this approach in her study of effective advocacy groups. She surveyed governmental decision makers to determine which interest groups were most influential. She then studied these organizations to determine what kind of strategies and tactics they employed.

◆ *Activity-based approaches.* These final approaches examine groups of organizations, asking what types of strategies they used. The more commonly used strategies are often considered effective because many users have found them valuable enough to use.

It is important to design new and effective interventions that make full use of these new tools. One of the most useful—and, unfortunately, underutilized—methods is the *design and development* strategy advanced by Rothman and Thomas (1994). This approach applies research and development theory to the creation of new social interventions. Using social science knowledge, the design and development team creates a new intervention, which it tests and then modifies according to the results. This allows for a structured approach to practice-theory development and validation. This also creates the need for new technology to assist researchers in collaborating and sharing knowledge (Lohmann 1997, 2000). Technology is likely to spark a major redesign of the ways in which we conduct and disseminate scholarship and research.

A related issue is the eventual need to develop new methods for the study of cyberphenomena (Jones 1999). Although most current research relies on traditional methodology, there are new developments that will add to our understanding of advocacy and technology. The development of evidence-based social work advocacy practice is clearly within our grasp—new tools and a commitment to social and economic justice can make it a reality.

THE QUEST FOR SOCIAL JUSTICE IN CYBERSPACE

Today's social workers face a challenge that is much like that faced by the original social workers of more than a century ago. Social workers of that time faced a new economy that promised to rip apart the social fabric of their agrarian society. In the midst of new forms of poverty, inequality, and injustice, they struggled to form a new profession, develop methods of intervention, and create a new social welfare system.

Today, social workers are again faced with many of these same challenges. The move to an information society has created a whole new range of social problems—not that the traditional issues were ever solved. In fact, the advent of an information society has only added to their seriousness and intractability.

We are in the process, however, of inventing new tools to deal with these problems and new workplaces to house the interventions. Technology has made possible such cyberinterventions as electronic advocacy and therapy over the Internet, as well as the virtual organizations that will house social work of the future. New social policy frameworks are also emerging.

We are entering a fascinating time in the history of the profession. It is our challenge to blend the tools and challenges of the future with the commitments and traditions of the past. We must be prepared to meet these challenges and take our place in the new information society.

Suggested Readings

Brainard, L. A., & P. D. Siplon. 2000. *Cyberspace challenges to mainstream advocacy groups: The case of healthcare activism.* Paper presented at the annual meeting of the American Political Science Association, 31 August–2 September, Washington, D.C.

Connell, J. P., A. C. Kubisch, L. B. Schorr, & C. Weiss (eds.). 1995. *New approaches to evaluating community initiatives.* Washington, D.C.: Aspen Institute.

Dertouzos, M. 1997. *What will be: How the new world of information will change our lives.* New York: Harper-Collins.

FitzGerald, E., & J. G. McNutt. 1999. Electronic advocacy in policy practice: A framework for teaching technologically based practice. *Journal of Social Work Education* 35 (3): 331-341.

Haynes, K. S., & J. S. Mickelson. 2000. *Affecting change* (4th ed.). Needham, Mass.: Allyn and Bacon.

Hick, S., E. F. Halpin, & E. Hoskins. 2000. *Human rights and the Internet.* London: Macmillan.

Jansson, B. S. 1999. *Becoming an effective policy advocate: From policy practice to social justice* (3rd ed.). Belmont, Calif.: Brooks/Cole.

Jones, S. (ed.). 1999. *Doing Internet research: Critical issues and methods for examining the Net.* Thousand Oaks, Calif.: Sage.

Lohmann, R. 1997. *Digital science: Electronic association and groupware in facilitating third sec-*

tor research. Paper presented at the twenty-sixth annual meeting of the Association for Research on Nonprofit Organizations and Voluntary Action, 5 December, Indianapolis, Ind.

————. 2000. *Furthering the scholarly common.* Paper presented at the twenty-ninth annual meeting of the Association of Voluntary Action Scholars, 15-18 November, New Orleans, La.

McNutt, J. G. 1996. National information infrastructure policy and the future of the American welfare state: Implications for the social welfare policy curriculum. *Journal of Social Work Education* 6 (3): 375-388.

McNutt, J. G., & K. M. Boland. 1998. Teaching about advocacy and the Internet: Strategies for social welfare policy courses. *Social Welfare Policy: The Newsletter of the Social Welfare Policy and Practice Group* 4 (1): 3–6.

McNutt, J. G., & K. Burke. 2001. *Electronic advocacy.* Presentation at the 2001 Salem State College Cyberadvocacy Conference, 12 February, Salem, Mass.

Menzies, H. 1996. *Whose brave new world: The information highway and the new economy.* Toronto: Between the Lines.

Price, T. 2000. *Cyberactivism: Advocacy groups and the Internet.* Washington, D.C.: Foundation for Public Affairs.

Rees, S. 1998. *Effective non-profit advocacy.* Washington, D.C.: Aspen Institute/Non-profit Sector Research Fund. Available at [http://www.Aspeninstorg/dir/polpro/NSRF/enpatoc.html]. Retrieved on 1 November 1999.

Rogers, E. M. 1995. *The diffusion of innovation* (4th ed.). New York: Free Press.

Rothman, J., & E. Thomas (eds.). 1994. *Intervention research.* Binghamton, N.Y.: Haworth Press.

Schneider, R. L., & L. Lester. 2000. *Social work advocacy: A new framework for action.* Belmont, Calif.: Brooks/Cole.

Schoech, D.; Quinn, A.; Rycraft, J. R. 2000. Data mining in child welfare. *Child Welfare,* 79 (5): 633–650.

Schorr, L. B. 1997. *Common purpose: Strengthening families and neighborhoods to rebuild America.* Garden City, N.Y.: Doubleday.

Skocpol, T. 1999. Associations without members. *American Prospect* 10 (45). Available at [http://www.prospect.org]. Retrieved on 5 April 2001.

Slack, W. 1996. *Cybermedicine.* San Francisco: Jossey-Bass.

Turner, R. 1998. *Democracy at work: Non-profit use of Internet technology for public policy purposes.* Washington, D.C.: OMBWatch.

VandenBos, G. R., & S. Williams. 2000. The Internet versus the telephone: What is telehealth anyway? *Professional Psychology* 31 (5): 490-492.

Wang, H., and C. Wang. 2001. Open source software adoption: A status report. *IEEE Software* 18 (2): 90.

Weiss, C. 1972. *Evaluative research.* Englewood Cliffs, N.J.: Prentice Hall.

Contributors

David Barnhizer is professor of law at Cleveland State University, where he teaches environmental law, international trade strategy, and trial advocacy. He is senior advisor to the international program of the Natural Resources Defense Council, a board member of Earth Summit Watch, and steering-committee member of the Industrial Shrimp Action Network (ISA Net). He has worked on environmental and human rights activities in (among other countries) Mongolia, Thailand, Ecuador, Honduras, Russia, Bangladesh, Colombia, Ecuador, and Honduras, as well as in most European nations. He is author of *The Warrior Lawyer,* which applies Japanese and Chinese strategic thinking to law practice, and *Strategies for Sustainable Societies.* He is currently completing, for Ashgate Publishing, two books dealing with effective strategies for human rights protection.

Jennifer Bartron is senior planner at United Way of the Capital Area in Hartford, Connecticut. She supervises an outcome measurement initiative, researches and recommends program priorities, and directs grant administration. She holds an M.S.W. in community organization, policy, planning, and administration from Boston College, and a B.S. in family studies from University of Connecticut. She gained her policy expertise through experience in such organizations as United Way of Massachusetts Bay and the Worcester Office of Elder Affairs. Her contributions to studies of e-advocacy and e-fundraising have been presented at national conferences.

Katherine Mary Boland is a researcher with the Department of Institutional Research and Planning at Rowan University. She has been coinvestigator for a number of studies on electronic advocacy and has published and presented papers on a variety of related topics. She has also taken part in creating an online advocacy program for a regional organization that advocates for children and youth.

Nick Buxton is communications and networks executive for the Jubilee 2000 Coalition in the United Kingdom and has worked for the debt campaign since 1996, shortly after it was launched.

Craig Campbell is a graduate of the M.S.W. program in the school of social work at Indiana University, with a specialization in macro-practice. Currently, he is the member benefits and technology manager with Indiana Youth Services Association, and associate faculty in the B.S.W. program at Indiana University. His presentations and publications have focused mainly on technology and community practice.

Joe Clarke received his M.S.W. from Boston College. He works for Catholic Social Services of Philadelphia as an outreach worker to some twenty-one urban parishes.

He came to social work after a twenty-year career in information technology and now works to combine information management techniques with principles of community organizing. He is a board member of the Digital Miracles initiative, a joint effort cosponsored by the Center for Community Partnerships of the University of Pennsylvania, community organizations, schools, and other institutions to bridge the gaps in resource access in the surrounding communities of west and southwest Philadelphia.

George Haskett has been associate professor of social work at Marywood University since 1985 and has been actively involved in social welfare programs since 1967. He has worked as an administrator, researcher, lobbyist, and advocate. His recent research interests have included child welfare, family violence, poverty, and public welfare programs.

Steven Hick is an associate professor in the School of Social Work at Carleton University. His published books include *Land Our Life: a Study of the Struggle for Agrarian Reform in the Philippines* (1987), *Human rights and the Internet* (2000), *Social Work in Canada: An Introduction* (2002) and numerous journal articles and studies on social work, social policy, human rights, and new technology. His teaching of introductory social work on the instructional television (ITV) and on the Internet has won him a teaching award and numerous accolades.

On-Kwok Lai, professor in the School of Policy Studies, Kwansei Gakuin University, Japan, also holds an honorary professorship in social work and social administration as well as an honorary research fellowship at the Center of Urban Planning and Environmental Management, both at the University of Hong Kong. He gained his Dr.rer.pol at the University of Bremen, Germany and has both taught and researched in Germany, Hong Kong, and New Zealand. His research interests involve the comparative sociopolitical analysis of environmental, social, and urban issues.

John McNutt teaches policy, research, and macro-practice in the Graduate School of Social Work at Boston College. His research is in the area of advocacy and activism on the Internet. He chairs the technology symposium at the Council on Social Work Education Annual Program Meeting and has presented, copresented, or published more than 100 scholarly works.

Goutham M. Menon is assistant professor at the College of Social Work, University of South Carolina. His work focuses on the use of technology for social work practice and education. He is on the board of editors for the *Journal of Technology in Human Services* and reviews papers for *Social Development Issues*. He manages the Web sites for the Inter-University Consortium for International Social Development and the International Commission of the Council on Social Work Education, and oversees the working of the Social Work Access Network (SWAN). He also follows developments in the areas of international social development, immigration policy, and Asian mental health.

Irene Queiro-Tajalli is professor and director of the B.S.W. program at Indiana University School of Social Work. Her areas of practice and teaching are generalist and community practice. She devotes part of her time to presenting workshops, mainly on Latinos, aging, and technology and is the author of several publications. A focus area of her recent writings is organizing in an information society.

Emily Reich has a lifelong interest in the social aspects of computer networking. She holds a degree in computer science/technology and society from Amherst College, and an international M.B.A. She has rich experience developing Web-based applications in a variety of organizational settings. She has designed and maintained Web sites for nonprofit groups (with an emphasis on sites that let people "take action" and get involved in political issues), as well as intranets for global organizations with projects around the world. She is currently working as a project director for GroupJazz.

Edward Schwartz is president of the Institute for the Study of Civic Values, an organization he founded in 1973 to develop educational, research, and action programs that relate contemporary issues to America's historic ideals. Presently, the Institute sponsors a Social Contract Project that helps neighborhood organizations develop social contracts with local government by defining shared responsibilities for community improvement. He has served as a visiting lecturer at the University of Pennsylvania and has taught classes at Haverford College and Temple University. In 1984, he was elected a councilman-at-large in Philadelphia. In only thirty-two years, he emerged as a major force in developing innovative strategies for neighborhood economic development. As a councilman, he was the first Philadelphia elected official to use computer-generated databases to monitor the work of city departments, and as early as 1986 participated regularly in an online local computer bulletin board to exchange views on public issues with computer-literate constituents. In 1984, *Philadelphia Magazine* gave Schwartz an award as an "Honest Politician," and he won "Best of Philly" awards as "Best Local Politician" and "Best City Councilman" in succeeding years as well.

Jamal Shahin is senior research fellow at the International Institute of Infonomics in the Netherlands. His research concerns the impact of the Internet on structures of governance, and he is completing his Ph.D. (Hull, U.K.) on the relationship between the Internet and governance at the European-Union level. He coestablished the Unit for Internet Studies and has given presentations and published articles in the field.

Jan Steyaert, Ph.D., lectures on social infrastructure and technology at the Fontys University of Professional Education in Eindhoven (the Netherlands). He has published widely on the application of technology in human services as well as on the dynamics between technology and the social quality of society. His work focuses on research and developments projects for local agencies, local and national government, and international work for the European Union.

Ryan Turner directs nonprofit policy and technology projects at OMBWatch, an effort to provide a voice for nonprofits in the technology development and practices that affect their use of information and communications tools in public policy activities. This includes research, demonstration projects, information dissemination, and outreach work, along with the identification of emerging trends and model practices of nonprofit technology. Prior to joining OMBWatch, he worked as a research specialist with the Washington, D.C.-based Police Executive Research Forum, where he assisted in information analysis for a federally funded model-development program for the improvement of homicide investigation. He also was the projects coordinator and editor for the Character Education Partnership, a national nonprofit coalition of organizations and individuals providing resource information on moral education programs in the United States.

Stephen P. Wernet is professor of social work and public policy studies at Saint Louis University. He is a nationally recognized social work educator and researcher in the field of nonprofit and social work administration. His recent research program also focuses on Web-enhanced and -distributed learning in higher education, particularly in social work education. He has authored numerous articles and papers on nonprofit organizations, social work administration, and distributed learning. He recently completed an edited book, *Managed Care in Human Service,* and coauthored *Cases in Macro Social Work Practice* with David P. Fauri and F. Ellen Netting.

Index